Child Marriage, Rights and Choice

This book addresses the issue of agency in relation to child marriage.

In international campaigns against child marriage, there is a puzzle of agency: While international human rights institutions celebrate girls' exercise of their agency not to marry, they do not recognize their agency to marry. Child marriage, usually defined as 'any formal marriage or informal union where one or both of the parties are under 18 years of age', is normally considered as forced – which is to say that it is assumed that are not capable of consenting to marriage. This book, however, re-examines this assumption, through a detailed socio-legal examination of child marriage in Indonesia. Eliciting the multiple competing frameworks according to which child marriage takes place, the book considers the complex reasons why children marry. Structural explanations such as lack of opportunities and oppressive social structures are important, but not exhaustive, explanations. Exploring the subjective reasons by listening to children's perspectives, their stories show that many of them decide to marry for love, desire, to belong to the community, and for new opportunities and hopes. The book, then, demonstrates how the child marriage framework – and, indeed, the human rights framework in general – is constructed on too narrow a vision of human agency: One that cannot but fail to respect and promote the agency of all, regardless of gender, race, religion, and age.

This book will be of interest to scholars, students, and practitioners in the areas of children's rights, legal anthropology, and socio-legal studies.

Hoko Horii is a lecturer at the Van Vollenhoven Institute in Leiden University, and a post-doctoral fellow at Kobe University. Her expertise lies in the field of socio-legal studies, legal philosophy, human rights law, and children's rights. Combining knowledge from these fields, her research interest concentrates on law, rights, and righteousness. In her research she observes court cases and interviews legal practitioners, social activists, youth, and others.

Child Marriage, Rights and Choice

Rethinking Agency in International Human Rights

Hoko Horii

Routledge
Taylor & Francis Group
LONDON AND NEW YORK

First published 2022
by Routledge
2 Park Square, Milton Park, Abingdon, Oxon OX14 4RN

and by Routledge
605 Third Avenue, New York, NY 10158

Routledge is an imprint of the Taylor & Francis Group, an informa business

British Library Cataloguing-in-Publication Data
A catalogue record for this book is available from the British Library

Library of Congress Cataloging-in-Publication Data
A catalog record has been requested for this book

ISBN: 978-1-032-02669-5 (hbk)
ISBN: 978-1-032-02672-5 (pbk)
ISBN: 978-1-003-18454-6 (ebk)

DOI: 10.4324/9781003184546

Typeset in Bembo
by Deanta Global Publishing Services, Chennai, India

Contents

Acknowledgements

Reading has always been my favourite activity. When I was little, I would trade my cup of ice-cream for reading my books. And not long after, knowing, or the pursuit of knowledge, has become another joy in and added meaning to my life. And this activity, which is conventionally called research, could not have been done alone. Researching and writing for this book was a truly collective project.

VVI and KITLV were the two main support bases for this project. Born and raised in Japan, the Netherlands has been a mother of my academic self and it has become my second home.

The continuous support of and numerous discussions with my supervisors, Adriaan Bedner and Gerry van Klinken, have stimulated, encouraged, and guided me through the making of an academic knowledge. Thank you for your willingness to debate ideas, and for having trust in me.

I have also spent a great amount of time with my other colleagues at VVI and KITLV, sharing ideas, draft papers, as well as coffee, boardgames, beers and tears. Santy, Bernardo, Fachrizal, Feby, Yance, Willem v.d. Muur, Annelien, Bruno, Arsjad, Maryla, Roxane, Hannah, Neske, Fayola, Laure, Laura, Erik, Monika, Katja, Lennie, Stacy, Sanne, Christian, Sarthak, Fenna, Matthew, Grace, Taufiq, Roel, Ward, James, Alana, Fridus, Marieke, Tom B., Tom H., Willem v.d. Molen, Kathy, Wouter, Bart, David Kloos, Henk, Gert, Rosemarijn, Katrien, Stephanie, Ton, Jan Michiel, Nadia, Carolien, Danielle, Daniel, Jacqueline, Nick, Suliman, Nienke, Mareike, Erik, Janine, Maartje, Yayah, Jeanette, Sikko, Ellen, Kari, Kora, Dennis, Pauline, Dyah, Stijn, Sulis, Pinky, Edward, Nicolas, Shiela, Fujimoto sensei, and Yoshida sensei, you and the shared stimulating discussions are the reason why I continue to be in academia and have kept my motivation to complete this book.

Mies Grijns has a special place in my work and in my heart. We have done so many things together. We were in the field together, both in West Java and in Bali. We co-authored articles. We attended conferences. We organized workshops. We published an edited volume. We went on a summer holiday. We shared so many meals, conversations, satisfaction, and excitement, as much as frustrations. I am forever grateful to you for being the most stimulating colleague, and the warmest friend, providing me a roof and a chocolate when it's tough.

Another dearest place in my heart is Indonesia, which I visited numerous times for volunteer work, fieldwork, and workshops.

Yogi and Dwi were more than research assistants to me, but colleagues and friends. It was thanks to them and through them that I came to know the most intimate part of Balinese adolescents' lives. I pay enormous respect to Anggreni, a woman with a big and tender heart, with a firm resolution for doing societal good, and with unlimited generosity. Another amazing woman I met in Bali was Viebeke, who inspired me with her thoughts and actions. Sita's presence was the reason I dared to start my fieldwork there. Grounded in Bali for decades, her wisdom and deep knowledge on Balinese life have been an such a valuable resource for this project. Finally, although I cannot thank them in names, I am most grateful to my informants for confiding in me to share their intimate life stories. Thank you for trusting me, and for opening your hearts to me.

I have been away from my home country, but the connection has always been there. Akira Fujimoto has provided me continuous support and encouragement. I am also thankful to the Toyota Foundation, and people from there, who invested in my project. Their support was beyond financial, as they encouraged me to create meaningful connections between my work and its value to the wider society.

My family in Japan has always been 'the home'. The reason why I can take challenges, and go on an untraveled path, is because I have the home I can come back to. My mother has especially been an unchanging support. Thank you for giving me life, and showing the kind of mother that I could be myself and that I want to be for Michi.

I had another family in France that I came to be connected to through our loving and loved girl. Papou and Mamou, the fact that I could always rely on you has been a source of faith in continuing in this project. Alex, without your encouragement I probably would not have dared to act on my academic ambitions. Thank you for co-parenting, and I am grateful for the trust you all have in my motherhood.

My dearest Michi. It is you, staying with you, talking with you, caring for you, and thinking for you, that I have come to understand what it is to be a child. You were five months old when I started my academic journey on socio-legal research, human rights, and Indonesian law. You were two years old when I came with you to Leiden to start this research project. You were only three years old when I decided to go with you to Bali for fieldwork. With all the changes of environment, I decided that I, as your mother, would be 'the home' for you. Thank you for trusting me, thank you for coming to different places along with me, and thank you for existing. With you, and for you, I can do anything.

Glossary

ACRWC: African Charter on the Rights and Welfare of the Child.
***Adat*:** Social rules and practices of a community; also custom or tradition.
***Adat* law:** *Adat* rules with legal value.
***Akta kelahiran*:** Birth certificate.
***Akta tunggal*:** Single birth certificate, without the name of the father. A child with *akta tunggal* is considered to be an 'illegitimate child' (*anak luar kawin*).
***Badan Kependudukan dan Keluarga Berencana Nasional*:** The governmental family planning institute in Indonesia.
BKKBN: See *Badan Kependudukan dan Keluarga Berencana Nasional.*
CEDAW: Convention on the Elimination of All Forms of Discrimination against Women.
CEDAW Committee: UN Committee on the Elimination of Discrimination against Women.
Child Protection Law: Indonesian Child Protection Law No.23 of 2002, *UU Nomor 23 Tahun 2002 Tentang Perlindungan Anak.*
CRC: Convention on the Rights of the Child.
CRC Committee: UN Committee on the Rights of the Child.
CSO: Civil Society Organization.
***Fatwa*:** Legal opinion given by Islamic authorities.
FGD: Focus Group Discussion.
***Fiqh*:** Islamic doctrine.
Girls Not Brides: The platform of international organizations working against child marriage.
ICCPR: International Covenant on Civil and Political Rights.
***Kantor Urusan Agama* (KUA):** Office of Religious Affairs (Indonesia).
***Kantor Catatan Sipil* (KCS):** Civil Registry Office (Indonesia).
***Katrol usia*:** Manipulation of the age registered in the state civil registry. Increasing the age of the bride or groom by changing the birthdate in the required documents enables them to receive their official marriage certificates right after the religious ceremony.
KCS: See Kantor Catatan Sipil.
KHI: See Kompilasi Hukum Islam.

***Kompilasi Hulum Islam* (KHI):** Compilation of Islamic Law (Indonesia).

KUA: See Kantor Urusan Agama.

KUHAP: Indonesian Criminal Procedure Code.

KUHP: Indonesian Penal Code.

LBH Apik Bali: *Lembaga Bantuan Hukum Asosiasi Perempuan Indonesia untuk Keadilan Bali* (Legal Aid Association of Indonesian Women for Justice). This is a local branch of the national CSO providing legal assistance for vulnerable people, such as women and children from low-income families.

Marriage Law 1974: Indonesian Marriage Law No.1 of 1974, *UU Nomor 1 Tahun 1974 Tentang Perkawinan.*

***Pacaran*:** Dating, courtship, or a romantic relationship formed before marriage.

***Parisada Hindu Dharma Indonesia*:** A major organization involved in rallying for the preservation of Hindu and *adat* customs.

***Penghulu*:** The district-level head of the Islamic bureaucracy whose functions include local marriage registration.

***Perkumpulan Keluarga Berencana Indonesia*:** A civil society organization for family planning in Indonesia.

***PKBI*:** See *Perkumpulan Keluarga Berencana Indonesia.*

PHDI: See *Parisada Hindu Dharma Indonesia.*

***Reformasi*:** The period of political, legal, economic, and social reforms that followed President Suharto's resignation in 1998.

UNICEF: United Nations Children's Fund.

UNFPA: United Nations Population Fund.

***Upacara*:** *Adat* ceremonies.

***Zinah*:** Fornication, adultery, and sin in Islamic law. Adultery includes extra-marital and pre-marital sexual intercourse.

Chapter 1

Introduction

When discussing child marriage, choice is an important yet uncomfortable topic. At Girls Advocacy Alliance's event in Amsterdam that I attended, they introduced their projects as aiming to support girls in Africa in "*having their own voice to be heard*". This suggests that the ultimate goal is to support their *choices*. Their representative was a girl from Ethiopia, selected to *be heard* in Geneva. The girl was chosen because she could tell "vibrant stories" of why she opposes child marriage practice with "capacity and confidence". Their presentation focused on supporting the girl and other girls' *choice not to marry*. What then, if, girls are *choosing to marry*? What about their *agency to marry*? Discussion on these questions was simply absent. I tried to raise the issue by asking what their approach is to children who themselves want to marry. They replied to me that they were in "constant dialogue with local communities to change customs and traditions". "It is difficult to fight with that kind of perception", they said. In their eyes, children *cannot possibly want to marry*, so they blame such scenarios on bad customs and traditions that they need to combat.

This book, with close-up narratives of child marriages in Indonesia, investigates the puzzle of agency in the working of international human rights, and the role of international human rights law in local contexts essentially. Is the law acting as a resource, or rather a constraint (Merry 1997), for those who are supposed to benefit from it? As this chapter will demonstrate, answering this question needs a good empirical study on how concepts such as agency, autonomy, freedom, and choice are constructed and how they work out in practice.

Over the past decade, organizations such as UNICEF and Girls Not Brides started to frame child marriage as a human rights violation and an obstacle to development (United Nations Children's Fund Innocenti Research Centre 2001; Girls Not Brides n.d.-a; UNFPA 2012; Equality Now 2014; United Nations Children's Fund 2014; United Nations Development Programme n.d.). They define child marriage as "any formal marriage or informal union where one or both of the parties are under 18 years of age" (Girls Not Brides n.d.-b). This definition is uniformly used and unchallenged. Within this established framework, children are considered incapable of deciding to marry.

DOI: 10.4324/9781003184546-1

Thus, a child's consent to marriage is merely an outcome of prevailing social norms. Such a marriage is forced, i.e., without consent.

Notwithstanding, marriage under the age of 18 has always occurred independently of how international institutions frame it. Countries with high child marriage prevalence[1] today are mostly in the 'Global South' – the top five being Niger, Central African Republic, Chad, Bangladesh, and South Sudan (Girls Not Brides n.d.-c). However, it has been historically and globally commonplace to marry young, including in the West. For instance, in the 1950s and 1960s, the median age for a woman's first marriage in the US was 20 (United States Census Bureau n.d.). Gradually, a number of social developments in modern society, such as an increase in years of education, have increased the average marriage age.

This change in the average marriage age corresponds with the global rise in the legal marriageable age. In England, for instance, the legal marriageable age was 14 for boys and 12 for girls until 1929 (Cretney 2005: 57–62). The minimum age changed to 16 under the influence of the League of Nations, which actively tried outlawing child marriage in parts of the world they deemed 'less-civilized' (Glendon 1989: 47). In this process of modernizing the legal marriageable age, marriage below the age of 18 has become "deviant behaviour". In Volpp's (2000) words, this change represents "the clash of cultures between 'modern' and 'backward' peoples" in the eyes of the colonial governments (Blackburn and Bessell 1997: 108). Policymakers also used the marriageable age as an instrument to control population growth (Ibid: 132). In other words, marital age was an area for significant colonial intervention (Bunting, Lawrance, and Roberts 2016: 19).

Alongside the increase in the minimum age for marriage, marriage by choice has also become the standard. Behind this normativization of marriage by choice is the modern core ideal: The importance of emancipation and autonomy, especially for women. The liberation of women has become a crucial marker of a state's level of civilization. At the same time, what Jenks (2005: 57–58) calls "the Apollonian" image of children has been influential in modern Western societies. Childhood is a time for play and should be a happy time. Children need protection and are pure and innocent. Within this model, children have become an object for protection, whereby their agency – their capacity to choose – has been compromised. The conceptual development of marriage and children has spanned the last few centuries and has, over the last few decades, crystalized the idea and discourse of child marriage as a human rights violation.

The transformation of norms around marriage suggests the concept has a fluid nature. It is important to understand that marriage has different meanings, norms, and consequences attached to it in every historical time and society.

1 Percentage of ever-married women aged 20 to 24 married before age 18.

For instance, in contemporary Indonesia, marriage is the threshold of any valid sexual relationship. Thus, banning marriage under a specific age means practically banning sexual relationships under that age altogether. And even within the same country, marriage has different consequences. I will study how Indonesia's framework operates in practice as a case study in this book. In patrilineal Bali, where I conducted the main part of the fieldwork, divorce has heavy social and practical consequences. By contrast, in West Java, divorce is quite common and relatively easy. Changing what it means to exit marriage also changes what it means to enter into marriage.

Considering the varied meanings of marriage in different contexts, can all marriages under the age of 18 be in the same category of 'child marriage' (as a human rights violation)? When we look at how international institutions frame child marriage, there is a general tendency to highlight only specific types. For instance, Volpp (2000), in her analysis of the American narratives of 'culture', compares the public narratives of two groups of female adolescents who marry older men: White and immigrants of colour. She discovers that the migrant girls' marriage is described as problematic and "cultural", while a white girl's marriage is described as an isolated instance of atypical behaviour. Her finding shows that race and ethnicity are two dimensions in identifying what to 'blame' as the cause of the practice. Another dimension is gender. Indonesian cases of girls marrying older men outrage human rights advocates. However, when a boy married an older woman in Indonesia, the news was received as a heart-warming love story (BBC News 2017). This specific way of presenting child marriage is related to the generalizing tendency of the campaigns against child marriage. They tend to present child marriage as a forced marriage between an early-teenage girl and a much older man. This portrayal creates 'a stereotypical child marriage' that appears on Google Images under the keyword 'child marriage'.

How representative of reality is the stereotypical child marriage? Certain studies mention a growing number of "love marriages" between teenagers because of increasing educational opportunities and mobility (Chaudhuri 2015; Grijns et al. 2016). However, international discourses and narratives tend not to focus on such examples or the wider diversity of 'child marriage' cases. This absence could be because of CSOs' strategic simplification. For the sake of their campaign, and to attract the attention of the world's populations to the issue, they *need to* simplify the narratives to match extreme and sensational cases. They may also consider children as lacking the necessary cognitive maturity and moral development to decide to marry, thus not recognizing their agency to marry. Child marriage then becomes an outcome of social structures instead of the child's or children's agency. Bodineau (2014: 124) studied the international narrative about child soldiers and concluded that policies and programmes do not reflect the diversity of children's experiences. This disconnect occurred because the diverse experiences challenged the representation of childhood at the foundation of children's rights. The same disconnect seems applicable to child marriage programmes.

While they do not recognize children's agency *to marry*, international human rights institutions emphasize certain autonomous choices made by women and celebrate when girls exercise their agency *not to marry* (See for instance: United Nations Population Fund 2018; Reiss 2018; Child Helpline International n.d.). Here, the discourse shows two contradictory views on agency. Children's agency is dismissed when they do not do "the right thing" (Hanson 2016), as is also observed in child labour or child soldier cases (see Section 1.1 and Section 6.1). Due to such contradictions, Hopgood (2017), with the example of female genital mutilation, describes such intervention as "international paternalism".

Such a normative approach is based on specific assumptions about what it is to be a child, e.g., "the Apollonian" image of children. However, "the idea of childhood as a universal category does not meet the real experiences of children across the globe", i.e., there is no single 'childhood' but "the proliferation of childhood*s*" (Jenks 2004: 5–6). Indeed, anthropological literature has observed the diversity of childhood*s* throughout the world (see Section 1.1).

There is currently an increasing amount of investment, human resources, time, and passion spent on ending child marriage. However, the definition of child marriage and its assumptions are unchallenged, and the approach to end child marriage is uncritically accepted. In other words, while child marriage is *constructed* by international institutions, it is currently *uncontested* among international institutions working on this issue. Thus, it is a crucial time to reinvestigate and reconstruct the taken-for-granted framework. The key puzzle in the reinvestigation process is the contradictory views on agency. One of the assumptions underlying the international approach of prohibiting and outlawing child marriage is that children under the age of 18 are *incapable* of choosing to get married. But are they really incapable? If they are, why would they be *capable* of choosing not to get married? To explore these contradictory views, this book explores *why children marry*. They do so not just because of the structural factors that human rights institutions present, e.g., poverty, oppressive culture, and lack of education. To understand *why children marry*, we need to ask *what for them are the reasons for getting married*. We need to listen to their perspectives, acknowledging that they are capable of thinking and acting on their own.

The central questions of this book are (1) *why children marry*, and (2) *how this practice both informs and is treated within the multiple competing normative frameworks that are in place*. The question considers both structural (e.g., poverty, oppressive culture, lack of education) and subjective (i.e., *what for them are the reasons to get married)* reasons. Thus, it is crucial to examine 'child marriage' from different angles at different levels of society. This examination should relate to how actors at each level are dealing with different sets of rules in the context of legal pluralism (i.e., the second part of the question). Starting from analysing child marriage discourse at the international level, I then move to discuss the political contestation over child marriage at the national level. There, I use a case study on Indonesia, where the tension over the issue arises between the conservative Muslim organizations and liberal groups of human rights advocates. To zoom in further, I investigate child marriage as a social practice on the Indonesian island of Bali, where I conducted fieldwork over six months.

To unpack the multi-layered reasons why children marry, each chapter addresses and provides evidence to answer the sub-questions listed below:

- Under the international discourse, since when and how did people under 18 become too young to marry, and why did the age limit become 18? (Chapter 2)
- How does the Indonesian government regulate a social reality where children continue to marry under its law while setting goals to comply with human rights standards to end child marriage? How is the state law implemented in practice and by which state and local actors? (Chapter 3)
- How do state legal agents in Bali navigate state law through local concerns and customary law, dealing with child marriage arising from teenage pregnancy? (Chapter 4)
- Why do some children marry under the age of 18 in Bali? What are the contexts in which they decide to marry by themselves? (Chapter 5)
- When children consent to a marriage, is such a decision really the child's choice, considering the social pressure from and power dynamics between their parents, their extended family, and local leaders? And even when it is the child's autonomous decision to marry, to what extent should policymakers take their voices seriously? (Chapter 6)

By answering these questions, this book offers important insights into the ongoing debates on the literature of human rights and children's rights. The next section summarizes the state of the art in these sets of literature and how this study engages with the current debates.

1.1. Emerging particularism in human rights and children's rights

Human rights are, in principle, universal. The Universal Declaration of Human Rights claims and prescribes universality (Henkin 1989). Created in the aftermath of the Second World War, the declaration was a political idea with moral foundations, aiming at ensuring that such a catastrophe would never take place again. All human beings, "with no distinction given to their race, colour, sex, language, religion, political or other opinion, national or social origin, property, birth or other status" (Article 2 of the UDHR), were equally acknowledged to have these basic rights stipulated by the Declaration. The Vienna Declaration (para. 1) describes the universality of human rights "beyond question". In short, human rights law is built on the normative premise that all human beings should enjoy all of these rights.

The problem with this claimed 'universality' has been widely addressed. The American Anthropologist Association (1947) issued the famous Statement on Human Rights with cultural relativist claims. They were concerned that the claimed universality of human rights was undermining cultural differences. Merry (2003: 56–57) points out that while some regard relativism as tolerance without limits (i.e., "anything goes"), others see it as a more nuanced recognition that tolerance of difference is an important ethical consideration. Arguing the latter, Merry (Ibid) criticizes external reform movements that try to change cultural practices without sufficient respect for differences. Some cultural anthropologists have charged that human rights is the imposition of the Western idea of natural rights and therefore is a form of cultural imperialism. Dembour (2001: 56–58) points out that an approach assuming the righteousness of human rights standards risks "arrogance" as it excludes the experience of the "other". Cowan (2006: 10) similarly points out the one-sidedness of human rights standards, arguing that just as local practice is a product of 'culture', human rights in a way are a 'culture', "an increasingly pervasive structuring discourse [...] that shapes how the world is apprehended".

Different disciplines offer varied perspectives on this debate. Legal philosophers such as Donnelly (1984; 2003) assessed the cultural relativist claims and concluded that weak cultural relativism (instead of radical cultural relativism or universalism) was the answer: Human rights are fundamentally universal, possibly with limited cultural variations. Human rights scholars like David Kennedy (2005) call for carefully assessing the negative impact of international humanitarian interventions, calling human rights the centre's (the West) criticism of the periphery (the rest). Political scientists like Stammers (1999) argue that proponents of human rights (as civil and political rights) are those with power who fail to see violations of economic, social, and cultural rights. These criticisms pose a serious question on the legitimacy of the international human rights system and indicate the need for reform.

So-called post-colonial scholars such as Santos and Rorty, as well as TWAIL (Third World Approach to International Law) scholars such as Mutua and Baxi, also criticize and deconstruct human rights from a historical viewpoint (see Section 2.4). In brief, post-colonial studies call for a counter-hegemonic conception of human rights (Santos 2015: 9). This historical approach to deconstructing human rights highlights that human rights are a product of a specific historical background and are 'man-made' and so are imperfect and hardly universally relevant.

What the above-mentioned historical approach does not consider is that *the practice* of human rights could be different from *the idea* of human rights. Some scholars focus on this distinction. Macdonald (2013: 26) argues that the human rights idea is not flawed because of its inherent characteristics but because of what it has been turned into by its proponents. Legal anthropologists (Cowan, Dembour, and Wilson 2001: 6) point out that, in spite of the law's positivist approach of essentializing social categories, legal principles are actually constantly readjusted to the demands of local contexts. Ignatieff (2003) called for a careful assessment of what human rights proponents wish to achieve, importantly distinguishing between a "minimalist" approach and an expansionist approach of interventions in the name of human rights. These arguments underscore that international law is a social process with many different actors involved in the adaptation process (Merry 2006a: 111). This means that, when human rights frameworks are put in context, their function, meaning, and consequences are often different from how they are designed. Therefore, the attempt to evaluate and reconstruct the current frameworks from bottom-up is crucial.

In response to these critics, scholars have deployed various approaches to reconstruct human rights. Rorty (1998) proposes a pragmatic approach to sentimental human rights education: Teach that we must treat other people well because we feel sympathy for them, not because they are morally our equals. Scholars such as An-Na'im (1992: 3), Flynn (2013) and Harris-Short (2003: 175) call for "cross-cultural dialogue", or "intercultural dialogue", for enhancing the "cultural legitimacy" of human rights (see Section 2.4).

These are all interesting propositions. The need for dialogue, in particular, suggests the need for attention to differences, i.e., the need for empirical evidence that investigates real and situated practices. Merry (2006b) has demonstrated how human rights norms get translated in the local context, a process she calls the "vernacularization of human rights". In a normative sense, this suggests that human rights need to be adapted to local understandings and conditions to be effective. International human rights law in theory grants state parties broad discretion in how to realize rights domestically, for "culturally sensitive approaches to human rights" (Fraser 2018). As law is a normative discourse that aims to regulate an often elusive reality (Alves 2000: 499), the local supersedes the universal, no matter how globally one may try to think. Everything becomes relative, localized, and ephemeral (Ibid: 491). Anthropological research on human rights illustrates their function in plural normative orders and how they are perceived, e.g., concerning violence against women (Merry 2006b), female genital mutilation (Boyle and Corl 2010; Gunning 1992), and polygamy (Campbell 2013). These studies demonstrate both the limitations and potentials of international human rights law and ideas, suggesting that paying attention to different socio-cultural contexts can make human rights relevant and less subject to the inequality of global power.

This need for the localization of human rights highlights the necessity of an anthropology of human rights (Freeman 1994). To conduct a fruitful debate about the universality of human rights, the discussion should focus on how human rights are applied in local contexts. If one asks how *universal* human rights are, we ought to ask: How *relevant* are human rights to people in each context? For instance, Ignatieff (2001: 111, 116) describes poor rural women in Pakistan who criticize honour killings. It is an example of how human rights go global by going local, empowering the powerless, and giving a voice to the voiceless as a language that creates the basis for deliberation. But when are rights indeed being used as a resource, and when do they start to become a constraint? In other words, there is a need to investigate the consequences of the human rights framework on people's lives. This book studies exactly that.

In so doing, I aim to take a constructive approach to studying and writing about human rights in context and eventually to make pragmatic suggestions. As Goodale (2006: 4) put it, "to study what human rights do is also to study what human rights are". These dimensions should be examined and analysed together. Thus, we need an ethnography of human rights that describes what human rights do and then reflects on what human rights are, reconceptualizing human rights at the basic theoretical level.

Some scholars have formulated a critical view of the international approach to children's rights, which arguably is based on modern Western ideas about childhood. Hanson et al. (Hanson et al. 2015) have challenged the dominant abolitionist approach to child labour and instead suggest focusing on children's rights to work in dignity. With the example of child labour, Nieuwenhuys (1996: 238) points out that modern society places children in the position of dependency and passivity. Desmet (2012: 5) likewise suggests that some provisions of the Convention on the Rights of the Child (hereafter CRC) are "patronizing" and focused excessively on "protection".

Such arguments may have to do with the origin of the CRC. The basis of the CRC is found in the 1924 Declaration of Children's Rights, which was drafted and championed by a British social activist, Eglantyne Jebb. Her ideas reflected her time and socio-cultural disposition (Hart 2006: 5). The philosophy behind the CRC is informed by a particularly Western conceptualization of childhood, which is characterized as irrational, natural, and universal (James and Prout 1997) (see Section 2.1.2). Child development psychology research from the early twentieth century has supported this model. However, the research is contentious because those psychological concepts, often taken as objective and scientific evidence, actually rest on a set of implicit assumptions and particular methods (Henrich et al. 2010; James and Prout 1997). Boyden (1997) interprets the adoption of the CRC as the export of a stereotyped childhood from the industrial world to the South. The protection-focused policies concerning children are deeply embedded in a liberal paternalistic view of childhood, which the following chapters will clarify.

The "localisation of human rights" approach is one method for studying real experiences, their diversity, and how they relate to the human rights framework (De Feyter and Parmentier 2011; Vandenhole 2012). The approach suggests investigating the use and relevance of human and children's rights in local communities and translating the findings into the current international norms (Ibid). For instance, Ngira's (2019) research in Kenya revealed that the systematic condemnation of child labour by international children's rights institutions is counterproductive, as it ignores the role of some forms of 'child labour' in integrating the child in the family and in guaranteeing their rights to education. Overall, the recognized challenge is to document and verify the effects and the consequences of policies concerning children's rights in real-life contexts (Reynolds, Nieuwenhuys, and Hanson 2006: 295). This challenge emphasizes the role of anthropology in the study of children's rights (Hart 2006). Montgomery (2007) conducted fieldwork to study child prostitution in Thailand. She expressed uneasiness with her view of "protecting children", as she became increasingly aware of how it differed from the children's accounts of their lives. Godoy (1999: 437) studied street children in Guatemala. She criticized CRC rights as based on a "Northern construct of childhood", with limited relevance for children who live according to the traditional roles assigned to them.

Those anthropological studies reveal that internationally constructed 'children's rights' are not always relevant to local conceptions and realities of childhood. For instance, Maithreyi (2019), from her ethnography of children's education programmes in India, concludes that children can be "strategically opportunising actors" who seek to make meaning of their lives despite structural and discursive constraints. Again, the key to disentangling this discrepancy between the local and the global is *agency* and *autonomy*. On the one hand, global human rights institutions assume that children (i.e., everybody under the age of 18) are not and cannot be fully *autonomous*. On the other hand, the very same institutions believe in and aspire towards *full autonomy* of human beings above the age of 18.

This idea of *full autonomy* is based on the ideals of modernity, the liberal understanding of agency that we all should be able to decide on our own lives instead of submitting to the traditional order. Relational autonomy, by contrast, suggests that such a conceptualization of agency is an illusion, as our 'selves' are all embedded in social interactions and relationships with others. This conceptual framework of agency, autonomy, and choice is crucial for this book, as well as for understanding the puzzle of agency surrounding human rights and child marriage (see Section 1.5).

Through this book, I deconstruct and challenge the taken-for-granted definition and assumptions in the child marriage framework, reconstruct the framework, and make it more relevant, efficient, and ethical. To do so, I use a case study approach, zooming in to study child marriage in Indonesia. Indonesia makes an excellent case to study how actors deal with different sets of rules regarding child marriage practices, for several reasons explained in the next section.

1.2. Case study: Indonesia

The first reason is that Indonesia is a Muslim majority country with a strong presence of Islamic organizations and norms. The Indonesian government is actively involved in international conventions and has set development goals that aim to end child marriage and comply with human rights standards.

It simultaneously faces social and political resistance and a complex reality. Resistance towards policies and laws against child marriage, which at times comes from conservative Muslim groups, present a sharp contrast with groups with more liberal ideas such as organizations for women's rights and child protection. For instance, in 2014, these organizations requested a judicial review of the 1974 Marriage Law at the Constitutional Court. The event triggered heated debates about the minimum age for marriage. The debates went beyond the minimum age for marriage: They were about human rights and development, as well as religious faith and sexual morality (see Chapter 3).

Second, the Indonesian legal system is pluralistic, which studies have documented exhaustively (see, e.g., Hooker 1975; Lev 1972, 1973; Lukito 2013). Many studies related to legal pluralism in Indonesia centre around how the extra-judicial system works at local levels and how it affects particular policy making (see, e.g., Vel and Bedner 2015; Muur 2018; Crouch 2013; Safitri 2011). The plurality of norms and types of law is particularly evident in family law. While van Huis (2015) and O'Shaughnessy (2009) take on the issue of divorce, Butt (2008) examines polygamy and mixed marriage cases, and Benda-Beckmann (1984) and Bowen (2003) and consider inheritance disputes. In comparison, child marriage in Indonesia remains an underexplored area of study. Still, the extensive literature on the pluralistic Indonesian legal system is useful towards disentangling the complex relationships between the different legal systems and actors involved.

Third, Indonesia has regional variations. Jones (2001) has documented regional differences and changes in the average marriage age. The BPS report (Badan Pusat Statistik (BPS) 2016) has recorded child marriage prevalence in each province (*provinsi*) and district (*kabupatan*) (see Section 1.3). Due to this regional variation, the research on child marriage in Indonesia is both challenging and compelling. To study child marriage in Indonesia in different regions, I organized a series of workshops in Jakarta together with both Dutch and Indonesian colleagues. The workshops resulted in a 12 chapter edited volume that complements studies of contemporary child marriage in Indonesia. The volume focuses on South Sulawesi, South and West Sumatra, West Nusa Tenggara, West, Central, and East Java, and DI Yogyakarta (Grijns et al. 2019). Yet, child marriage practices in Indonesia's Muslim-minority areas are still under-researched.

Therefore, to zoom in further, I chose to conduct fieldwork in Bali, a Muslim-minority area of Indonesia with mainly Hindu populations. At the national debates about the minimum age for marriage, the national Hindu organization representing their region (PHDI, *Parisada Hindu Dharma Indonesia*) seems to support the international norm of the marriageable age of 18 (Parlina 2014). This stance contrasts with the Islamic religious organizations' opposition to raising the marriageable age and the dominance of the *zinah* discourse in national and local debates among Indonesian Muslims. The prevalence of child marriage is relatively low in Bali. The data between 2008 and 2012 shows that 15.6% of ever-married women aged 20 to 24 in Bali were first married before age 18, while the national average is 25.4% (Badan Pusat Statistik (BPS) 2016: 59). In 2017, the average age of first marriage in Bali (23.0%) is also above the average of Indonesia (21.8%) (Badan Pusat Statistik (BPS) n.d.) While child marriage in Bali may not be as pronounced as in other provinces of Indonesia, it is one of the nine provinces where child marriage prevalence has been increasing recently (Badan Pusat Statistik (BPS) 2016; see also Section 1.3). Thus, the study of child marriage in Bali challenges the common assumption that child marriage is linked to orthodox Muslim beliefs. It also allows me to explore other possible explanations. Although the main area of my study is Bali, I occasionally refer to conditions in West Java, where I previously conducted relatively short fieldwork (see Horii 2020). The comparison between the two areas reveals the role of cultural practices and beliefs in child marriage patterns (discussed in Chapters 4 and 5).

Lastly, there are complex relations between changing marriage patterns and the persistently high rate of child marriage, which are worth investigating. The next section discusses them in detail.

1.3. Child marriage in Indonesia and changing marriage patterns

The most prominent record on marriage age in Indonesia to date is demographic research conducted by Gavin Jones. He emphasized the regional differences in marriage patterns. He concluded that of all Indonesians, West Javanese Muslims had the youngest female age of marriage (age 16.6) until the late 1960s. But since then, their marital age has started to rise, and Madurese speakers have become the earliest-marrying group (age 17.6 in the 1980s) (Jones 2001: 4). There have been other notable changes in marriage patterns, such as the increase in women marrying someone of lower or the same education level, associated with the increase in female labour participation and improved educational opportunities (Utomo 2014: 6; Malhotra 1997: 448). These changes suggest that the number of women who marry young decreases in the natural course of modern social changes, in line with research in other countries (see, e.g., Saardchom and Lemaire 2005; Garenne 2004).

Indeed, Cammack et al. (1996) found a significant decline in the early marriage of women and a corresponding rise in female marriage age. All women getting married below age 16 fell from about 40% in 1961 to about 20% in 1985. According to UNICEF, this decline has continued, with the percentage of women marrying below age 16 declining to 5.5%. They also associated these changes with modernization. The generation of new ideas about marriage became based more on female autonomy. This change occurred due to education, exposure to different cultural practices, and the destabilization of institutionalized beliefs regarding parental authority and female autonomy. According to the authors, the enactment of the Marriage Law 1974 had a slight effect on the decline of marriages in cities by having contributed to the destabilization of ideas but overall had no significant independent effect (Cammack, Young, and Heaton 1996: 71–72).

Yet, according to the 2013 national household survey, 25% of all women aged 20–24 who had ever been married, still got married before the age of 18. This percentage even increased slightly between 2010 and 2012 (Badan Pusat Statistik (BPS) 2016). This rise is associated with an increase in child marriage prevalence in urban areas since 2008. In rural areas, child marriage prevalence has been steadily decreasing: 33.5% in 2008 to 29.2% in 2012. By contrast, in urban areas it rose from 18.8% in 2008 to 19.0% in 2012 (Ibid) (see Section 5.5.1). What UNICEF Indonesia (2016) finds worrying is the recorded increase in marriage among girls aged 16–17 between 2008 and 2012. The increased child marriage prevalence in urban areas, as well as the rise of female (mid- to late-) teenage marriage, seems at odds with what we would expect from the modernization changes mentioned above.

What are the factors affecting the prevalence of child marriage? The UNICEF report and the BPS report show that low education levels and poverty are closely linked with child marriage prevalence. In 2015, girls who married below the age of 18 were six times less likely to complete upper secondary school compared to girls who married after the age of 18 (45.4 % and 8.9 % respectively). The data also shows that many married adolescent girls do not complete education beyond the primary school level. It is two times more likely for married girls to drop out of or never attend primary school compared to unmarried girls (9.9% and 4.5% respectively) (UNICEF Indonesia & UNICEF 2016). However, it is difficult to determine whether girls stop going to school because they marry early or whether those who leave school early have little choice but to marry. To determine whether or not a causal relation exists requires qualitative assessment. Another UNICEF report finding is that, perhaps surprisingly, while child marriage is generally strongly associated with poverty, prevalence is still high among the wealthy. About one in eight girls marry before age 18 among wealthy households[2] in Indonesia. This prevalence indicates that the practice may be heavily influenced by other factors, including social and cultural norms that are accepted across all economic levels.

One of the UNICEF report's five recommendations is to "address social norms and cultural norms" by, e.g., "engaging local leaders" and "encouraging parents to make better investments in their daughters" (UNICEF Indonesia 2016: 6). Other organizations make a similar suggestion. Reports from the implementing committee of the Convention on the Elimination of All Forms of Discrimination against Women (hereafter CEDAW) invariably mention cultural norms as one of the most difficult challenges to address, particularly

2 The richest household among the five categories (poorest, poorer, middle, richer, and richest) by level of expenditure (UNICEF Indonesia, 2016).

when associated with religious interpretation (Committee on the Elimination of Discrimination against Women 2011). Plan International points out the strong influence of social norms playing a role in decision-making for marriage (Plan International Asia Regional Office & Coram International 2015). However, those reports tend to generalize what they call 'social norms'. They rarely discuss the content, mechanism, and diversity of the cultural, social, and religious norms. The way they use the term as a container category is not helpful towards addressing the issue and even risks misguiding possible solutions.

The most relevant work to date that addresses social norms regarding child marriage is the ethnographic study conducted by Mies Grijns in a West Javanese village. The study suggests that a key element in most child marriage cases is a fear of committing *zinah* (the sin of pre-marital sexual relations) (Grijns et al. 2016). A strong influence of religious norms on people's inclination to conclude and accept child marriages is also evident in the attempts to legalize child marriage. Parents ask the Islamic court for marriage dispensation to avoid *zinah*, and judges grant the dispensation referring to *zinah* (elaborated in Chapter 3). Marcoes (2016) has elaborated on the moral and social factors influencing the practice of child marriage. These factors include fear of being ridiculed by neighbours, fear of sin, the obligation for girls to relieve the burden on their parents, and fear of becoming an "old maid". These findings suggest that Islamic teaching and norms, such as *zinah*, have been an influential factor contributing to the prevalence of child marriage. However, Indonesian CSO Rumah Kita Bersama's extensive research project explained that Islamic texts do not actually promote the practice of child marriage (Ali et al. 2015).

Grijns has also developed a typology of underage marriage, which provides a useful point of departure for comparative purposes (Grijns et al. 2016):

1. Marriage according to orthodox values: For instance, girls are expected to marry simply because it is a family tradition to marry around the age of 15. In this case, parents usually do not see the use of continuing their education after elementary school and see being a good wife and mother as their ultimate destiny.
2. Marriage to escape serious problems at home, such as poverty or domestic violence: This is a type of marriage that mainly happens upon the initiative of the girls themselves. Examples include extreme poverty, where girls try to escape by marrying a boy with some economic perspective to create a better situation for themselves and to reduce the burden for their parents who have to raise more children.
3. Marriage of social orphans: This is child marriage that emanates from the neglect of girls by their parents and the wider community. This often starts because of broken homes or the absence of migrant parents. The parents do not raise their children but place them in the care of a grandmother or other relative.

4. Love matches (*suka sama suka*): These are becoming more popular and frequent due to increased mobility, attending secondary school outside of the village, and the possibilities of getting to know others via social media, Facebook in particular.
5. MBA (married by accident): This is an aggravating factor in all of the above cases. Usually the fear of being accused of *zinah* is enough for girls to take steps to get married.

This typology suggests that *zinah* is an underlying factor that plays different roles in each type of child marriage. Her findings are of particular importance because they show that underage marriage does not conform to the 'traditional' pattern of an arranged marriage and that new forms of underage marriage have emerged. Grijns suggests that the level of agency exercised by the married children varies depending on the types of child marriage.

The existing literature reviewed above indicates the strong influence of social norms on child marriage practice, amongst other factors. This influence means that, from the perspective of reformists, the issue seems difficult to resolve without addressing social needs (e.g., getting married to avoid stigma). This difficulty reminds me of the legal reform debates during the colonial era. Benda-Beckmann and Benda-Beckmann (2011) explain that Dutch scholars on Indonesian *adat* law (e.g., Van Vollenhoven and Snouck Hurgronje) proposed a gradual development within a community. They argued that gradual change was the only way for appropriate social and economic progress to occur without damaging the local social order. In today's context, only a gradual integration of human rights could bring about the intended outcomes in harmony with the local social order. Bedner and van Huis (2010) also argue that local concerns must be considered for the vernacularization of women's rights to be effective. Furthermore, Cammack, Bedner, and Van Huis (2015) have noted that since *Reformasi*[3] there have been important developments in the field of women's rights in Indonesia. However, they are argued in terms of different interpretations of Islamic law rather than human rights (Ibid). For reformists and advocates of women's rights (including child marriage activists), it is also important to consider that the transition from traditional to modern (and more westernized) societies may not systematically lead to progress regarding women's rights (Malhotra 1997:435). These discussions hint at the necessity of child marriage research that focuses on the nuanced understanding of socio-cultural conditions and the careful assessment of the consequences of the reformists' movements. This research project has been designed with attention to these elements; therefore the choice of ethnographic methods was necessary.

3 The period of political, legal, economic, and social reforms that followed President Suharto's resignation in 1998.

1.4. Doing children's rights' ethnography: Some notes on methodology

The challenges in doing ethnographic work include the time and resource required, ethical concerns, and troubled subjectivities. Let alone when the work involves adolescents. This section highlights some of the methodological issues in the relevant fields of study: (1) being 'lied to' by informants and attentive qualitative method, (2) value judgements in doing human rights ethnography, and 3) research with adolescents. These methodological explorations, in fact, offer some insights on the philosophical and ethical questions about subjectivity and engagement with local informants and adolescents in conducting research.

1.4.1. Being 'lied to' by informants and attentive qualitative method

Initially, I planned to combine qualitative with quantitative methods. The survey that I prepared with my colleagues and assistants was ready to be distributed to adolescents in several schools in Bali. However, while preparing the survey, I came to understand several limitations of quantitative methods in this research. Firstly, in the survey I was planning to distribute, I would not be able to use contexts and nuances both to ask questions and to understand their answers. The topic I was dealing with was personal and complex. I found it very difficult to design a user-friendly questionnaire that would be clear and easily understandable by adolescents. Secondly, the topic I was dealing with was a sensitive one, and the answers most likely included the most private and intimate information about the respondents' lives and beliefs. This type of information is not easily disclosed, and respondents in the survey would have had little motivation to answer the questions truthfully. There would be no reason for them to answer honestly. This expectation also came from my experience in the field: Informants occasionally 'lied' to me.

At the beginning of my fieldwork, I came to know Yuri,4 one of the informants. She was a courageous, smart, and hardworking woman in her 20s. We started to form a friendship as we met regularly. In the beginning, when the two of us were chatting at a café, I asked her if it was common for young people in Bali to have sex before marriage, and if she did herself. She said, "I had never had sex with my boyfriends. I want to keep it until I know about my boyfriend". At that time, I just thought, "So, she is a kind of 'the good girl' who follows social norms then". One day, about three months after we started our meetings, we were having lunch together at a *warung* (street-food stand). She was talking about some intimate experiences with her ex-boyfriends. The time

4 All of the informant names in this book are pseudonyms.

I needed to leave for the next appointment was approaching. I was thinking about how I should say that I needed to leave. But I hesitated. She was sharing a personal story, and I felt that she wanted to talk about it to me. So I stayed. It had been about one hour since we started to talk on the sofa by then. Then, she asked, "Do you have to leave? What time is your next appointment?" When I said, "It's okay –", before I finished the sentence, she continued, "Because actually, there is another thing I wanted to tell you". Then she continued, "I was not comfortable to tell this to anybody before, but I have been pregnant before", and started sharing her true experience, which included an abortion.

Such 'lies' turned out to be the most revealing information once different versions of the same story came about. I had two versions of the story from the same person because the relationship between us changed. This kind of revelation would not be possible in questionnaires. Of course, there is no certainty that the information I have collected through qualitative methods was the 'truth'. Margaret Mead is a famous and established anthropologist who has been lied to. Her study in Samoa, which has established her fame, has turned out to be based on lies by informants, as a way of mocking a foreigner. This revelation shook the whole discipline of anthropology. People asked: Is interviewing a reliable method? How do researchers deal with lies?

These were also the questions I asked myself when I discovered these 'lies'. The discovery made me question my research integrity, the relationship with my informants, and the accuracy of my previous and future interviews. But I also realized that their 'lies' are also their 'truth'. This was how they decided to tell (or not tell) me what had happened. They are not 'lies', but only 'the act of lying'. To increase the accuracy of my data, I cross-checked the information I collected from interviews with various actors, as well as with reports and court judgements. Although I can never be sure of the complete accuracy of the information I collected, 'the attentive qualitative method' allowed me to read the information in a more detailed *context.*

The attentive qualitative method pays attention to the contexts and nuances and uses them both to ask questions and to understand their narratives. I always took extensive notes both during and after the interviews. The notes included what had been said but also situations, gestures, facial expressions, tones, pauses, paces of speech, and my feelings as an observer. Two of the examples from my field notes read:

> When we came in, Nina was cheerful, smiling and hosting us. When she talks, she uses some gestures that are very teenager-like, such as touching her hair and ears or putting her hands together. It felt a bit strange, as it seemed that she possesses both the innocence of teenagers and the sensibility of grown-ups at the same time.

> When D was talking, he was very clear in the way he talked and in what he said. He also remembered in detail the date of the events, etc. I wondered

> why, maybe it was because he thought about it a lot or he repeated it a lot during the legal process. S was from the beginning very nervous and obviously not content to be in that room. He constantly was moving nervously, touching his ears and hands. He also constantly looked away, his eyes moving all the time from here to there. He also answered very shortly, only with a few words.

When I worked with research assistants, I also instructed them to make extensive notes on these details. I always accompanied them for the interviews they conducted to see the details myself. The survey would have been limited in its capacity to extract information in such detail.

1.4.2. Value judgements in doing human rights ethnography: Multivocality and reflexivity

One of the challenges in conducting an anthropological study of human rights is dealing with our own value judgement. Collecting and analysing data from a one-sided perspective is one of the greatest risks that many ethnographers of human rights face. For instance, Montgomery, based on her experience of conducting ethnographic research on child prostitutes in Thailand, explains that researchers themselves have their moral values about children's rights and that these values affect how they perceive the situation (Montgomery 2007: 427). I myself, at the beginning of this research project, saw child marriage as a human rights violation, just as the human rights discourse framed. Slowly and gradually, I started to realize that this discourse was based on certain assumptions about what 'child' and 'marriage' mean and that those meanings were not necessarily universally relevant.

There are at least two ways to tackle this issue. One is multivocality, i.e., including multiple and various voices in qualitative methods (Tracy 2010: 844). And in order to include the various voices, collaboration with local actors was particularly important for this project. Throughout my fieldwork in Bali, I was working with LBH Apik Bali (*Lembaga Bantuan Hukum Asosiasi Perempuan Indonesia untuk Keadilan Bali*, Legal Aid Association of Indonesian Women for Justice), a local branch of a national CSO providing legal assistance for vulnerable people, e.g., women and children from low-income families. The association was interested in my topic and supported my research. For instance, they introduced me to a 17-year-old-girl and her family, who was in the process of a legal case against her ex-boyfriend, who made her pregnant (see Chapter 4). Working with them gave me access to key interviewees (such as children, local leaders, and judges) and opportunities for participant observation. During the latter, I observed how these intermediaries 'translate' (Merry 2006b) rights norms into local terms through legal awareness programmes and how they use various legal systems to strategize their objective to protect their clients.

With LBH Apik, I organized a workshop at the end of my fieldwork. In the workshop, I first presented my findings and discussed the issues related to child marriage in Bali with local actors. The topics included: (1) Causes and consequences of teenage pregnancy, (2) prosecution for pre-marital sexual intercourse between adolescent lovers, (3) marriage dispensation, (4) the legal position of unwed mothers, (5) laws and policies on contraceptive means, and (6) child marriage cases not resulting from pregnancy. I shared the real-life examples of problems that pregnant teenagers faced in Balinese society, particularly in relation to their legal rights under both state and customary law. The participants were all key persons in Bali for the topic, such as staff from the Marriage Registration Office (*Kantor Catatan Sipil*), members from religious/*adat* organizations, and organizations for the protection of women and children.

I organized this workshop for three reasons. First, to 'give back' to the local community, I wanted to share the findings for local actors to utilize in some ways. For that purpose, instead of making a report and presenting problems and solutions from my perspective, I wanted the local actors to formulate what they thought were the problems and solutions. Second, I aimed to use this workshop as an FGD, and as an opportunity to collect further information. I prepared a set of questions for each participant and assigned a research assistant to make notes of all the discussions and opinions shared during the workshop.

Third, the workshop was my way of contributing to LBH Apik's goal. Their clients include victims of domestic violence, women who need legal recourse and advice about divorce and custody proceedings, and child victims of sexual violence. Sharing the interview results with them and other stakeholders and discussing concrete solutions was consistent with their goals. As local key persons, the participants had the potential to impact local practice with the workshop's insights.

I also worked closely with local research assistants. They were two young women and one young man, all Balinese and in their 20s, whom I hired as research assistants. Over time, they also became my friends and colleagues. I held regular meetings with them, where I encouraged them to take the initiative and freely express their opinions about the research approach, methods, and interpretations. With time, they also started to confide in me enough to share the most intimate and private information about young Balinese life. They were of great help in expanding my network in Bali for looking for informants. I conducted most interviews with one of them, although sometimes with more than one, and sometimes alone. During the interviews, they helped me linguistically (especially when informants talked in Balinese), in understanding the social codes, and in interpreting what informants had said.

Overall, working with the local organization and the assistants was a crucial part of this research. It gave me opportunities to consider locally sensitive solutions to the issue, instead of blindly imposing a foreign standard that could be irrelevant to the local situation. In other words, such collaboration provided me with differently "situated knowledge" (Haraway 1988) that I otherwise had limited access to because of my positionality.

Situating knowledge, or reflexivity, for this research project was another way to grapple with the value judgement. The myth of silent authorship has been proven false (Charmaz and Mitchell 1996) and reflexivity is a standard practice in today's anthropology of writing through which researchers identify themselves. However, reflexivity is not only about writing about ourselves to reflect on how our subjectivities play a role in our research but also an attitude towards fair accounts and storytelling.

As a part of the reflexive effort, when I interviewed those who married before the age of 18, I deliberately did not apply the label 'child bride' to them. I consider this label as one of the "Western diagnostic labels" (Wikan 1990: 137) that prevent researchers like myself from truly understanding local reality. Such labels obscure fair accounts in studying individual cases. Montgomery (2007) also describes how such labels overshadowed her understanding of the children in Thailand. She claims it is crucial to acknowledge that such anthropological work on children does not always give researchers the answers that we expect and that our ideas about children may be profoundly challenged (Ibid: 429). Other examples of prejudices in relation to my informants include 'traditional practices are harmful to women', 'child marriage is bad for children', and 'child brides are victims, and their families are poor and uneducated'. By seeing the early-married girls without these labels, it became apparent to me that married children were not simply passive victims of a child marriage that had been forced upon them. Contrary to the stereotype of child marriage involving a young girl, there were many boys who married before the age of 18. About 75% of my case studies involve both girls and boys as underage parties, half of which are cases where boys are younger than girls.

Reflexivity also sheds light on relational aspects of fieldwork. Fieldwork involves intense relational work (Coffey 1999: 39), all the more if the research deals with intimate topics such as marriage and pregnancy. Interpretivism rests on the idea that information varies depending on the context in which the information was retrieved. Under this assumption, the relationship between the researcher and the researched should be a part of the analysis. For instance, I brought my then three-year-old daughter to my fieldwork, and her presence had some impact on the relational work there. When establishing local relationships, a child's presence was the best reason for both sides to start a conversation. We became more accessible to each other. When meeting informants who have small children, I sometimes brought my daughter with me so that they could relate to us and let their children play with her. In this sense, having a child helped me get to know people and enter the community, and it helped deepen and maintain my relationships with them.

Concerning the relational aspects of data collection, positionality is also relevant, i.e., the researcher's role, image, representation, self-identification, and identification by others. My daughter's presence in the field naturally accentuated my positionality as a mother. My being a mother and motherhood coincided with that of young mothers. In interviews with some of my informants,

I consciously shared my personal profile and stories, that I am a young unmarried mother. Despite some painful differences between us, such as class and education, I focused on finding and emphasizing commonalities. For instance, there was a moment when Ratna, one of the informants, opened up to me, after which she started to share her intimate and private experiences. Our conversation at that moment went as follows:

Ratna: Wow, M (my daughter's name) is so smart.
Author: Because her mother also studies! (Ratna was a teenage single mother, who continued her education regardless of the situation)
Ratna: Haha yes, that is true ... Hoko, if you live in the Netherlands now, are your parents far away?
Author: Yes, my parents live in Japan, so I come back to Japan once every year to see them. You have a very nice mother. She supports you all the time.
Ratna: yes, that is right. She is a very nice mother.
Author: My mother too. When I heard your story yesterday, I remembered my story and my mother.
Ratna: We are the same, aren't we, Hoko?
Author: Yes, we are the same.

Being a mother myself also impacted how I interpreted the informants' accounts. Fieldwork is also personal, emotional, and identity work (Coffey 1999: 1). When I listen to and write the stories of the young mothers in Bali, I do so through my own experiences of becoming a mother, making life choices, dealing with daily tasks, feeling vulnerable, and finding strength. Retrospectively, the (re)construction of my identity during the fieldwork was itself more than a tool for collecting information but became part of the information itself. My identity as a young, educated, and single mother is an uncommon one in most places, including and perhaps particularly in my home country of Japan and in my fieldwork site, Bali. During my fieldwork, I sent several emails to friends, one of which shows how this identity sometimes played an informative role:

> *Also, while having lunch with D (one of my Balinese friends), she asked me about M (my daughter) and her father, so I shared my story. I always answer openly when people ask me that kind of question, but people usually do not ask and keep wondering where the father is, or just assume that he works and lives away, etc. Apparently, it took her 3 months to ask me that question.*

When people in Bali assumed that I was married given that I had a child, in certain contexts, I sometimes chose not to deny it and let them continue to see me as a 'normal' mother. I did so partly consciously, knowing that being a 'normal' (married) mother would probably enable a smoother process in connecting with them, without raising unnecessary suspicion, discomfort, or gossip. And perhaps also unconsciously, I did so by sensing the atmosphere and the need to be accepted there. How I experienced my identity through local interactions further confirmed that strong social structures around the shame of being an unmarried mother existed in Bali. This structure was exactly the reason why local teenagers were marrying.

This is the "outward" part of reflexivity in the double reflexive gaze (Rose 1997). While the inward gaze explores the identity of the researcher, the outward gaze tries to locate the self in knowledge production. Concerning knowledge production, the fact that the author has the power to interpret and write about the stories is a significant determiner of power relations between the research and the researched. Trying to flatten this inherent power imbalance by engaging with the perspectives of the researched is a complex task. My perspective was dynamic and fluid, floating between theirs, others, and mine. It kept changing throughout the process, through gaining access to informants, interviewing, leaving the field, analysing, and writing. Such a process was confusing, and integrating all of the perspectives was indeed "a god-trick" (Haraway 1988: 581). Such an outcome may even be undesirable, as aligning one's perspective too closely with those of the researched arguably limits a critical stance and self-awareness (i.e., the risk of over-familiarization and immersion (Coffey 1999: 34)).

Distancing one's perspectives to flatten the power imbalance is bound to fail. A person cannot see north and south at the same time. Instead, one can go back and forth between two (or more) positions repeatedly. Engaging with 'their' perspectives was an intense enough task for me during fieldwork. I needed time and distance after returning from fieldwork to make space to view the different perspectives. I needed to distance myself both physically, metaphysically, spatially, and temporally. This is not the solution to the problem of the power imbalance in knowledge production. Still, if reflexivity's goal is set to produce humble knowledge that learns from other kinds of knowledge, one must allow oneself distance in every sense to create space for reflexivity.

1.4.3. Research with adolescents and ethics

Research involving children is methodologically challenging. ERIC (Ethical Research Involving Children) is an international guideline for researchers who conduct ethical research involving children. It ensures that the children's rights and wellbeing are respected in every phase (Graham et al. 2013). The guideline covers four main concerns: (1) Harms and benefits, (2) informed consent, (3) privacy and confidentiality, and (4) payment and compensation. All of these concerns are applicable to research in general, but some contain particular or additional challenges in research involving children.

For instance, one such issue is the limits of interviews. As a researcher interviewing children on sensitive subjects, I often needed to decide how far I could go in listening to them and asking them questions. While some were willing and even eager to talk, others were occasionally reluctant or hesitant to do so.

Any scholars ought not to force informants to talk in any way. This concern is especially important when interviewing children, for whom it might be more difficult to express their unwillingness due to a lack of experience and their perceived social position. Considering that listening to children can be intrusive and cause distress (Roberts 2000), I carefully observed them for signs of reluctance or hesitance. For instance, when I saw one of the informants nervously shaking his legs and never touching the food during the interview at a restaurant, I considered it a sign of reluctance and did not ask him for another interview. On another occasion, when a teenage girl with a traumatic experience started crying as she described distressing nightmares, I told her she could contact me if she needed somebody to talk to, but never contacted her again myself.

Another issue is informed consent. Some might ask whether children are capable of providing consent at all. One might assume that children lack the cognitive and moral capacity to make informed decisions about their participation in research. However, such an assumption has been challenged by studies showing that children, including those who are very young or have learning difficulties, can make informed decisions when provided with appropriate information (Powell et al. 2012: 13–21). Therefore, resolving this issue is perhaps less about determining whether children are capable of providing consent and more about whether researchers can provide information in a way that children understand the consequences of their consent (Graham et al. 2013: 59).

This ethical concern points to the essence of this book: The complexity of 'listening to children'. Komulainen (2007) warns researchers who aim to 'listen to [a] child's voice' that voices are always social and thus that researchers have to consider the social dynamics in interactions with children. A power imbalance is present in any relationship between researchers and the researched, but it is of particular importance when interviewing children. As I described above, I paid particular attention to signs of reluctance because I assumed that 'it might be more difficult for children to express unwillingness due to lack of experience and their perceived social position'. This relational aspect shall be carefully considered when 'listening to children's voices'. However, the intention of 'protecting' children, if taken too far, could result in liberal paternalism, which is exactly what I challenge in this research. In short, this need and wish to protect children from harm should not overshadow their agency. Chapter 6 will elaborate on the agency of children and the thin line between the protection and empowerment of children.

To 'listen to children', we need to recognize them as subjective agents. This is not as self-evident as it might sound. It was only in the 1970s when scholars started to challenge the assumptions embedded in what is implied in the concept of 'a child' (Garnier 2015). Before, children were regarded as a passive object for protection, with neither 'voice' nor 'agency'. The whole field of 'childhood studies' is marked by orienting studies on children towards the social sciences, started by recognizing them as active agents worth being studied in their own light. The sociology of childhood has experienced a paradigm shift by regarding children as active agents and recognizing their voices (James and Prout 1997; Leonard 2015).

Subjectivity is the precondition of agency. As described in the research question, when I try to understand '*why they marry*', I am also trying to understand '*what for them are the reasons to get married*'. Here, I am focusing on their subjectivity. Put simply, I am taking them seriously. Ethnographic investigations of children's subjectivity can offer new ways of understanding and explaining children's experiences (Williams 2016: 344).

I use the category of 'children' in this book to analyse the international framework, which defines a child as a person who is below 18 years old. However, during fieldwork, I did not consider informants as *children*. Somewhat instinctively, I treated them as equals and not as less knowledgeable, mature, or capable. I believe this made all the difference. From the viewpoint of constructivism, subjectivity is dependent on relations (Hill 2006: 70). Therefore, if informants are treated as incompetent or as victims, they are more inclined to act like one. Blazek (2016: 34) also points to the dynamic, interactive, and flexible approach to fieldwork, destabilizing the boundaries between the researcher and the researched and challenging the imagination of the passive field and the active researcher. Foucault (1998: 291) explains that subjectivities are "not something invented by the individual himself". Instead, subjectivities are "the models that he finds in his culture and that are proposed, suggested, imposed upon him by his culture, his society and his social group". By this logic, unequal relations reinforce the subjectivity of children even when they are not necessarily incompetent or victims. For instance, their response might have been different if I interviewed them explicitly as 'child brides'.

This approach simultaneously deconstructs the concept of childhood and adulthood. Discussing children's agency is difficult because of this underlying dichotomy. Agency, as an anthropological and sociological concept, is based on the idea of reasoning and rationality (Giddens 1979). Rationality is what is considered to distinguish adulthood from childhood (see Section 2.1.2). However, such dichotomic categorization is not realistic (Johansson 2012: 112), and children are constantly in transition between the two. Two of the case studies illustrate this ambiguity well.

In one case, a 17-year-old boy decided to marry his girlfriend when she became pregnant. From how he described the decision-making process, it was evident that his decision at that time was informed by social structure: The social norms, connections, and expectations surrounding him. He said, "I was a bit scared, but my father told me that I just need to accept the fate and marry her". At the same time, he believes that "you have to marry when there is pregnancy of your child". In this sense, his decision was informed by social structure in two ways: He wanted to be a good son and a good father.

In the second case, I met a 14-year-old girl for the first time just after she gave birth. She was holding her two-week-old baby in her arms while being engaged in household chores. Then she looked like a young mother in her late teens. However, when she said she was very happy about having a baby and wanted another child, her shy and innocent smile reminded me that she was still 14.

1.5. Key concepts and terminologies

It would be useful in this chapter to outline the definitions I use for the key concepts and terminologies in this book: *Tradition, modernity, choice (agency, autonomy), structure, child marriage framework, children, international/local.*

1.5.1. Tradition

The international human rights framework categorizes child marriage as a 'harmful traditional practice' (The Fourth World Conference on Women 1995). In this book, I challenge such an essentialized way of using the word 'tradition' and critically examine the way the international human rights framework uses the term. While the international human rights community often criticizes 'harmful traditional practices', it hardly discusses 'non-harmful traditional practices'. This contrast is because tradition is a mirror image of modernity: Discourse on tradition reflects the ideology and beliefs of the creators of the discourse, subsuming the reverse image of modernity as something undesirable. Therefore, it is important to pay attention to the *modernification* of discourse on tradition, which (re)produces the stereotypes of tradition without considering each context. It is even likely that what is called 'tradition' is somewhat 'invented' by the international community. This possibility of "invented tradition" was first coined by Hobsbawn and Ranger (1983), whose work transformed the anthropological notion of tradition in the 1980s. Hence, the way the international human rights discourse uses 'tradition' is factually and anthropologically obsolete (see Chapter 2).

1.5.2. Modernity

'Modernity' is an important concept in this book, but it is also a loaded concept that needs careful specification. In this book, I use modernity to mean a changing social condition. I borrow Gidden's idea that the modern world is where social life is "open" with multiple lifestyle choices (Giddens 1991: 6). He understands modernity as a post-traditional order in which lifestyle choice is increasingly important in the constitution of self-identity and daily-activity (Ibid: 6, 13). In this study, this choice is exemplified in increasing educational opportunities, engagement in career planning, and consequent mobility, with children having more opportunities and spaces to meet and mingle with the opposite gender. An increased prevalence of mobile-phone usage gives youngsters access outside of their communities and provides tools to communicate with their love interests via texts. Chapter 5 engages more with this concept.

1.5.3. Choice, agency, autonomy, and structure

The modern world is then where individuals' choices become and are considered increasingly important. The human rights framework subscribes to this ideal: Ignatieff (2003) and Merry (2009: 385, 404) demonstrate that the protection of agency is the core principle in human rights discourse (see Section 2.3). Santos (2015: 6) also argues that collective rights are not part of the original canon of human rights, and the priorities continue to be accorded to individual rights over collective rights. Indeed, the ideals of modernity are at the base of international advocacy to 'end child marriage'. The ideal is that individuals should be fully autonomous and emancipated, 'free' from social norms that chain them. This approach is what Mackenzie (2013) calls a libertarian understanding of autonomy.

In contrast, this book's analysis rests on the relational understanding of agency. According to Gidden's theory of agency and structure, agency is the capacity to observe one's experience and give reasons for one's actions (Tucker 1999: 80). Another influential concept of agency in anthropology is "agentival capacity". This idea encompasses acts that resist norms and the multiple ways one inhabits norms (Mahmood 2004: 15). For instance, the recent debates over the regulations on headscarves have revealed that what seems like a symbol of oppression to an outsider can be a Muslim woman exercising her autonomy. According to these understandings, agency is an ability to choose by making internal reconciliations with structure, i.e., patterned arrangements that influence or limit available choices. And such choice, limited by one's sense of moral community, is not less rational than that of the imagined full autonomy (Rorty 1998: 178).

In his concept of liquid modernity, Bauman (2000: 8) points out that individuals do not become free from structures. Traditional structures do not disappear but are replaced by self-chosen ones. This point also highlights that the structure that actors interact with is not the essentialized 'culture' or 'tradition' but persons with whom they are in relationships. To unpack the social connection that constitutes 'structure', I use the socio-psychological concept of 'reference network', which I will explain in Chapter 5. This understanding of structure and agency is crucial for discussions on consent in marriage.

The recognition of everyone's agency is an important topic among critical scholars of international human rights and development. The dominant discourse has often misrepresented or underrepresented the agency and subjectivity of "Third World Woman" (Mohanty 1984; Spivak 2010). Engle similarly points out the failure of the international human rights' to engage with the "Exotic Other Female" (Engle 1992). The agency of girls in the Third World is in the most precarious position in international development discourse (see Section 5.8). The relational understanding of autonomy or agency is crucial to challenging the paternalistic notions of development.

1.5.4. Child marriage framework, child marriage, early marriage, forced marriage, arranged marriage, underage marriage, and marriage

In this book, the '*child marriage framework*' means the basic structure upon which international organizations deal with child marriage practice, including its definition, discourse, and the relevant legal rules. According to the definition of international institutions, 'child marriage' means "any formal marriage or informal union where one or both of the parties are under 18 years of age". In this book, I use this definition of 'child marriage' to evaluate this framework. 'Early marriage' in international discourse is often used in the same sense. The international child marriage framework frames all child marriage as 'forced marriage', i.e., as marriage without 'consent'. However, throughout the book, I will demonstrate that there is an important difference between the two. Bunting et al. (2016) elaborates on the difference between forced marriage and arranged marriage. Families may arrange marriages that are still based on the full and free consent of the two spouses. By contrast, forced marriage is conducted without such consent. According to these researchers, real autonomy means an ability to say no under the conditions of social, economic, and gender equality, which needs to be distinguished from habitual acquiescence, assent, silent dissent, submission, or enforced submission. I will discuss the meaning of autonomy under social, cultural, and economic constraints later in this book.

I use 'underage marriage' to mean a marriage under the minimum age for marriage under the respective state law. It can be a civil marriage that is somehow registered illegally or a customary or religious marriage without state registration (see Chapters 3 and 4). Thus, this book's definition of 'marriage' is not limited to civil marriage or state-registered marriage but refers more broadly to a socially approved relationship, including customary and religious marriage. It is also noteworthy that, in spite of the varied meanings and forms of marriage throughout human history, no international treaty currently includes a good definition of 'marriage'. Does it mean only a civil marriage, or does it also include religious marriage without state registration? Does it imply a direct consummation or cohabitation? If it includes 'informal' customary marriage, what about cohabitation of teenagers in the West? These are important questions to ask when discussing 'child marriage'. Chapter 7 will return to this point.

1.5.5. Children, adolescents, and teenagers

'Children' in this book refers to the category of those who are below 18 years old, adopting the international definition of children (see Section 2.1.2). I use this category to assess to what extent this large cohort as a homogenous category contributes to the realization of 'children's rights', as laid down in international instruments such as children's rights conventions. 'Adolescents' (from the Latin 'adolescere', meaning 'to grow up') or 'youth' is the broadest category I use here, referring to those who are 10 to 24 years old. They are the protagonists of this book. Most of the informants whose accounts I relied on for analysis fall into the category of adolescents. I also refer to those who are 13 to 19 years old as 'teenagers'. When appropriate, this group is divided into three sub-categories: Early teenage (13 and 14), mid-teenage (15 and 16), and late-teenage (17 to 19).

1.5.6. International/local

The 'child marriage framework' that I refer to in this book is an '*international*' one. Merry's theory of 'vernacuralization' helps to clarify what international and local mean here. She explains that a key dimension of the vernacuralization process is the people in the middle, who work to negotiate between local, regional, national, and global systems of meaning (2013: 211). These different levels, defined in both geographical and socio-economic terms (e.g., social class, education, mobility, and cosmopolitan awareness of elites), are relevant for the analysis of the transformation of the norms at each level (Ibid). Structures at the international level, such as international human rights conventions, are made to adopt universal moral frameworks. These frameworks face tensions and contradictions with the particularities of each locality. I am also aware that there are several local programmes and movements on the issue of child marriage. These initiatives are informed by the international framework and 'vernacularized', 'localized', or 'translated' to a varied extent in each context. For the sake of analysis, I use these terms to define the 'child marriage framework' as an international one, constructed by various international institutions, including UN institutions (e.g., UNICEF, UNFPA, CEDAW, and CRC) and international CSOs (e.g., Girls Not Brides, Plan International, and Equality Now).

1.6. Multi-layered analysis

Through the case study approach, I assess international trends and perspectives and how they differ from the diversity of provincial, and individual practices of child marriage. All chapters have implications and connections with international debates about child marriage, while empirical data is collected at various levels. Accordingly, each chapter uses different data sets, as shown in Table 1.1.

Chapter 2 examines in two parts how child marriage is constructed at the international level. The first step traces the establishment of child marriage as a discursive practice since the 1960s, analysing international conventions and general recommendations regarding child marriage. The second step unpacks

Table 1.1 Level of analysis, methods, scope, and types of data sets used in each chapter

Chap.	*Level of analysis*	*Methods*	*Scope of data*	*Types of data*
2	international	legal analysis and discourse analysis of international documents	international	1) conventions and general recommendations regarding child marriage that were issued by international human rights institutions since the 1960s 2) reports about child marriage published by major international organizations in the period between 2001 and 2016
3	national, provincial	socio-legal analysis of Indonesian law-making and implementation, social practice in West Java	national, provincial	1) legal texts in Indonesia and their historical conception 2) interviews and case analysis at religious courts in West Java 3) ethnographic research in a village in West Java (conducted by Grijns)
4	provincial	fieldwork in Bali, legal case-study analysis of court decisions	provincial	1) interviews and case analysis from civil courts in Bali 2) interviews with judges, marriage registrars, *adat* law scholars, and children and their families who were involved in legal cases
5	provincial, individual	fieldwork in Bali, interviews and Focus Group Discussions with actors, analysis of case studies	provincial	1) interviews and Focus Group Discussions with Balinese adolescents, legal practitioners, CSO staff members, government officials, health care personnel, and teachers 2) case studies of child marriage or/and teenage pregnancy among the Balinese Hindu populations
6	individual, international	fieldwork in Bali, analysis of case studies and interviews with early-married couples	provincial	1) case studies of child marriage among the Balinese Hindu populations 2) interviews with those between 14 and 28 years old who married below the age of 18

the dominant child marriage discourse by analysing the use of specific languages in reports about child marriage published by major international organizations.

Chapter 3 analyses the way the Indonesian government and state agents deal with the social reality that children continue to marry, focusing on two levels: (1) law-making at the national level (Indonesia) and (2) the implementation of the law at the provincial level (West Java). At the national level of society, child marriage is a political contestation, as illustrated in the long-lasting debates on the marriageable age. To study how the state rules are implemented in practice, I use the case study of West Java, focusing on the role of intermediary actors in facilitating underage marriage to accommodate local needs and concerns.

Chapter 4 focuses on the provincial level (Bali), investigating how state authorities try to enforce their rules and norms. I focus on Balinese Hindu practices to identify the role of their *adat* law. Courts are where judges try to compromise between state law, religious law, and social norms. Therefore, they are a particularly interesting place to observe the tension between different legalities (Bowen 1998: 385). I accordingly investigated cases related to marriage dispensation and sex crimes at the *Pengadilan Negeri* (civil court).

Chapter 5 investigates child marriage practices in Bali and the socio-cultural conditions in which children marry. It analyses the link between child marriage and adolescents' sexuality in Bali, based on interviews and Focus Group Discussions (FGD) that I conducted during my fieldwork in 2017. I also refer to some of the cases of child marriage, specifically to examine the relationship between teenage pregnancy and child marriage. By investigating the data collected in Bali, I also clarify what these area-specific data mean for the transnational movements and policies about child marriage.

Chapter 6 then focuses on children's subjectivities. It looks at individual cases of child marriage in Bali, focusing on how children exercise their agency in deciding their marriage, relying on interviews with those between 14 and 28 years old that married below the age of 18. Based on these empirical data in Bali, I evaluate the current international children's rights scheme, in which agency is an increasingly pressing matter.

1.7. Readership and social relevance

Following this Introduction, Chapters 2 to 5 were originally written as articles in different journals, although all have been substantially revised here (see Appendix 1 for the list of original articles). Thus, each chapter engages with different scholarly discussions. Chapter 2, originally an article published in *The International Journal of Human Rights*, engages with (critical) theories of human rights. Chapter 3, based on an article co-authored with Mies Grijns in *Asian Journal of Law and Society*, is a contribution to socio-legal studies of Indonesian family law. Chapter 4 was published previously as an article in *Journal of Legal Pluralism and Unofficial Law* and discusses the literature on legal pluralism and human rights. Chapter 5 was originally written as an article in the Special

Issue "Early Marriage" in *Progress in Development Studies*, situating agency and modernity in development studies. Chapter 6, an article published in *Childhood* journal, engages in the scholarly discussion on children's rights. Throughout the book, I have researched all types of material on child marriage, e.g., scholarly, advocacy, reports, and legal texts. My study aims to offer an alternative way of approaching the issue of child marriage.

As such, I hope this book reaches a varied readership. Firstly, it is relevant for scholars in various disciplines, including human rights, socio-legal studies, legal pluralism, legal anthropology, children's rights, youth studies, and Indonesian and Southeast Asian studies. I hope both the content and methodology are of interest and use and become a point of discussion. Secondly, I strongly believe that its relevance is not limited to the world of academics; it also applies to so-called practitioners. The practitioners include legislators, such as the UN treaty bodies and national legislative bodies, and those who support the process of legislative changes. For instance, national legislative bodies in several countries have now raised the minimum age for marriage under the national law, supported and celebrated by (mainly international) campaigns against child marriage. I hope my empirical findings can inform those policies.

Finally, I am confident that the findings and arguments in this book will benefit organizations and individuals who are engaged with projects to protect or enhance the human rights of people out there. The organizations can be large and both national and international: E.g., UNICEF, UNFPA, Ministries of Foreign Affairs, Plan International, Girls Not Brides. They can also be small CSOs who work at a national scale. I know many of these organizations and individuals who work most ardently and effectively, and I pay them enormous respect. Child marriage has become increasingly invested in the international women's rights and children's rights agenda. It is now crucial to re-examine, reflect, and discuss the general approach to child marriage, so that the invested time, human resources, finances, and passions are used constructively and effectively. I hope this book will be of use for that process.

Bibliography

Ali, M., Gunawan, R., Hilmi, A., & Mohammad, J. (2015). *Fikih Kawin Anak* (L. Marcoes & R. Gunawan, Eds.). Jakarta: Yayasan Rumah Kita Bersama.

Alves, J. A. L. (2000). The declaration of human rights in postmodernity. *Human Rights Quarterly, 22*(2), 478–500. https://doi.org/10.1353/hrq.2000.0018

An-Na'im, A. A. (1992). Introduction. In A. A. An-Na'im (Ed.), *Human Rights in Cross-Cultural Perspectives: A Quest for Consensus* (pp. 1–15). Philadelphia, PA: University of Pennsylvania Press.

Badan Pusat Statistik (BPS). (2016). *Kemajuan yang Tertunda: Analisis Data Perkawinan Usia Anak di Indonesia*. BPS.

Badan Pusat Statistik (BPS). (n.d.). Median Usia Kawin Pertama Perempuan Pernah Kawin Umur 25–49 Tahun Menurut Provinsi, 2012 dan 2017, https://www.bps.go.id/dynamictable/2018/06/06%2000:00:00/1445/median-usia-kawin-pertama-perempuan-pernah-kawin-umur-25-49-tahun-menurut-provinsi-2012.html (accessed on April 20, 2021).

Bauman, Z. (2000). *Liquid Modernity*. Cambridge, UK; Malden, MA: Polity.

BBC News. (2017) Teenager Weds Woman in Her 70s, https://www.bbc.com/news/world-asia-40529590 (accessed on April 20, 2021).

Bedner, A., & Van Huis, S. (2010). Plurality of marriage law and marriage registration for Muslims in Indonesia: A plea for pragmatism. *Utrecht Law Review*, *6*(2), 175–191.

Benda-Beckmann, F. von, & Benda-Beckmann, K. von (2011). Myths and stereotypes about adat law: A reassessment of Van Vollenhoven in the light of current struggles over adat law in Indonesia. *Bijdragen Tot de Taal-, Land- En Volkenkunde*, *167*(2/3), 167–195.

Benda-Beckmann, K. von (1984). *The Broken Stairways to Consensus: Village Justice and State Courts in Minangkabau*. Dordrecht, the Netherlands: Foris Publications.

Blackburn, S., & Bessell, S. (1997). Marriageable age: Political debates on early marriage in twentieth-century Indonesia. *Indonesia*, *63*, 107–141. https://doi.org/10.2307/3351513

Blazek, M. (2016). *Rematerialising Children's Agency: Everyday Practices in a Post-socialist Estate*. Bristol: Chicago: Policy Press.

Bodineau, S. (2014). Vulnerability and agency: Figures of child soldiers within the narratives of child protection practitioners in the democratic republic of Congo. *Autrepart*, *72*(4), 111–128.

Bowen, J. R. (1998). "You may not give it away": How social norms shape Islamic Law in contemporary Indonesian Jurisprudence. *Islamic Law and Society*, *5*(3), 382–408.

Bowen, J. R. (2003). *Islam, Law, and Equality in Indonesia: An Anthropology of Public Reasoning*. Cambridge, UK; New York, NY: Cambridge University Press.

Boyden, J. (1997). Childhood and the policymakers. In A. James & A. Prout (Eds.), *Constructing and Reconstructing Childhood: Contemporary Issues in the Sociological Study of Childhood* (pp. 184–215). London, UK: Falmer Press.

Boyle, E. H., & Corl, A. C. (2010). Law and culture in a global context: Interventions to eradicate female genital cutting. *Annual Review of Law and Social Science*, *6*(1), 195–215. https://doi.org/10.1146/annurev-lawsocsci-102209-152822

Bunting, A., Lawrance, B. N., & Roberts, R. L. (2016). Something old, something new? In A. Bunting, B. N. Lawrance, & R. L. Roberts (Eds.), *Marriage by Force?: Contestation Over Consent and Coercion in Africa* (pp. 1–40). Athens, OH: Ohio University Press.

Butt, S. (2008). Polygamy and mixed marriage in Indonesia: Islam and the Marriage Law in the courts. In T. Lindsey (Ed.), *Indonesia: Law and Society* (pp. 266–287). Leichhardt, N.S.W.: The Federation Press.

Cammack, M., Bedner, A., & Huis, S. van (2015). Democracy, human rights, and Islamic family law in post-soeharto Indonesia. *New Middle Eastern Studies*, *5*, 1–24.

Cammack, M., Young, L. A., & Heaton, T. (1996). Legislating social change in an Islamic Society-Indonesia's Marriage Law. *The American Journal of Comparative Law*, *44*(1), 45–73. https://doi.org/10.2307/840520

Campbell, A. (2013). Wives' tales on research in Bountiful. In R. Provost & C. Sheppard (Eds.), *Dialogues on Human Rights and Legal Pluralism* (pp. 247–268). Dordrecht; Heidelberg; New York; London: Springer.

Charmaz, K., & Mitchell, R. G. (1996). The myth of silent authorship: Self, substance, and style in ethnographic writing. *Symbolic Interaction, 19*(4), 285–302. https://doi.org/10.1525/si.1996.19.4.285

Chaudhuri, E. R. (2015). *Thematic Report: Unrecognised Sexual Abuse and Exploitation of Children in Child, Early and Forced Marriage*. ECPAT International, Bangkok.

Child Helpline International. (n.d.). *A Story from Malawi: Escaping Child Marriage to Find Empowerment in Education*. Child Helpline International. https://www.childhelplineinternational.org/youth/blog-youth/escaping-child-marriage-education-malawi/ (accessed on April 20, 2021).

Coffey, A. (1999). *The Ethnographic Self: Fieldwork and the Representation of Identity*. London; Thousand Oaks; New Delih: SAGE Publications.

Committee on the Elimination of Discrimination Against Women. (2011). *Consideration of Reports Submitted by States Parties under Article 18 of the Convention on the Elimination of All Forms of Discrimination against Women, CEDAW/C/IDN/6-7.*

Cowan, J. K. (2006). Culture and rights after culture and rights. *American Anthropologist, 108*(1), 9–24. https://doi.org/10.1525/aa.2006.108.1.9

Cowan, J. K., Dembour, M.-B., & Wilson, R. A. (2001). Introduction. In J. K. Cowan, M.-B. Dembour, & R. A. Wilson (Eds.), *Culture and Rights: Anthropological Perspectives*. Cambridge; New York: Cambridge University Press.

Cretney, S. (2005). *Family Law in the Twentieth Century: A History*. Oxford; New York: Oxford University Press.

Crouch, M. (2013). *Law and Religion in Indonesia: Conflict and the Courts in West Java*. Routledge.

De Feyter, K., & Parmentier, S. (2011). Introduction: Reconsidering human rights from below. In K. De Feyter, S. Parmentier, C. Timmerman, & G. Ulrich (Eds.), *The Local Relevance of Human Rights* (pp. 1–11). Cambridge University Press.

Dembour, M.-B. (2001). Following the movement of a pendulum: Between universalism and relativism. In J. K. Cowan, M.-B. Dembour, & R. A. Wilson (Eds.), *Culture and Rights: Anthropological Perspectives*. Oxon; New York: Cambridge University Press.

Desmet, E. (2012). Implementing the convention on the rights of the child for 'youth': Who and how? *International Journal of Children's Rights, 20*, 3–23.

Donnelly, J. (1984). Cultural relativism and universal human rights. *Human Rights Quarterly, 6*(4), 400–419. https://doi.org/10.2307/762182

Donnelly, J. (2003). *Universal Human Rights in Theory and Practice*. New York: Cornell University Press.

Engle, K. (1992). Female subjects of Public International Law: Human rights and the exotic other female symposium on feminist critical legal studies and postmodernism: Part two: The politics of gender identity. *New England Law Review, 26*, 1509–1526.

Equality Now. (2014). *Protecting the Girl Child: Using the Law to End Child, Early and Forced Marriage and Related Human Rights Violations*. New York; Nairobi; London: Equality Now.

Flynn, J. (2013). *Reframing the Intercultural Dialogue on Human Rights: A Philosophical Approach*. New York: Routledge.

Foucault, M. (1998). *Ethics: Subjectivity and Truth* (P. Rabinow, Ed.). New York: The New Press.

Fraser, J. (2018). *Every Organ of Society* [Doctoral Thesis]. Utrecht University.

Freeman, M. (1994). The philosophical foundations of human rights. *Human Rights Quarterly, 16*(3), 491–514. https://doi.org/10.2307/762434

Garenne, M. (2004). Age at marriage and modernisation in sub-Saharan Africa. *Southern African Journal of Demography, 9*(2), 59–79.

Garnier, P. (2015). The "Agency" of children. The "Childhood Studies" scientific and political project. *Éducation et société, 2*(36), 159–173.

Giddens, A. (1979). *Central Problems in Social Theory: Action, Structure, and Contradiction in Social Analysis*. Berkeley: University of California Press.

Giddens, A. (1991). *Modernity and Self-Identity: Self and Society in the Late Modern Age*. Stanford, Calif: Stanford University Press.

Girls Not Brides. (n.d.-a). *About Child Marriage*. Girls Not Brides. https://www.girlsnotbrides.org/about-child-marriage/ (accessed on April 20, 2021).

Girls Not Brides. (n.d.-b). *Where Does It Happen*. http://www.girlsnotbrides.org/where-does-it-happen/ (accessed on April 20, 2021).

Girls Not Brides. (n.d.-c). *Why Does Child Marriage Happen?* Girls Not Brides. https://www.girlsnotbrides.org/why-does-it-happen/ (accessed on April 20, 2021).

Glendon, M. A. (1989). *The Transformation of Family Law*. Chicago: The University of Chicago Press.

Godoy, S. A. (1999). `Our right is the right to be killed' making rights real on the streets of Guatemala city. *Childhood, 6*(4), 423–442. https://doi.org/10.1177/0907568299006004003

Goodale, M. (2006). Introduction to "Anthropology and human rights in a new key". *American Anthropologist, 108*(1), 1–8.

Graham, A., Powell, M. A., Anderson, D., Fitzgerald, R., & Taylor, N. (2013). *Ethical Research Involving Children*. Florence: UNICEF Office of Research – Innocenti.

Grijns, M., Horii, H., Irianto, S., & Saptandari, P. (Eds.). (2019). *Marrying Young in Indonesia: Voices, Laws and Practices*. Jakarta: Yayasan Pustaka Obor Indonesia.

Grijns, M., Limijaya, S., Restuningrum, N. H., Fathurrohman, I. H., Damayanti, V. R., & Harahap, R. A. (2016). Pernikahan Anak di Sukabumi Jawa Barat: Diri dan Agensi Anak Perempuan. *Journal Perempuan, 21*(1), 9–33.

Gunning, I. R. (1992). Arrogant perception, world-travelling and multicultural feminism: The case of female genital surgeries. *Columbia Human Rights Law Review, 23*(2), 189–248.

Hanson, K. (2016). Children's participation and agency when they don't 'do the right thing'. *Childhood, 23*(4), 471–475.

Hanson, K., Volonakis, D., & Al-Rozzi, M. (2015). Child labour, working children and children's rights. In W. Vandenhole, E. Desmet, D. Reynaert, & S. Lembrechts (Eds.), *Routledge International Handbook of Children's Rights Studies*. New York: Routledge.

Haraway, D. (1988). Situated knowledges: The science question in feminism and the privilege of partial perspective. *Feminist Studies, 14*(3), 575–599. https://doi.org/10.2307/3178066

Harris-Short, S. (2003). International Human Rights Law: Imperialist, inept and ineffective? Cultural relativism and the UN Convention on the rights of the child. *Human Rights Quarterly, 25*(1), 130–181. https://doi.org/10.1353/hrq.2003.0004

Hart, J. (2006). Saving children: What role for anthropology? *Anthropology Today, 22*(1), 5–8. https://doi.org/10.1111/j.1467-8322.2006.00410.x

Henkin, L. (1989). The universality of the concept of human rights. *The Annals of the American Academy of Political and Social Science, 506*(1), 10–16.

Henrich, J., Heine, S. J., & Norenzayan, A. (2010). The weirdest people in the world? *The Behavioral and Brain Sciences, 33*(2–3), 61–135. https://doi.org/10.1017/S0140525X0999152X

Hill, M. (2006). Children's voices on ways of having a voice: Children's and young people's perspectives on methods used in research and consultation. *Childhood, 13*(1), 69–89. https://doi.org/10.1177/0907568206059972

Hobsbawm, E., & Ranger, T. (Eds.). (1983). *The Invention of Tradition*. Cambridge: Cambridge University Press.

Hooker, M. B. (1975). *Legal Pluralism: An Introduction to Colonial and Neo-Colonial Laws*. Oxford: Clarendon Press.

Hopgood, S. (2017). Modernity at the cutting edge: Human rights meets FGM. In M. N. Barnett (Ed.), *Paternalism Beyond Borders* (pp. 256–291). Cambridge, UK: Cambridge University Press. https://doi.org/10.1017/9781316799956.009

Horii, H. (2020). Legal reasoning for legitimation of child marriage in West Java: Accommodation of local norms at Islamic courts and the paradox of child protection. *Journal of Human Rights Practice, 12*(3), 501–523, https://doi.org/10.1093/jhuman/huaa041.

Ignatieff, M. (2001). Attacks on human rights, the essay. *Foreign Affairs, 80*, 102–116.

Ignatieff, M. (2003). *Human Rights as Politics and Idolatry* (A. Gutmann, Ed.). Princeton: Princeton University Press.

James, A., & Prout, A. (1997). A new paradigm for the sociology of childhood? Provenance, promise and problems. In A. James & A. Prout (Eds.), *Constructing and Reconstructing Childhood: Contemporary Issues in the Sociological Study of Childhood* (pp. 7–33). London: Falmer Press.

Jenks, C. (2004). Editorial: Many childhoods? *Childhood, 11*(1), 5–8. https://doi.org/10.1177/0907568204040179

Jenks, C. (2005). *Childhood*. London; New York: Routledge.

Johansson, B. (2012). Doing adulthood in childhood research. *Childhood, 19*(1), 101–114. https://doi.org/10.1177/0907568211408362

Jones, G. W. (2001). Which Indonesian women marry youngest, and why? *Journal of Southeast Asian Studies, 32*(01), 67–78. https://doi.org/10.1017/S0022463401000029

Kennedy, D. (2005). *The Dark Sides of Virtue: Reassessing International Humanitarianism*. Princeton: Princeton University Press.

Komulainen, S. (2007). The ambiguity of the child's 'voice' in social research. *Childhood, 14*(1), 11–28. https://doi.org/10.1177/0907568207068561

Leonard, M. (2015). *The Sociology of Children, Childhood and Generation*. Los Angeles: SAGE Publications.

Lev, D. S. (1972). *Islamic Courts in Indonesia: A Study in the Political Bases of Legal Institutions*. Berkley: Los Angeles: University of California Press.

Lev, D. S. (1973). Judicial unification in post-colonial Indonesia. *Indonesia, 16*, 1–37. https://doi.org/10.2307/3350645

Lukito, R. (2013). *Legal Pluralism in Indonesia: Bridging the Unbridgeable*. Oxon; New York: Routledge.

Macdonald, R. (2013). Pluralistic human rights? Universal human wrongs? In R. Provost & C. Sheppard (Eds.), *Dialogues on Human Rights and Legal Pluralism* (pp. 15–36). Dordrecht; Heidelberg; New York; London: Springer.

Mackenzie, C. (2013). The importance of relational autonomy and capabilities for an ethics of vulnerability. In C. Mackenzie, W. Rogers, & S. Dodds (Eds.), *Vulnerability: New Essays in Ethics and Feminist Philosophy* (pp. 33–59). New York, NY: Oxford University Press.

Mahmood, S. (2004). *Politics of Piety: The Islamic Revival and the Feminist Subject*. Princeton, N.J: Princeton University Press.

Maithreyi, R. (2019). Children's reconstruction of psychological knowledge: An ethnographic study of life skills education programmes in India. *Childhood, 26*(1), 68–82. https://doi.org/10.1177/0907568218798014

Malhotra, A. (1997). Gender and the timing of marriage: Rural-urban differences in Java. *Journal of Marriage and Family, 59*(2), 434–450. https://doi.org/10.2307/353481

Marcoes, L. (2016). Child marriage thrives in urban areas too. *The Jakarta Post*. http://www.thejakartapost.com/news/2016/11/12/child-marriage-thrives-urban-areas-too.html

Merry, S. E. (1997). Global human rights and local social movements in a legally plural world. *Canadian Journal of Law and Society, 12*, 247–272.

Merry, S. E. (2003). Human rights law and the demonization of culture (and anthropology along the way). *PoLAR: Political and Legal Anthropology Review, 26*(1), 55–76. https://doi.org/10.1525/pol.2003.26.1.55

Merry, S. E. (2006-a). Anthropology and international law. *Annual Review of Anthropology, 35*(1), 99–116. https://doi.org/10.1146/annurev.anthro.35.081705.123245

Merry, S. E. (2006-b). *Human Rights and Gender Violence Translating International Law into Local Justice*. London; Chicago: University of Chicago Press.

Merry, S. E. (2009). Relating to the subjects of human rights: The culture of agency in human rights discourse. In M. Freeman & D. Napier (Eds.), *Law and Anthropology: Current Legal Issues Volume 12* (pp. 385–407). London; Oxford: Oxford University Press.

Merry, S. E. (2013). Transnational human rights and local activism: Mapping the middle. In R. Provost & C. Sheppard (Eds.), *Dialogues on Human Rights and Legal Pluralism* (pp. 207–228). Dordrecht; Heidelberg; New York; London: Springer.

Mohanty, C. T. (1984). Under western eyes: Feminist scholarship and Colonial discourses. *Boundary 2, 12/13*, 333–358. https://doi.org/10.2307/302821

Montgomery, H. (2007). Working with child prostitutes in Thailand: Problems of practice and interpretation. *Childhood, 14*(4), 415–430.

Ngira, D. O. (2019). *Examining the Role of Informal Justice Systems in Child Rights Protection in Kenya: A Case Study of the Kipsigis* [Doctoral Thesis]. Utrecht University.

Nieuwenhuys, O. (1996). The paradox of child labor and anthropology. *Annual Review of Anthropology, 25*(1), 237–251. https://doi.org/10.1146/annurev.anthro.25.1.237

O'Shaughnessy, K. (2009). *Gender, State and Social Power in Contemporary Indonesia: Divorce and Marriage Law*. Oxon; New York: Routledge.

Parlina, I. (2014). Minimum age for marriage debated at Constitutional Court. *The Jakarta Post*. http://www.thejakartapost.com/news/2014/12/03/minimum-age-marriage-debated-constitutional-court.html

Plan International Asia Regional Office, & Coram International. (2015). *Getting the Evidence: Asia Child Marriage Initiative*. https://plan-international.org/getting-evidence-asia-child-marriage-initiative#download-options

Powell, M. A., Fitzgerald, R., Taylor, N., & Graham, A. (2012). *International Literature Review: Ethical Issues in Undertaking Research with Children and Young People (Literature review for the Childwatch International Research Network)*. Lismore; Dunedin: Southern Cross University, Centre for Children and Young People/University of Otago, Centre for Research on Children and Families.

Reiss, F. (2018). *I Escaped Forced Marriage—Now Is the Time to Outlaw Child Marriage in Florida*. Global Citizen. https://www.globalcitizen.org/en/content/child-marriage-florida/

Reynolds, P., Nieuwenhuys, O., & Hanson, K. (2006). Refractions of children's rights in development practice. *Childhood, 13*(3), 291–302.

Roberts, H. (2000). Listening to children: And hearing them. In P. Christensen & A. James (Eds.), *Research with Children: Perspectives and Practices* (pp. 225–240). London: Falmer Press.

Rorty, R. (1998). *Truth and Progress: Philosophical Papers*. Cambridge: Cambridge University Press.

Rose, G. (1997). Situating knowledges: Positionality, reflexivities and other tactics. *Progress in Human Geography, 21*(3), 305–320. https://doi.org/10.1191/030913297673302122

Saardchom, N., & Lemaire, J. (2005). Causes of increasing ages at marriage: An international regression study. *Marriage & Family Review, 37*(3), 73–97. https://doi.org/10.1300/J002v37n03_05

Safitri, M. (2011). Langkawana's community forest: Decentlization and legal pluralism in Indonesian State Forestlands. In W. Zips & M. Weilenmann (Eds.), *The Governance of Legal Pluralism: Empirical Studies from Africa and Beyond* (pp. 235–256). Münster: LIT Verlag Münster.

Santos, B. de S. (2015). *If God Were a Human Rights Activist*. Stanford, California: Stanford University Press.

Spivak, G. C. (2010). "Can the subaltern speak?" revised edition, from the "History" chapter of Critique of Postcolonial Reason. In R. Morris (Ed.), *Can the Subaltern Speak?: Reflections on the History of an Idea* (pp. 21–80). New York: Columbia University Press.

Stammers, N. (1999). Social movements and the social construction of human rights. *Human Rights Quarterly, 21*(4), 980–1008. https://doi.org/10.1353/hrq.1999.0054

The Executive, American Anthropological Association. (1947). Statement on human rights. *American Anthropologist, 49*(4), 539–543.

The Fourth World Conference on Women. (1995). *Beijing Declaration and Platform for Action*, A/CONF.177/20 and A/CONF.177/20/Add.1. http://hrlibrary.umn.edu/instree/e5dplw.htm

Tracy, S. J. (2010). Qualitative quality: Eight "Big-Tent" criteria for excellent qualitative research. *Qualitative Inquiry, 16*(10), 837–851. https://doi.org/10.1177/1077800410383121

Tucker, K. (1999). *Anthony Giddens and Modern Social Theory* (1 edition). London; Thousand Oaks, Calif: SAGE Publications Ltd.

UNFPA. (2012). *Marrying Too Young: End Child Marriage*. New York: UNFPA.

UNICEF Indonesia, & UNICEF. (2016). *Child Marriage in Indonesia: Progress on Pause*. Jakarta: UNICEF Indonesia.

United Nations Children's Fund. (2014). *Ending Child Marriage: Progress and Prospects*. New York: UNICEF.

United Nations Children's Fund Innocenti Research Centre. (2001). *Early Marriage: Child Spouses*. Florence: United Nations Children's Fund Innocenti Research Centre.

United Nations Development Programme. (n.d.). *Sustainable Development Goals*. United Nations Development Programme. https://www.undp.org/content/undp/en/home/sustainable-development-goals.html (accessed on April 20, 2021).

United Nations Population Fund. (2018). *Escaping Child Marriage in Sierra Leone*. United Nations Population Fund. https://www.unfpa.org/news/escaping-child-marriage-sierra-leone (accessed on July 30, 2021).

United States Census Bureau (n.d.). Table MS-2. Estimated median age at first marriage, by sex: 1890 to the present, https://www.census.gov/data/tables/time-series/demo/families/marital.html (accessed on April 20, 2021).

Utomo, A. (2014). Marrying up? Trends in age and education gaps among married couples in Indonesia. *Journal of Family Issues, 35*(12), 1683–1706.

Van der Muur, W. (2018). Forest conflicts and the informal nature of realizing indigenous land rights in Indonesia. *Citizenship Studies, 22*(2), 160–174. https://doi.org/10.1080/13621025.2018.1445495

Van Huis, S. (2015). *Islamic Courts and Women's Divorce Rights in Indonesia: The cases of Cianjur and Bulukumba* [Doctoral Thesis]. Leiden University.

Vandenhole, W. (2012). Localizing the human rights of children. In M. Liebel (Ed.), *Children's Rights from Below: Cross-Cultural Perspectives* (pp. 80–93). Basingstoke: Palgrave Macmillan.

Vel, J. A. C., & Bedner, A. W. (2015). Decentralisation and village governance in Indonesia: The return to the nagari and the 2014 Village Law. *The Journal of Legal Pluralism and Unofficial Law, 47*(3), 493–507. https://doi.org/10.1080/07329113.2015.1109379

Volpp, L. (2000). Blaming culture for bad behavior. *Yale Journal of Law & the Humanities, 12*, 89–116.

Wikan, U. (1990). *Managing Turbulent Hearts: A Balinese Formula for Living*. Chicago: University of Chicago Press.

Williams, T. P. (2016). Theorizing children's subjectivity: Ethnographic investigations in rural Rwanda. *Childhood, 23*(3), 333–347. https://doi.org/10.1177/0907568216644031

Chapter 2

Discourse

Child marriage is a new and old phenomenon. It is new in that the term, defined as marrying below the age of 18, caught international attention as a human rights issue. It is old in that marrying below the age of 18 was more common than marrying at a later age in many societies throughout human history. Yet today, it is believed to be something that has to end. Human rights organizations across the globe are advocating that communities "End Child Marriage". The movement has gained momentum over the last decade. In this sense, child marriage itself is a discursive practice. It is a specific way of talking about its causes and consequences in a condemning manner. This way of talking started in international human rights communities with a specific background and agenda based on a particular vision of childhood and proper human development.

Thus, child marriage is a construction and one that is currently hardly contested. Various human rights organizations have published reports and launched campaigns against child marriage, while their definition of child marriage is uniformly used and remains unchallenged. Academic research on the topic is limited, and only a handful of the research has pointed out the dominant and sometimes unproductive characteristics of child marriage discourse (Archambault 2011; Boyden, Pankhurst, and Tafere 2012; Bunting and Merry 2007).

The lack of critical study on the topic can be partially explained by Dembour's (2010) classification of the four schools of human rights. The natural school frames human rights as given. The deliberate school frames human rights as agreed upon. The protest school frames human rights as a way to redress injustice. Finally, the discourse school frames human rights as a language (ibid). The natural and deliberate schools are the major two schools of thought, deferring to the existing human rights system. In contrast, the discourse school considers rights as talked about, as a culture, and a construction, opposing the natural school, which sees rights as given. In Cowan's (2006: 10) words, the discourse itself is "human rights culture", which is "an increasingly pervasive structuring discourse […] that shapes how the world is apprehended". Calavita (2010: 97) also pointed out the pervasive nature of supranational legal institutions,

DOI: 10.4324/9781003184546-2

impinging on local practices as globalization progresses. This view of seeing human rights as 'a culture' is uncomfortable for human rights, as it challenges the stable core of the human rights system – their universality. In other words, the discourse school is confronting for those who believe in or rely on the universality of human rights.

This chapter applies the discourse school to study and deconstruct human rights. The school challenges the taken-for-granted assumptions to transform the existing human rights framework from which the dominant schools depart. This deconstruction approach to the dominant discourse, considering the global power structure, also has the potential to bring diversity into the idea of human rights. I take this approach in two steps.

The first step traces the establishment of child marriage as a discursive practice by analysing conventions and general recommendations about child marriage that international human rights institutions have issued since the 1960s. This part of the analysis aims to understand how child marriage has been formed into a discursive practice by international legal institutions and to establish the assumptions underlying the concept's development. The second step unpacks the dominant child marriage discourse by analysing the use of specific words in 10 reports about child marriage published by major international organizations between 2001 and 2016. The publications were selected to investigate the dominant discourse in the international arena and the implications of this dominance.

The analysis is based on the Foucauldian assumption that ideology is embedded in language. The underlying idea here is that the construction of global human rights texts has both relied on and resulted in promoting a specific type of knowledge. Consequently, the construction has subjugated other types of knowledge. This chapter aims to clarify different types of knowledge that played a role in this process. Legal texts are of particular importance. They are constructed based on ideas and discourse in society and then reinforce these ideas by becoming the frame of reference for future discourse.

The next section discusses how the term 'child marriage' has developed over the last few decades, including the idea of it being a human rights violation. This section highlights the assumptions behind this development: (1) The concept of an innocent childhood and (2) the ideal that modern marriages are based on individual choices and romantic love. Section 2.2 examines the first assumption by discussing different terms related to child marriage, including arranged marriages and forced marriages. The international organizations' use of these different terms underlines liberal paternalistic concepts of childhood and children's agency. Section 2.3 focuses on the second assumption by using the dichotomic concepts of 'modernity' and 'tradition' to reveal how the problem of child marriage is *traditionalized* in the dominant discourse. Section 2.4 discusses the implications of the dominant discourse. The conclusion reflects on alternatives to the current approach to child marriage.

2.1. Emergence of the concept 'child marriage' in the international arena

2.1.1. Child marriage as a human rights violation

Marrying young has long been commonplace. For centuries, it was normal to marry below 18 years of age in the Western world, and this is still the case in many places. The average marriage age has gone up in the course of social developments in modern society. However, in many countries, including developed countries, it still is possible to marry at or below age 16 with parental consent or judicial approval. Exceptions to rules about marriageable age are also common. For instance, until 2015, the Dutch civil law allowed girls of 16 years old to get married if they had fallen pregnant (Warendorf and Curry-Sumner 2003: 36).

Today, a 'child marriage' is considered a human rights violation. In 2001, the United Nations Children's Fund Innocenti Research Centre (2001) pointed out that the modern women's rights and children's rights movements had paid scant attention to early marriage. They had also not examined early marriage as a human rights violation itself. Since then, we can observe a growing movement against child marriage. 'End Child Marriage' has been a slogan of international organizations such as UNICEF, UNFPA, Council on Foreign Relations, Anti-slavery International, Plan International, Equality Now, and Girls Not Brides (Evenhuis and Burn 2014; Girls Not Brides, n.d.-c; Turner 2013; UNFPA 2012; United Nations Children's Fund 2014; Vogelstein 2013).

In 2013, the UN Human Rights Council (2013) passed a resolution aimed at "strengthening efforts to prevent and eliminate child, early and forced marriage". In 2014, this was followed by another resolution on the same topic by the UN General Assembly (2015). More recently, the United Nations listed the elimination of child marriage as a target in the newly established Sustainable Development Goals (no. 5.3), supported by 116 member states. Child marriage is now considered an impediment to development. Throughout their campaigns, those international organizations heavily emphasize what they consider negative consequences of child marriage (e.g., female genital mutilation, domestic and sexual violence, exploitation as domestic servants, reduced educational opportunities, health hazards, and sex trafficking) (Equality Now 2014: 5). Bunting and Merry (2007: 330) have argued that child marriage is salient by being at the intersection of various themes on the human rights agenda (e.g., slavery, health hazards of traditional harmful practices, violence against women, and child welfare).

2.1.2. The first assumption: What it is to be a 'child'

When and how did people under 18 become too young to marry, and why was 18 the relevant age? The first international instrument mentioning a minimum age for marriage is the 1957 Supplementary Convention on the Abolition of

Slavery, the Slave Trade, and Institutions and Practices Similar to Slavery. This Convention states that 'the State Parties undertake to prescribe, where appropriate, suitable minimum ages of marriage' (Article 2). However, in the drafting process, several intergovernmental organizations and some states expressed that the Convention should set a suitable minimum age, and give these provisions a more mandatory form (Gutteridge 1957). Subsequently, the 1964 United Nations Convention on Consent to Marriage, Minimum Age for Marriage, and Registration of Marriages stipulated the right for 'men and women of full age' to marry 'with free and full consent'. From 1966, the International Covenant on Civil and Political Rights (ICCPR) recognizes the right of men and women of 'marriageable age' (A23(2)) to get married. These conventions and the ICCPR merely require state parties to set a minimum age for marriage in national legislation, without specifying an age limit. In 1979, the issue emerged again in international conventions when the UN General Assembly adopted the Convention on the Elimination of All Forms of Discrimination against Women (hereafter CEDAW). In Article 16(2), CEDAW requires that all parties take the necessary actions to set a minimum age of marriage and to make marriage registration compulsory but again without establishing an age limit.

While the international instruments listed above have not specified a lower age limit, this was specified in certain accompanying documents and regional conventions. In 1965, UN General Assembly (1965) resolution 2018 required member states to specify a minimum age of marriage that was no less than 15 years of age. By 1994, the UN Committee on CEDAW recommended that the minimum age of marriage should be 18 years for both men and women. This recommendation was based on the impact of marriage on minors' education, health, and economic autonomy (UN Committee on the Elimination of Discrimination against Women 1994). Interestingly, the African Charter on the Rights and Welfare of the Child 1990 (hereafter ACRWC) (A21) and the 2003 Protocol to the African Charter on Human and Peoples' Rights on the Rights of Women in Africa (A6) both set 18 as the minimum age for marriage (Sloth-Nielsen 2012). The Charter and the Protocol are the only binding global legal instrument to explicitly prohibit child marriage (African Union 2003; Organization of African Unity (OAU) 1990). Taken together, the changes in international conventions between 1957 and 1994 increasingly imposed substantive standards and demonstrated an on-going process of globalization.

It is then worth discussing how 18 became the specified age. The documented discussions from the CRC drafting process show that there was no clear consensus among the member states about the definition of a child (Office of the United Nations High Commissioner for Human Rights 2007: 305). In the CRC draft working group, some delegates worried that the age of 18 was quite old to still be a 'child', in light of some states' legislation (ibid). The alternative suggested age limit was 14; in many countries, that was the legal marriageable age for girls and the age of finishing compulsory education (ibid). The Nepalese representative suggested the lower age limit be 16, considering "the concerns of poorer States who may not be able to shoulder the burdens imposed by this convention for children up to 18 years of age" (ibid: 311). However, the working group eventually defined a child as "every human being below the age of eighteen years unless, under the law applicable to the child, majority is attained earlier", as stipulated in Article 1 of the CRC. While the argument about compulsory education seems a particularly sensible one, the available documents do not explain why this opinion was overruled.

Differences in opinions about the age limit defining a child are attributable to how experiences of childhood can differ globally. Childhood studies, a disciplinary field that took shape in the 1990s, can help unpack the concept of a 'child' underlying the development of the child marriage framework. Childhood scholarship has established that childhood has been defined differently over time and in different places with sometimes contradicting definitions (James, Jenks, and Prout 1998: 21). The historian Aries' (1996: 6) described 'childhood' as a modern European invention. Stephens (1995: 13, 19) followed by noting that the child/adult distinction was central to the development of modern capitalism and modern nation-states. James, Jenks, and Prout (1998) explain that there are different versions of imagined childhood: "The evil child", "the innocent child", "the immanent child", "the naturally developing child", and "the unconscious child". According to them, "the innocent child" is "what we have come to imagine as modern, Western childhood", although Freudian's "unconscious child" with sexual drives and instincts has also significantly impacted psychology. Jenks quotes Robertson, who claimed the idea of an innocent child is based on the philosophy of the eighteen-century European Enlightenment, Rousseau's calling attention to the needs of children (Jenks 2005: 57, 58). According to Jenks (ibid), the "the Apollonian" image of children has been influential in modern Western societies and has become increasingly dominant throughout the world. That image is of childhood as a time for play, when children need protection, are pure and innocent, and should be happy.

This thinking is also embedded in international policy-making (Ansell 2005). According to James and Prout (1997: 9, 10), the philosophy behind the CRC is informed by psychological explanations of child developmental psychology from the early twentieth century. The explanations contain three dominant themes: 'Rationality', 'naturalness', and 'universality'. These concepts are so dominant that they are "incorporated into the everyday understanding of children in Western societies that it is difficult to think outside of it" (ibid: 11). Boyden (1997: 193) interprets the adoption of the CRC as the export of stereotyped childhood from the industrial world to the South.[1]

1 It is important to note that the CRC is not necessarily the simple 'export'. As well as ACRWR that prohibits marriage under the age of 18, many laws in Africa have seen widespread acceptance

Boyden (Ibid) argues that it has been the explicit goal of children's rights specialists to crystalize in international law a universal system of children's rights based on these post-enlightenment ideas of childhood. By this logic, the fixed minimum standard for marriage age has emerged within this 'crystalized system'.

2.1.3. The second assumption: Modern ideals of 'marriage'

The previous section has shown that child marriage has emerged as a discursive practice based on modern assumptions about childhood. This section will discuss an assumption about marriage. In most parts of the world today, people increasingly perceive marriage to be about romantic love and companionship, although this perception is a recent phenomenon. Glendon (1989: 287) states that the idea of marriage as a vehicle for individual self-fulfilment became prominent only in the twentieth century. Modern family law has stimulated the transformation of ideas about marriage, internalizing tension between the ideas that family involves a community and that it facilitates the personal fulfilment of individuals (ibid: 143). The decision-making about marriage became less collective and more individualistic, and in this process, age and 'maturity' of the spouses have become relevant (Blackburn and Bessell 1997: 108). Moses (2017: 1) suggests that this change of ideas and laws on marriage has resulted in a "fragility of marriage", meaning that marriage has now become optional rather than an unavoidable rite of passage.

Through processes connected with 'modernization' (i.e., trade, mass migration, and growing empires in the eighteenth and nineteenth centuries), individuals encountered new cultures that seemed vastly different from their own (ibid: 7). These encounters promoted a 'normativization' of a particular marriage ideal, a celebration of one type of marriage over another. 'Modernity' in marriage implies "being 'civilized'" and is "denoted by monogamous marriage based on love involving an adult man and woman" or "companionate, affectionate and consensual relationships" (ibid: 1, 9). One of the examples of 'normativization' includes seeing an arranged marriage as a traditional practice. Majumdar (2009: 1) contests this idea by arguing that the institution of arranged marriage came to be solidified as a traditional practice that is juxtaposed against "love marriages", i.e., marriage based on romantic love.

of international and regional treaties (Sloth-Nielsen, 2012). Imoh's (2019: 181) research showed that the Ghanaian society has localized global frameworks of childhood, "leading to constructions of childhoods that are neither completely local nor purely global". Furthermore, Grugel (2013) argues that the discrepancy results from the CRC's persistent reliance on welfare model, which is a product of a particular moment in Northern European history. This explanation suggests that the CRC is a weak legal tool not necessarily due to the irrelevant childhood model but to lack of reflection on how to effectively bring children's rights and children's welfare together.

Banning child marriage is part of the normativization of marital practices today. Child marriage gradually became deviant behaviour after the rise of modernity in the Western world. It was followed by the idea of modern marriage being based on romantic love and individual choices: The autonomy of women, instead of 'arranged marriage'. In other words, child marriage as a discursive practice has emerged out of a modern and specific idea of marriage.

However, the main purpose of marriages varies significantly over time, culture, and social class (e.g., the regulation of duties and responsibilities of the spouses and marriage's relation to sexual activity). Until today, "despite globalization – through improved communications technologies, travel and trade, the rise and fall of vast new empires, and new international organizations – marriage [has] continued to exist in a variety of configurations and remained imbued with diverse meanings" (Moses 2017: 1). Considering this variety and the fluid nature of marriage mores, the practical consequences of the child marriage framework also vary. For instance, in a society where pre-marital sexual intercourse is a religious sin, prohibiting marriage under a certain age is also the prohibition of sexual activities under the same age.

The ideal age for childbirth is another relevant assumption underlying the concept of child marriage. Campaigns often argue that one of the negative impacts of child marriage is higher maternal mortality rates in young pregnancies. Such campaigns rely on the claimed consequences to justify their interventionist approach to prohibit *all* child marriages. However, I found that these claimed negative consequences are not necessarily well supported by the evidence. The reports at times lack sources to prove higher maternal mortality rates in mid- to late-teenage pregnancies. Moreover, their claims frequently rely on previous international reports.[2] This cross-referencing between transnational organizations seems a sign of self-legitimation. While there is a physical and emotional limit to childbirth (e.g., childbirth at the age of 12 is dangerous), these campaigners fail to provide convincing evidence that all childbirth before the age of 18 has negative consequences. Additionally, the quantified measurement itself likely contains problems and political aspects (Merry 2016). Similarly, with her research on cousin marriage among British Pakistanis, Shaw (2006: 214) demonstrates that what the dominant discourse considers "numerical biological risk" can be in fact a matter of culture, politics, and morality.

Scientific discussion about the ideal age for childbirth has varied opinions. For instance, Mirowsky (2002) argues that the best biological and physical age for carrying a healthy pregnancy is in the late teens or early twenties. The recent general concern focuses on how to balance the biologically ideal and socially ideal ages for childbirth, considering increasing social constraints

2 See, for instance, Girls Not Brides n.d.d; World Health Organization 2011; World Health Organization 2017; United Nations Population Fund 2013.

to delay it.[3] Furthermore, campaigns against child marriage assume that early pregnancy is caused by child marriage, while often the opposite is true. Child marriage can be motivated by an extra-marital pregnancy (Grijns and Horii 2018). Blackburn and Bessel (1997: 108, 112) have noted that although physical readiness for sexual intercourse and child-bearing is a consideration for raising the marriageable age, marriage, and sexual intercourse are two separate matters. The consummation of marriage can be arranged much later than the wedding.[4] These alternative scenarios indicate the generalizing tendency of the international discourse, which does not consider the diversity of forms, motivations, and consequences of child marriage.

In sum, fixed ideas of childhood and marriage underlay the development of the 'child marriage' concept. In the next two sections, an analysis of international discourse will show how these ideas influence the way international reports present child marriage.

2.2. 'Child marriage' in international discourse: Childhood and agency

2.2.1. *Use of terms related to child marriage*

The assumptions about childhood in the child marriage discourse can be identified in how international organizations define different terms related to child marriage. This section discusses 'child marriage', as well as 'early marriage', 'forced marriage', and 'arranged marriage'. The platform of international organizations working against child marriage, Girls Not Brides (n.d.a) defines child marriage as "any formal marriage or informal union where one or both of the parties are under 18 years of age". 'Early marriage' is often used in the same sense. 'Forced marriage' is commonly defined as "marriage in which one or both of the parties is married without his or her consent or against his or her will". 'Arranged marriage' is "marriage in which both parties consent to the assistance of their parents or a third party, such as a matchmaker, in identifying a spouse, although the consent may be uninformed" (Greene 2014). International organizations use these terms often to emphasize that children who are married, particularly girls, are usually not in a position to give their free, full, and informed consent to marriage, and are often subject to marriage under pressure and coercion (Evenhuis and Burn 2014).

Most human rights advocates argue that child and early marriages are by definition 'forced marriages', even when the child appears to give his or her consent (Equality Now 2014: 53). The reasoning behind this argument varies. The

3 See, for instance, Bellieni (2016).

4 This type of marriage is called "*kawin gantung*" (suspended marriage), practised in colonial times in some parts of Indonesia.

United Nations Children's Fund Innocenti Research Centre (2001) bases its argument on the UDHR, which recognizes "the right to free and full consent to a marriage" and claims that consent cannot be "free and full" when at least one partner is "immature". The CEDAW Committee comments that "[w]hen men and women marry, they assume important responsibilities. Consequently, marriage should not be permitted before they have attained full maturity and capacity to act" (UN Committee on the Convention of the Elimination of All Forms of Discrimination against Women 1994: para 36). UNICEF Indonesia clarifies that even if the child consents to their marriage, it is to be considered a forced marriage, as such 'consent' is an outcome of prevailing social norms whereby children are expected to marry as children (Irdiana 2015).

Some organizations even maintain that child marriage is a form of slavery (International Planned Parenthood Federation 2015). Anti-Slavery International's 'servile marriage', based on Article 1 (C) of the 1956 Supplementary Convention on the Abolition of Slavery, identifies the following practices relating to women in marriage as akin to slavery:

> promise or giving of a woman, without her having the right to refuse, by her parents, family or others in marriage in return for consideration in money or in kind; the handing over of a woman to another person by her husband or his kin for 'value received or otherwise;' or widow inheritance, whereby a married woman is transferred to become the wife of another man upon the death of her husband.
>
> (Turner 2013: 22)

As children are in a weaker position than adults to give full and informed consent, their marriage easily becomes a form of servile marriage (ibid: 17). This categorization of child marriage as slavery can be strategic, as it puts more legal weight on the anti-child marriage campaigns (Asghari 2019).

Some women's rights advocates have recently begun advocating reconsidering and changing the term 'child marriage'. They argue that 'marriage' is inappropriate as it suggests an official and joyful occasion, while they consider it to be sexual abuse and marital rape (Mihara and Abrahams 2017). For that reason, the African Union Goodwill Ambassador on Ending Child 'Marriage', Gumbonzvanda (2017), urged people to reconsider and change the term 'child marriage', yet without suggesting an alternative. These discussions show the significance and sensitivity of the (ab)use of terms.

2.2.2. 'Childhood' imagined in the international reports

UNICEF argues that child marriage cuts childhood short (United Nations Children's Fund Innocenti Research Centre 2001: 1). Child marriage is often presented as an "abrupt", "premature", or "unnatural" end of childhood (Turner 2013; UNFPA 2012: 11, 57; United Nations Children's Fund Innocenti

Research Centre 2001; Vogelstein 2013: 13). It is also described as a "harsh transition from childhood to adulthood" (Evenhuis and Burn 2014: 13) and therefore "abruptly sanctions the end of childhood and prematurely ushers in adulthood" (Chaudhuri 2015: 2). The CRC regards childhood as a process of development (United Nations Children's Fund Innocenti Research Centre 2001: 6). Thus, child marriage leads to "the denial of childhood and adolescence, the curtailment of personal freedom and the lack of opportunity to develop a full sense of selfhood" (ibid: 9). It also violates childhood (Chaudhuri 2015: 66). Child marriage "deprives", "robs", and "pushes [girls] out" of childhood (Chaudhuri 2015: 3; UNFPA 2012: 11; United Nations Children's Fund Innocenti Research Centre 2001: 6). The idea behind this common discourse is that childhood is a privilege (Chaudhuri 2015: iv) to which girls are entitled (UNFPA 2012: 12).

The ideas of childhood and children's agency are closely interlinked. In the current childhood model scheme, how much agency children exercise in deciding to marry is a difficult question. The CEDAW and CRC committees co-published a general comment in 2014 that seemingly attempts to create some space for exceptional cases, "as a matter of respecting the child's evolving capacities and autonomy in making decisions that affect her or his life"(Committee on the Elimination of Discrimination against Women and Committee on the Rights of the Child 2014: para 20). The general comment endorses "a marriage of a mature, capable child below 18 years of age" with or without parental consent in exceptional circumstances, under two conditions (Ibid). First, the child is at least 16 years old. Second, "such decisions are made by a judge based on legitimate exceptional ground defined by law and on the evidence of maturity, without deference to culture and tradition" (Ibid). This general comment is in line with the recent attention paid to the 'evolving capacity' of children in the realm of the CRC based on Articles 5 (evolving capacity) and 12 (right to be heard), as a response to the criticism that the notion of best interests of the child is 'paternalistic' (Cantwell 2016). As such, other international organizations are also increasingly recognizing, somewhat reluctantly, the need to balance between the "growing demand for autonomy and self-determination" and the "intrinsically harmful nature" of child marriage (ECPAT International, Plan International, Save the Children, UNICEF, & World Vision 2014).

International children's rights literature has supported this increasing attention to children's autonomy. A number of scholarships have extensively discussed the concept of children's evolving capacities and their participation in decision-making process (Lundy 2018; Shier 2001; Tisdall 2017; Tobin 2015; Varadan 2019), right to be heard (Lundy 2007; Lundy, Tobin, and Parkes 2019; Daly 2018; Tisdall 2016), voice in research (Hill 2006; Komulainen 2007; Liebel 2012b; Spyrou 2016), and right to development as "freedom" (Peleg 2013).

These crucial legal concepts are often overlooked or set aside by international institutions. Why is this the case? A possible explanation would be that the CRC lacks serious discussions and reflection on the tensions between demanding rights in a post-welfare age (Grugel 2013: 22). Another explanation could be that, as Hanson (2016) mentions, when children do not "do the right thing", their autonomy and agency become severely limited. 'The right thing' here means what is 'right' for children to do or not do according to UN institutions. These institutions hold that it is not right for children to marry, work, engage in armed conflict, or commit a criminal offence (ibid). The international human rights regime imposing its moral authority is described as "international paternalism" (Hopgood 2017). The same goes for women's rights. There are some forms of behaviour which are considered to be so destructive to women that they could not possibly consent to them, and child marriage is one such form of behaviour (Merry 2009).

Liebel (2012a: 103) suggests focusing on what children *can* instead of what they *cannot* do. While the "freedom to marry" (Glendon 1989) was promoted as a basic human right in Europe from around 1800, the international community has turned this freedom in the context of child marriage into the 'freedom not to have to marry' and even the prohibition of marriage below the age of 18. According to Merry (1997), "[r]ights generally act as a resource rather than a constraint". That said, the prohibition from marrying below 18 often serves as the denial of children's right to marry (a constraint), rather than as their right not to have to marry (a resource).

2.3. 'Child marriage' in international discourse: Modernity and tradition

The analysis so far has established that child marriage as a discursive practice is a construction derived from a specific vision of childhood, marriage, and human development. Another prominent discourse found in the analysis is the use of the word 'tradition'. Before introducing the analysis, this section explains the complementary relation between the terms 'tradition' and 'modernity'.

'Modernity' and 'tradition' are often used as a contrast in various forms. Giddens (1991: 6, 13) has identified autonomy over lifestyle choice as the core of modernity: He understood modernity as a post-traditional order in which lifestyle choice is increasingly important in the constitution of self-identity and daily-activity. In other words, 'tradition' and 'modernity' are two sides of one coin; "the constructs of traditional and modern society are themselves products of modernity, in which tradition is the 'other' to modernity" (Merry 2009: 401).

Jacobson (2012) explains the dichotomic relationship between modernity and tradition. He suggests that globalization creates tensions in patriarchal societies, prompting a battle between the community and the self and between patriarchy and modernity (Ibid: 4, 5). According to him, an honour society is where patriarchal and tribal traditions dictate that a woman's body belongs to and serves the community. An interest-based society privileges the self-determination of women and the sovereignty of the individual over her body (ibid). According to Appadurai (1996: 23), this tension between the two different normative systems is the challenge for modernizing society: Will emerging cultural heterogeneity accommodate norms and values that do not require strict adherence to the modern West's liberal social norms? Child marriage is a typical case of such battles. As Bunting (2005: 26) also expressed, "early marriage can be a part of a struggle over cultural traditions and the future meaning of those customs".

Human rights are an institution of modernity in that its movement is designed to achieve individual sovereignty, modernity's core ideal. The creation of the 1948 Universal Declaration of Human Rights (hereafter UDHR) was based on the perception of the individual as an autonomous being (Jacobson 2012: 11). Ignatieff (2003) demonstrates that the protection of agency is the core principle of human rights. Merry (2009: 385, 404) points out that the notion of agency is deeply enshrined in the human rights discourse. She argues "the human rights system is premised on the idea that it can facilitate the creation of modern subjectivity, in which utilitarian choices take precedence over obligations rooted in custom, tradition, and relationships". She found that, in documents generated at global conferences, the CEDAW Committee typically talks about culture as a barrier to progress, understanding culture as a static tradition (Merry 2003).

In reports, legal texts, and advocacy campaigns against child marriage, this specific conceptualization of 'tradition' is also observed. The 1995 Beijing Declaration and Platform for Action explicitly addressed child marriage as a harmful traditional custom (The Fourth World Conference on Women 1995). This reference derives from Article 24(3) of the CRC. It obliges State Parties "to abolish traditional practices prejudicial to the health of children". As well as these legal texts, the analysis of the selected ten reports in the next section reveals the persistent use of 'tradition' as being a 'harmful tradition'. For instance, one of the United Nations Children's Fund's (2005) reports is titled "Early marriage: A harmful traditional practice". All of the reports mention 'tradition', though with varying frequency and explicitness.

2.3.1. *'Tradition' invented in the international reports*

To start with, the United Nations Children's Fund Innocenti Research Centre's (2001) report mentions 'tradition' 23 times over 30 pages. It encourages governments to conduct "a serious examination of customary marriages that contravene existing legislation", as "harmful traditional practices are allowed to continue in spite of laws that forbid them" (ibid: 19). It argues that "marriage at or shortly after puberty is common among those living traditional lifestyles" and "[e]arly marriage lingers on as a culturally and socially sanctioned practice according to some traditional sets of values" (ibid: 2). The report includes several descriptions of "traditional societies". These are where "the idea of an adolescent period between puberty and adulthood is alien". Such societies are where many parents still believe that investment in a girl's education is wasted when she is simply going to be married and work in another household (ibid: 6, 11). It also describes the difference in family patterns "between the traditional 'familist' system and the modern 'individualist' systems", the latter being "the norm in industrialized countries" (ibid: 6). It claims that to end child marriage, "societies must re-examine traditional gender roles" (ibid: 19). It also discusses the "resilience of traditional practices and custom" despite demographic transitions, explaining that "[f]amilies in the process of transition may, therefore, be caught between traditional and modern values" (ibid: 7).

The UNICEF report (United Nations Children's Fund 2005), "Early Marriage: A harmful practice", uses "tradition" 22 times over 31 pages, excluding the title. Most uses refer to "traditional method of contraception" (ibid). The report introduces statistics about child marriage practice and its correlation with polygamy, domestic violence, and reproductive health. It contains no explicitly ideological message about tradition, except for the claim that customary laws condoning the practice are one of the factors influencing child marriage rates (ibid).

(Image: The cover page of the report (United Nations Children's Fund 2005))

In 2008, UNICEF published another report about "Child Marriage and the Law" (de Silva-de-Alwis 2008). It begins by describing child marriage as "a tradition which constitutes one of the most severe forms of child abuse". It emphasizes "the right to be protected from harmful traditional practices" (ibid: 1, 2). The term 'tradition' appears 39 times over 76 pages, including sentences such as "the tradition of child marriage has a disproportionately negative impact on the girl child", and "[u]nderlying causes of early marriage" include "traditional notions of the primary role of women and girls as wives and mothers" (ibid: 32). The report calls for legislative reform "to review local traditions and customs in light of international standards" and to adapt to such standards. Notably, this report also draws its argument from international conventions and the related documents (ibid: 19). It refers to Article 24(3) of the CRC about the States' obligation to abolish "traditional practices prejudicial to the health of children", including child marriage (ibid: 3, 22). It also refers to three institutional comments. The CEDAW Committee "expressed its concern about traditional customs and practices detrimental to women and girls, such as child marriage". The Human Rights Committee's General Comment 28 states, "Inequality in the enjoyment of rights by women is deeply embedded in tradition, history and culture including religious attitudes". The ICCPR Concluding Comments recommend steps "to prevent certain traditions and customs, such as forced marriage that are inconsistent with the equal rights of women" (ibid: 14).

The United Nations Population Fund's (2012) report "Marrying Too Young: End Child Marriage", argues that child marriage is a human rights violation and a deterrent to development. It says that child marriage "may be part of local tradition", and that "persistent traditions in favor of early marriage [...] set conditions in which the practice continues". In total, it mentions "tradition" 8 times throughout its 60 pages (ibid: 4, 50). It also refers to traditional gender roles, stating: "[t]raditionally the family and elders of the community have made the decision whether, when and whom a girl will marry". It concludes that "[c]hallenging harmful traditions that do not comply with human rights standards is an essential step" to address child marriage (ibid: 53).

The US Council on Foreign Relations' 31-page report includes 13 explicit references to child marriage as a 'tradition', often as a 'harmful tradition' (Vogelstein 2013). It argues "the practice of child marriage is driven by "deeply embedded cultural traditions". It then directly refers to child marriage as tradition, e.g., "[p]rogress in curbing this tradition [child marriage] has been slow" and "[t]oday, this tradition [child marriage] is motivated by poverty and social and cultural norms and is perpetuated by the low status of girls and women" (ibid: 1, 3, 7).

Equality Now (2014) is an international human rights organization that works to protect and promote the rights of women and girls. Its 2014 report refers to 'tradition' 16 times over 52 pages. The report begins by writing that "[c]hild marriage legitimizes human rights violations and abuses of girls under the guise of culture, honor, tradition, and religion" (ibid: 7). It also condemns justification based on tradition, saying that many practices (including child marriage) are often tolerated by governments and permitted in law because they are defined as cultural norms, traditions, or viewed as religious practices (ibid: 15). Therefore, it states, the "[s]tate must conduct a full review of customary and religious laws and traditional practices and evaluate how these laws and practices affect girls and women and perpetuate child marriage" (ibid: 16). It also identifies "traditional practices" as "one of the contributing factors in child marriage", together with gender inequality, poverty, lack of education, and the rule of law (ibid: 32).

Plan International Australia's report relatively carefully mentions 'tradition' four times (Evenhuis and Burn 2014). It describes "international action against harmful traditional practices including child, early and forced marriage". It claims that "child marriage is driven by beliefs about the rights and status of girls, who are too often seen as having little value outside the traditional roles of wife and mother" (ibid: 8). Its more nuanced endnote states, "often what is regarded as 'traditional' may be a relatively recent change or variant in practices which were traditionally intended to protect girls and women. It is important to recognize that cultural beliefs and values can also be a source of support to end child marriage" (ibid: 46).

ECPAT International's report focuses on sexual abuse and exploitation of children in child marriage. It uses 'tradition' most carefully and with the least condemning tone, 46 times over 89 pages (Chaudhuri 2015). It first distinguishes various notions of marriage as "a social and economic institution which has long prevailed, especially in traditional societies", and refers to "traditional cultures" as "where early marriage is more prevalent" (ibid: 20, 21). It also recognizes the tension child marriage can cause, which I mentioned earlier in this section. "In societies where the practice is widespread, new policies and legislation framed to contract child marriage may generate tension between an established notion of child marriage as a community tradition and the individual right to be free from child marriage" (ibid: 30). It also quotes Archbishop Desmond Tutu, "a champion in the movement against child marriage": "child marriage is not a religious practice – it is a tradition. There are many good traditions that bind communities together. But traditions are also not static – they evolve. Traditions that are harmful, that have outlived their purpose, must be challenged" (ibid: 71). This approach suggests that one should not presuppose that traditions *are* harmful but instead examine *if* some of them are harmful, and how.

2.3.2. 'Modernity' celebrated in the international reports

The use of 'tradition' contrasts with the use of words associated with modernity, such as freedom, choice, and autonomy. For instance, UNICEF claims that the right to make choices about one's reproductive health is contested by tradition (United Nations Children's Fund Innocenti Research Centre 2001: 18). UNICEF presents "the free consent of both partners" as the core of marriage in modern Europe (ibid: 5). It also celebrates the "independent sense of self", which is "seen as undesirable for adolescents in some societies" (ibid: 7). Their key concern about the practice of child marriage is "the curtailment of personal freedom and the lack of opportunity to develop a full sense of selfhood" (ibid: 9). Girls that marry young tend to leave the education system prematurely, resulting in them growing up without self-confidence, with "no sense of the right to assert her own point of view" and a "lack of self-esteem or of a sense of ownership of her own body" (ibid: 12). The report claims that "what passes for 'consent' in the eyes of custom of the law" does not count as real "consent" (ibid: 2).

In the 2008 report on child marriage and the law, UNICEF further criticized states that allow the practice of child marriage, claiming that they violate their commitment to guarantee women's fundamental freedoms (de Silva-de-Alwis 2008: 22). According to them, girl brides do not have the "autonomy to negotiate with their spouse" and find themselves in their new home "without much autonomy or decision-making power" (ibid: 4, 34). This, it claims, "results in the denial of the [girls'] right to decide freely and responsibly on the number and spacing of their children which is recognized in the CEDAW" (ibid: 4). It also points out that child marriage "discriminates against girls by denying them the same freedoms allowed to boys", as it is more common for girls than boys to marry below the age of 18 (ibid: 22).

UNFPA's (2012) report emphasized the 'choice' that girls lose when they marry. It writes, "[c]hoosing when and who to marry is one of life's most important decisions. […] For a girl, marriage can steal from her fundamental life choices" and child marriage "limits their life choices" (ibid: 4, 11). This is because when given a choice, girls marry later (ibid: 4). Equality Now (2014: 10) also states that their work is focused on "securing for women the rights they need to ensure they have future choices", and that "empowering girls to make their own choices/control their own lives" is necessary (ibid: 52).

However, the emphasis on choices, freedom, and autonomy seems occasionally contradictory. For instance, Plan International Australia considers that "[a]dolescence should be a period of physical, psychological and cognitive development for girls during which experimentation and risk-taking are a normal and fundamental part of developing decision making skills and autonomy" (Evenhuis and Burn 2014: 19). However, their autonomy cannot be exercised in the context of decision-making for marriage because "[w]hen child marriage abruptly ends a girl's education, it undermines her transition to adulthood and burdens her with all the responsibilities that marriage entails" (ibid: 19). The report also cites from the Human Rights Committee's General Comment No. 28: "human rights obligations require countries to protect children and to eradicate both through legislation and any other appropriate measures, all cultural or religious practices which jeopardize the freedom and well-being of female children, including child marriage" (ibid: 33).

ECPAT International's most recent report addresses this contradiction. It discusses

> the need to find a balance between recognition of the evolving capacities and sexual maturity of children – linked to the right to autonomously decide their emotional lives – and the vulnerability stemming from entering early unions, which may impact children's rights and jeopardise their interests.
>
> (Chaudhuri 2015: 20)

The articles on evolving capacities and the right to decide emotional lives recognize children's autonomy to decide to marry. The vulnerability stemming from early unions implies that "the condition of being subjugated to an older husband or in-laws and being victims of power imbalances within the family and the community limits the autonomy, agency and decision-making of girls" (ibid: 59).

2.3.3. *Blind spots in the dominant discourse*

Altogether, analysing the dominant child marriage discourse has shown it celebrates the autonomous woman and dismisses 'tradition' as a constraint on a woman's autonomy. Such a normative position is based on the modern ideals of autonomy, that we all should be able to decide about our own lives, which is especially important in the lives of women. While this sounds clear and convincing, sociological and anthropological literature has demonstrated the complexity of agency. Mahmood (2004: 15) suggests not considering agency as the capacity to realize one's interests against the weight of custom, tradition, or other obstacles. Instead, we should talk about one's "agentival capacity", that encompasses not only acts that resist norms but also the multiple ways one inhabits norms.

There are, inevitably, clashes between the imagined autonomous self and the "relational self" shaped by obligations to traditional kin and community (Merry 2009: 404). In Donnelly's (1984: 415) words, modern institutions "tend to create communities of relatively autonomous individuals, who lack the place and protections provided by traditional society". For instance, when a national court in Papua New Guinea adjudicated a case concerning a local dispute settlement that comprised a girl as compensation from one clan to another, the girl expressed her worry that the trial process might result in the loss of her tribal support (Strathern 2004). If the ultimate purpose of human rights is not only to enable persons to be autonomous agents but also to relate to other persons through mutual respect and cooperation (Freeman 1994: 507, 508), the imagined autonomous self and the 'relational self' need to be balanced.

Ironically, members of modern societies are also constrained by relationships and customs. "Man is an animal suspended in webs of significance he himself has spun" (Geertz 1977). This famous remark underlines that what is now understood as 'autonomy' is inseparable from social relationships around the self. Therefore, the modern ideal of complete 'autonomy' is an illusion. Thus, it is more useful to think of "relational autonomy", which suggests that social relationships are a necessary background, enabling conditions for autonomy (Mackenzie 2013). Autonomy's complexity also highlights the existence of multiple perspectives on an individual's decision. A decision that seems like a sacrifice of autonomy to an outsider is sometimes an act of relational autonomy for an insider. The current human rights system and black-and-white conceptualization of child marriage are insensitive to such possibilities.

In other words, the current human rights framework's ignorance of the possibility of exercising agency in 'traditional' settings is its blind spot. This blind spot exists both in the child marriage framework and in the broader human rights framework. A typical example is the issue of female genital circumcision, where a global set of institutions tend to overwhelm local claims of autonomy (Hopgood 2017: 259). Another blind spot is its dismissal of the possibility of children's agency to marry, based on a certain model of childhood prominent in modern Western societies. While international advocacy celebrates and emphasizes children's agency not to marry, the discussions about their agency to marry have been considerably limited. But if children lack the cognitive and emotional capacity to decide to marry, how are they capable of deciding not to marry?

These blind spots show that the discourse has been *modernifed*, i.e., built upon the premise of modern ideals and assumptions. Thus, the discourse on tradition reflects the ideology and beliefs of the discourse's creators, subsuming the reverse image of modernity as something undesirable. Given this, the next section turns to the discourse's implications.

2.4. Implications of the hegemonic discourse

The previous sections demonstrated the knowledge created about child marriage and the background of such knowledge. The analysis also showed that the recent campaigns against child marriage in the 2000s are built on legal documents produced by international legal institutions, which have been crafted under certain assumptions. According to Foucault, knowledge reproduces power relations. One major function of dominant discourse is to manufacture "hegemony", associated with consensus, acceptance, and legitimacy of dominance (van Dijk 1993: 255). The international discourse and the dominant schools of human rights (i.e., the natural and deliberate schools) manufacture legitimized 'hegemony' in terms of 'human rights culture'. They do so by deferring to the existing human rights system. This hegemony then continues to reproduce dominance, perpetuating the power hierarchy between North and South.

The blind spot found in the child marriage discourse analysis suggests that the current child marriage framework is based on implicit assumptions about gender, race, and 'progress'. In her essay on the American conception of 'culture', Volpp (2000) compares the narratives of two groups of female adolescents who marry older men: White and immigrants of colour. Although she does not use the term 'child marriage', she focuses on child marriage cases in the US. Volpp writes "we must recognize that our society tends more readily to identify those who deviate from the hegemonic norm, who are perceived to inhabit outsider communities, to inherit culture that we assume to be monolithic, fixed, and dysfunctional" (ibid: 98). In light of her account, the representation of child marriage is the 'othering' of a certain cultural practice. This assumption that immigrant women require liberation through induction into the progressive social mores and customs of the metropolitan West has been subjected to significant criticism (ibid). The same type of 'othering' is recognizable when international bodies call child marriage 'a harmful tradition'.

Giaquinta (2016: 1) and MacDonald (2016: 1) point out that "the girl child" has become the new favourite investment, symbol, and emblem of "a better future" from Westerners' perspective. Similarly, Mustonen (2017), critically examines the Finish Plan International's latest campaign about girl brides from a post-colonial studies perspective. She argues that this campaign is "situated within the nation's self-understanding as a 'developed' and 'progressive nation'", in the form of "celebrity humanitarianism" and relies on the "representation of third world women as passive and deprived of their agency" (ibid). Mohanty (1984: 336) warns Western feminist scholarship by drawing attention to the "explanatory potential" of particular analytic strategies employed by most Western feminist writings on women in the third world, and to their "political effects" in the context of such scholarship's hegemony. As hegemonic Western feminist scholarship tends to construct monolithic images of 'Third World Women', hegemonic child marriage discourse risks creating simplistic categories of 'Child Brides'.

The idea that culture is a problem for human rights is related to a more general tendency to culturalize problems. It is a way to interpret women's subordination in terms of cultural practices (Merry 2003: 63). Similarly, the current conceptualization of child marriage allows the *traditionalization* of problems. If human rights are a virtue and based on the idea of modernity, then 'tradition' automatically becomes a vice, as in the international child marriage discourse. This is dangerous, as the human rights system is dismissing the 'traditions' of 'the South' without attempting to investigate and discuss them. Majumdar (2009: 1, 34) criticizes the same kind of automatic negative association with the word: Although modern marriages do play out the theme of freedom, it would be problematic to equate the empty word 'tradition' with a lack of freedom. From her study in Vanuatu, Jolly (1996: 183) concludes that human rights are not necessarily inconsistent with their 'tradition', as tradition is not a static burden of the past but something created for the present. Lack of empirical work that refutes certain assumptions about 'tradition' prevents human rights systems from paying attention to context and crucial global power relationships.

Such distinction between tradition and the other is conceptualized as "abyssal lines", i.e., visible and invisible distinctions between knowledge from the South and the North, created and radicalized by modern Western "abyssal thinking" (Santos 2014). Abyssal thinking in human rights is demonstrated by the natural law theory developed by Thomas Hobbes, John Locke, Jean-Jacques Rousseau, Kant, and Hegel (Barreto 2014). Rorty (1998) argues that human rights activists rely too much on "rationality", a philosophical and normative assumption based on European Enlightenment. Baxi (1998: 129) emphasizes the role played by the non-European "subaltern discourse". Some scholars see reminiscences of colonialism. Mutua (2003: 901) describes the construction of human rights as "part of the colonial project that forms the unbroken chain of the Christian missionary, the early merchant of capital, and the colonial administrator". Merry (2006: 226) maintains that human rights are burdened by the colonialist understanding of culture.

Such limited knowledge also limits the legitimacy and validity of human rights, an "insufficiency of cultural legitimacy" in need of "cross-cultural dialogue" (An-Na'im 1992: 3). Flynn (2013) relies on Habermas' discourse theory and calls for "intercultural dialogue" about monological human rights concepts based on the natural law theory. Harris-Short (2003: 181) argues that this dialogue is insufficient within "a society of states for states" and "those at the grassroots must be given a direct voice". This chapter's dominant discourse analysis highlights the need for this both procedural and epistemological shift. While it is not easy to think of an alternative to abyssal thinking, one suggestion is, what Mingnolo (2001: 11) calls, "border thinking", which "engages the colonialism of Western epistemology from the perspective of epistemic forces that have been turned into subaltern (traditional, folkloric, religious, emotional, etc.) forms of knowledge".

The child marriage discourse analysis demonstrated an *a priori* view on what is called a 'harmful tradition'. Such a view would not exist if informed by anthropologically accurate accounts. Steps to rethinking and reworking human rights are twofold. An epistemological shift is needed throughout the campaigns striving to end child marriage practice. The above-mentioned 'border thinking' invites us to engage the currently hegemonic child marriage discourse with a perspective from 'the other' side, to avoid the simplistic representation of child marriage. The current challenge of the human rights framework is to recognize the agency of the "Exotic Other Female" (Engle 1992) or the "Third World Woman" which are caught between tradition and modernity, culturalism, and development (Mohanty 1984; Spivak 2010: 61). An accompanied procedural shift towards more inclusively making and applying human rights and to promoting multi-cultural dialogue would enable a more accurate understanding of local realities. Such efforts will help transnational organizations carefully consider the responsibilities of their intervention that aims at cultural changes (Hopgood 2017: 290). They have the potential to enable the child marriage framework to realize its capacity for emancipation and to move away from regulation and domination.

2.5. Conclusion: Towards overcoming the blind spot

Over the last decade, child marriage has become an increasingly hot topic on the human rights agenda. With the common marital age increasing in modern times, child marriage gradually became a deviant behaviour in the Western world. It then quickly became a human rights violation, an idea propagated by international organizations. Despite a large number of campaigns and reports on this topic, the child marriage framework remains uniform, unchallenged, and too simplistic. It might well be intentional 'strategic simplification'. However, in Koskenniemi's (2009: 16) words, "(t)he world's causalities are too complex, the strategic simplifications too crude".

The role of legal texts is significant. The international conventions have provided binding norms concerning child marriage. Their associated committees have further specified their opinions with general comments and recommendations. The increasingly imposing substantive standard specified in the international conventions between 1962 and 1994 is a suggestive form of globalization. The analysis showed that the recent campaigns against child marriage in the 2000s are built on the legal documents produced by international legal institutions, which have been crafted under certain assumptions. The international discourse and the dominant schools of human rights silence the assumptions underlying the framework by taking human rights as given, thus perpetuating the power hierarchy between the North and the South. The analysis provides proof of the power of accumulated self-legitimation, which helps justify the increasing strict norms imposed on child marriage.

The dominant discourse on child marriage has dismissed 'tradition' as something harmful while celebrating autonomous individuals and the ideals of 'modernity'. In fact, these two concepts are different sides of the same coin. The automatic dismissal of 'tradition' from 'the South' and the *traditionalization* of problems means one fails to recognize the possibility of autonomy existing in social settings in the Global South. Due to this blind spot, the human rights framework risks becoming self-defeating and failing to achieve an end goal: To protect the agency of human beings.

Finally, although potentially premature and experimental, I suggest ways to re-conceptualize the current child marriage (and broader human rights) framework. Reworking human rights requires a twofold shift in their construction and application: An epistemological shift to include perspectives from 'the other' side and a procedural shift to include multi-cultural dialogues. This alternative approach has the potential to aid the current black-and-white conceptualization of child marriage to overcome the blind spot. Consequently, it would help multi-lateral international organizations, and us researchers, move beyond using simplistic categorization. Only with such an inclusive approach can human rights become fully ethical, emancipatory, and efficient in practice.

One key to the inclusive approach, and towards overcoming the blind spot, is to pay attention to the context where human rights (are supposed to) work in practice. Thus the next chapter will focus on the concerns about and regulation of child marriage in Indonesia.

Bibliography

African Union. (2003). *Protocol to the African Charter on Human and Peoples' Rights on the Rights of Women in Africa.* https://www.refworld.org/docid/3f4b139d4.html

An-Na'im, A. A. (1992). Introduction. In A. A. An-Na'im (Ed.), *Human Rights in Cross-Cultural Perspectives: A Quest for Consensus* (pp. 1–15). Philadelphia: University of Pennsylvania Press

Ansell, N. (2005). *Children, Youth, and Development.* Abingdon, Oxon ; New York: Routledge.

Appadurai, A. (1996). *Modernity At Large: Cultural Dimensions of Globalization.* Minneapolis, MN: University of Minnesota Press.

Archambault, C. S. (2011). Ethnographic empathy and the social context of rights: "rescuing" maasai girls from early marriage. *American Anthropologist, 113*(4), 632–643. https://doi.org/10.1111/j.1548-1433.2011.01375.x

Aries, P. (1996). *Centuries of Childhood* (R. Baldick, Trans.). London, UK: Pimlico.

Asghari, S. (2019). Early marriage in Iran: A pragmatic approach. *Journal of Human Rights Practice, 11*(3), 569–588. https://doi.org/10.1093/jhuman/huz035

Barreto, J.-M. (2014). Epistemologies of the south and human rights: Santos and the quest for global and cognitive justice. *Indiana Journal of Global Legal Studies, 21*(2), 395–422.

Baxi, U. (1998). Voices of suffering and the future of human rights. *Transnational Law & Contemporary Problems, 8*(2), 125–170.

Bellieni, C. (2016). The best age for pregnancy and undue pressures. *Journal of Family and Reproductive Health, 10*(3), 104–107.

Blackburn, S., & Bessell, S. (1997). Marriageable age: Political debates on early marriage in twentieth-century Indonesia. *Indonesia, 63*, 107–141. https://doi.org/10.2307/3351513

Boyden, J. (1997). Childhood and the policymakers. In A. James & A. Prout (Eds.), *Constructing and Reconstructing Childhood: Contemporary Issues in the Sociological Study of Childhood* (pp. 184–215). London, UK: Falmer Press.

Boyden, J., Pankhurst, A., & Tafere, Y. (2012). Child protection and harmful traditional practices: Female early marriage and genital modification in Ethiopia. *Development in Practice, 22*(4), 510–522. https://doi.org/10.1080/09614524.2012.672957

Bunting, A. (2005). Stages of development: Marriage of girls and teens as an international human rights issue. *Social & Legal Studies, 14*(1), 17–38. https://doi.org/10.1177/0964663905049524

Bunting, A., & Merry, S. E. (2007). Global regulation and local political struggles: Early marriage in Northern Nigeria. In S. A. Venkatesh & R. Kassimir (Eds.), *Youth, Globalization, and the Law* (pp. 321–353). Stanford, CA: Stanford University Press.

Calavita, K. (2010). *Invitation to Law and Society: An Introduction to the Study of Real Law*. Chicago, IL: University of Chicago Press.

Cantwell, N. (2016). Are 'best interests' a pillar or a problem for implementing the human rights of children? In T. Liefaard & J. Sloth-Nielsen (Eds.), *The United Nations Convention on the Rights of the Child: Taking Stock after 25 Years and Looking Ahead* (pp. 61–72). http://booksandjournals.brillonline.com/content/books/b9789004295056s006

Chaudhuri, E. R. (2015). *Thematic Report: Unrecognised Sexual Abuse and Exploitation of Children in Child, Early and Forced Marriage*. Bangkok, Thailand: ECPAT International.

Committee on the Elimination of Discrimination against Women & Committee on the Rights of the Child. (2014). *Joint General Recommendation No. 31/General Comment No. 18 on Harmful Practices, CEDAW/C/GC/31–CRC/C/GC/18.*

Cowan, J. K. (2006). Culture and rights after culture and rights. *American Anthropologist, 108*(1), 9–24. https://doi.org/10.1525/aa.2006.108.1.9

Daly, A. (2018). *Children, Autonomy and the Courts: Beyond the Right to be Heard*. Brill Nijhoff. https://brill.com/view/title/35870

de Silva-de-Alwis, R. (2008). *Child Marriage and the Law: Legislative Reform Initiative Paper Series*. New York, NY: UNICEF.

Dembour, M.-B. (2010). What are human rights? Four schools of thought. *Human Rights Quarterly, 32*(1), 1–20.

Donnelly, J. (1984). Cultural relativism and universal human rights. *Human Rights Quarterly, 6*(4), 400–419. https://doi.org/10.2307/762182

ECPAT International, Plan International, Save the Children, UNICEF, & World Vision. (2014). *National Child Protection Systems in the East Asia and Pacific Region: A review and analysis of mappings and assessments*. Bangkok, Thailand: ECPAT International; Plan International.

Engle, K. (1992). Female subjects of public international law: Human rights and the exotic other female symposium on feminist critical legal studies and postmodernism: Part Two: The politics of gender identity. *New England Law Review, 26*, 1509–1526.

Equality Now. (2014). *Protecting the Girl Child: Using the Law to End Child, Early and Forced Marriage and Related Human Rights Violations*. New York; Nairobi; London: Equality Now.

Evenhuis, M., & Burn, J. (2014). *Just Married, Just a Child: Child marriage in the Indo-Pacific Region*. Melbourne: Plan International Australia.

Flynn, J. (2013). *Reframing the Intercultural Dialogue on Human Rights: A Philosophical Approach*. New York: Routledge.

Freeman, M. (1994). The philosophical foundations of human rights. *Human Rights Quarterly, 16*(3), 491–514. https://doi.org/10.2307/762434

Geertz, C. (1977). *The Interpretation of Cultures*. New York, NY: Basic Books.

Giaquinta, B. (2016). *Silenced Subjectivities & Missed Representations: Unpacking The Gaps of the International Child Marriage Discourse* [Master Thesis]. International Institute of Social Studies.

Giddens, A. (1991). *Modernity and Self-Identity: Self and Society in the Late Modern Age*. Stanford, CA: Stanford University Press.

Girls Not Brides. (n.d.a). *About Child Marriage*. Girls Not Brides. https://www.girlsnotbrides.org/about-child-marriage/ (accessed on April 20, 2021).

Girls Not Brides. (n.d.b). *Health*. Girls Not Brides. https://www.girlsnotbrides.org/themes/health/ (accessed on April 20, 2021).

Girls Not Brides. (n.d.c). *The World We Want: End Child Marriage*. https://www.youtube.com/watch?v=RvQjBjqmNLM (accessed on April 20, 2021).

Glendon, M. A. (1989). *The Transformation of Family Law*. Chicago, IL: The University of Chicago Press.

Greene, M. E. (2014). *Ending Child Marriage in a Generation: What Research is Needed?* Ford Foundation.

Grijns, M., & Horii, H. (2018). Child marriage in a village in West Java (Indonesia): Compromises between legal obligations and religious concerns. *Asian Journal of Law and Society*, 1–14. https://doi.org/10.1017/als.2018.9

Grugel, J. (2013). Children's rights and children's welfare after the Convention on the rights of the child. *Progress in Development Studies*, *13*(1), 19–30. https://doi.org/10.1177/146499341201300102

Gumbonzvanda, N. (2017). FreedomForFarirai, https://twitter.com/vanyaradzayi/status/922426611265409024 (accessed on April 12, 2021).

Gutteridge, J. A. C. (1957). Supplementary Slavery Convention, 1956. *The International and Comparative Law Quarterly*, *6*(3), 449–471.

Hanson, K. (2016). Children's participation and agency when they don't 'do the right thing.' *Childhood*, *23*(4), 471–475.

Harris-Short, S. (2003). International Human Rights Law: Imperialist, inept and ineffective? Cultural relativism and the UN Convention on the rights of the child. *Human Rights Quarterly*, *25*(1), 130–181. https://doi.org/10.1353/hrq.2003.0004

Hill, M. (2006). Children's voices on ways of having a voice: Children's and young people's perspectives on methods used in research and consultation. *Childhood*, *13*(1), 69–89. https://doi.org/10.1177/0907568206059972

Hopgood, S. (2017). Modernity at the cutting edge: Human rights meets FGM. In M. N. Barnett (Ed.), *Paternalism Beyond Borders* (pp. 256–291). Cambridge, UK: Cambridge University Press. https://doi.org/10.1017/9781316799956.009

Ignatieff, M. (2003). *Human Rights as Politics and Idolatry* (A. Gutmann, Ed.). Princeton: Princeton University Press.

Imoh, A. T.-D. (2019). Terminating childhood: Dissonance and synergy between global children's rights norms and local discourses about the transition from childhood to adulthood in Ghana. *Human Rights Quarterly*, *41*(1), 160–182. https://doi.org/10.1353/hrq.2019.0007

International Planned Parenthood Federation. (2015). Child marriage- it's modern slavery. International Planned Parenthood Federation. https://www.ippf.org/blogs/child-marriage-it-s-modern-slavery

Irdiana, N. (2015, June 9). *Ending Child Marriage: The Art (Challenge!) of Asking Difficult Questions*. Child Marriage, Sexual Moralities, and The Politics of Decentralization in Indonesia, Jakarta.

Jacobson, D. (2012). *Of Virgins and Martyrs: Women and Sexuality in Global Conflict*. Baltimore: Johns Hopkins University Press.

James, A., Jenks, C., & Prout, A. (1998). *Theorizing Childhood*. Cambridge: Polity Press.

James, A., & Prout, A. (1997). A new paradigm for the sociology of childhood? Provenance, promise and problems. In A. James & A. Prout (Eds.), *Constructing and Reconstructing Childhood: Contemporary Issues in the Sociological Study of Childhood* (pp. 7–33). Falmer Press.

Jenks, C. (2005). *Childhood.* London; New York: Routledge.

Jolly, M. (1996). "Woman Ikat Raet long human Raet O No?" Women's rights, human rights and domestic violence in Vanuatu. *Feminist Review, 52*, 169–190. https://doi.org/10.2307/1395780

Komulainen, S. (2007). The Ambiguity of the child's 'voice' in social research. *Childhood, 14*(1), 11–28. https://doi.org/10.1177/0907568207068561

Koskenniemi, M. (2009). The politics of international law – 20 years later. *The European Journal of International Law, 20*(1), 7–19.

Liebel, M. (2012a). Discriminated against being children: A blind spot in the human rights arena. In M. Liebel (Ed.), *Children's Rights from Below: Cross-Cultural Perspectives* (pp. 94–107). Basingstoke: Palgrave Macmillan.

Liebel, M. (2012b). The role of children in shaping new contexts of children's rights. In M. Liebel (Ed.), *Children's Rights from Below: Cross-Cultural Perspectives* (pp. 199–225). Basingstoke: Palgrave Macmillan.

Lundy, L. (2007). 'Voice' is not enough: Conceptualising Article 12 of the United Nations Convention on the rights of the child. *British Educational Research Journal, 33*(6), 927–942. https://doi.org/10.1080/01411920701657033

Lundy, L. (2018). In defence of tokenism? Implementing children's right to participate in collective decision-making. *Childhood, 25*(3), 340–354. https://doi.org/10.1177/0907568218777292

Lundy, L., Tobin, J., & Parkes, A. (2019). Article 12. The right to respect for the views of the child. In J. Tobin (Ed.), *The UN Convention on the Rights of the Child: A Commentary* (pp. 397–434). Oxford, New York: Oxford University Press.

MacDonald, K. (2016). Calls for educating girls in the Third World: Futurity, girls and the 'Third World Woman'. *Gender, Place & Culture, 23*(1), 1–17. https://doi.org/10.1080/0966369X.2014.991699

Mackenzie, C. (2013). The importance of relational autonomy and capabilities for an ethics of vulnerability. In C. Mackenzie, W. Rogers, & S. Dodds (Eds.), *Vulnerability: New Essays in Ethics and Feminist Philosophy* (pp. 33–59). New York, NY: Oxford University Press.

Mahmood, S. (2004). *Politics of Piety: The Islamic Revival and the Feminist Subject.* Princeton, NJ: Princeton University Press.

Majumdar, R. (2009). *Marriage and Modernity: Family Values in Colonial Bengal.* Durham: Duke University Press Books.

Merry, S. E. (1997). Global human rights and local social movements in a legally plural world. *Canadian Journal of Law and Society, 12*, 247–272.

Merry, S. E. (2003). Human rights law and the demonization of culture (and anthropology along the way). *PoLAR: Political and Legal Anthropology Review, 26*(1), 55–76. https://doi.org/10.1525/pol.2003.26.1.55

Merry, S. E. (2006). *Human Rights and Gender Violence Translating International Law into Local Justice.* Chicago: University of Chicago Press.

Merry, S. E. (2009). Relating to the subjects of human rights: the culture of agency in human rights discourse. In M. Freeman & D. Napier (Eds.), *Law and Anthropology: Current Legal Issues Volume 12* (pp. 385–407). London; Oxford: Oxford University Press.

Merry, S. E. (2016). *The Seductions of Quantification Measuring Human Rights, Gender Violence, and Sex Trafficking.* Chicago: University of Chicago Press.

Mihara, N., & Abrahams, J. (2017). DevExplains: Do we need a new term for "child marriage?" *Devex*. https://www.devex.com/news/sponsored/devexplains-do-we-need-a-new-term-for-child-marriage-90039

Mingnolo, W. (2001). Local histories and global designs: An interview with Walter Mingnolo. *Discourse, 22*(3), 7–33.

Mirowsky, J. (2002). Parenthood and health: The Pivotal and optimal age at first birth. *Social Forces, 81*(1), 315–349. https://doi.org/10.1353/sof.2002.0055

Mohanty, C. T. (1984). Under western eyes: Feminist scholarship and colonial discourses. *Boundary 2, 12/13*, 333–358. https://doi.org/10.2307/302821

Moses, J. (2017). *Marriage, Law and Modernity: Global Histories*. London; New York: Bloomsbury Publishing.

Mustonen, L. (2017). Is it time for Finnish celebrities to save the black girls of a "developing country"? *Allegra Lab: Anthropology, Law, Art & World*. http://allegralaboratory.net/finnish-celebrities-save-the-black-girls-of-a-developing-country/

Mutua, M. W. (2003). The transformation of Africa. In F. G. Isa & K. De Feyter (Eds.), *International Human Rights Law in a Global Context* (pp. 899–924). Bilbao: University of Deusto.

Office of the United Nations High Commissioner for Human Rights. (2007). *Legislative History of the Convention on the Rights of the Child*.

Organization of African Unity (OAU). (1990). *African Charter on the Rights and Welfare of the Child, CAB/LEG/24.9/49*. Organization of African Unity (OAU).

Peleg, N. (2013). Reconceptualising the child's right to development: Children and the capability approach. *International Journal of Children's Rights, 21*, 523–542.

Roberts, H. (2000). Listening to children: And hearing them. In P. Christensen & A. James (Eds.), *Research with Children: Perspectives and Practices* (pp. 225–240). London: Falmer Press.

Rorty, R. (1998). *Truth and Progress: Philosophical Papers*. Cambridge: Cambridge University Press.

Santos, B. de S. (2014). *Epistemologies of the South: Justice Against Epistemicide*. Boulder: Routledge.

Shaw, A. (2006). The arranged transnational cousin marriages of British Pakistanis: Critique, dissent and cultural continuity. *Contemporary South Asia, 15*(2), 209–220.

Shier, H. (2001). Pathways to participation: Openings, opportunities and obligations. *Children & Society, 15*(2), 107–117. https://doi.org/10.1002/chi.617

Sloth-Nielsen, J. (2012). Modern African childhoods: Does law matter? In M. Freeman (Ed.), *Law and Childhood Studies* (pp. 117–132). Oxford: Oxford University Press.

Spivak, G. C. (2010). "Can the Subaltern speak?" revised edition, from the "History" chapter of critique of Postcolonial reason. In R. Morris (Ed.), *Can the Subaltern Speak?: Reflections on the History of an Idea* (pp. 21–80). New York: Columbia University Press.

Spyrou, S. (2016). Troubling children's voices in research. In F. Esser, M. S. Baader, T. Betz, & B. Hungerland (Eds.), *Reconceptualising Agency and Childhood: New perspectives in Childhood Studies* (pp. 105–118). London: New York, NY: Routledge.

Stephens, S. (1995). Introduction: Children and the politics of culture in "'Late Capitalism'". In S. Stephens (Ed.), *Children and the Politics of Culture* (pp. 3–48). Princeton, N.J: Princeton University Press.

Strathern, M. (2004). Losing (out on) intellectual resources. In A. Pottage & M. Mundy (Eds.), *Law, Anthropology, and the Constitution of the Social: Making Persons and Things* (pp. 201–233). Cambridge; New York: Cambridge University Press.

The Fourth World Conference on Women. (1995). *Beijing Declaration and Platform for Action, A/CONF.177/20 and A/CONF.177/20/Add.1.* http://hrlibrary.umn.edu/instree/e5dplw.htm

Tisdall, E. K. M. (2016). Subjects with agency? Children's participation in family law proceedings. *Journal of Social Welfare and Family Law, 38*(4), 362–379. https://doi.org/10.1080/09649069.2016.1239345

Tisdall, E. K. M. (2017). Conceptualising children and young people's participation: Examining vulnerability, social accountability and co-production. *The International Journal of Human Rights, 21*(1), 59–75. https://doi.org/10.1080/13642987.2016.1248125

Tobin, J. (2015). Understanding children's rights: A vision beyond vulnerability. *Nordic Journal of International Law, 84*(2), 155–182. https://doi.org/10.1163/15718107-08402002

Turner, C. (2013). *Out of the Shadows: Child marriage and slavery.* Anti-Slavery International.

U.N. Committee on the Convention of the Elimination of All Forms of Discrimination against Women. (1994). *General Recommendation no. 21 concerning Article 16(2) on equality in marriage and family relations.* http://www.un.org/womenwatch/daw/cedaw/recommendations/recomm.html

UN Committee on the Elimination of Discrimination against Women. (1994). *CEDAW General Recommendation No. 21 on Equality in Marriage and Family Relations, CEDAW/C/GC/31–CRC/C/GC/18.* http://www.refworld.org/docid/48abd52c0.html

UNFPA. (2012). *Marrying Too Young: End Child Marriage.* New York: UNFPA.

United Nations Children's Fund. (2005). *Early Marriage: A Harmful Traditional Practice.* New York: United Nations Children's Fund.

United Nations Children's Fund. (2014). *Ending Child Marriage: Progress and Prospects.* New York: UNICEF.

United Nations Children's Fund Innocenti Research Centre. (2001). *Early Marriage: Child Spouses.* Florence: United Nations Children's Fund Innocenti Research Centre.

United Nations General Assembly. (1965). *General Assembly resolution 2018 (XX), Recommendation on Consent to Marriage, Minimum Age for Marriage and Registration of Marriage.*

United Nations General Assembly. (2015). *Resolution Adopted by the General Assembly on 18 December 2014 (69/156. Child, Early and Forced Marriage).*

United Nations Human Rights Council. (2013). *Resolution Adopted by the Human Rights Council, Strengthening Efforts to Prevent and Eliminate Child, Early and Forced Marriage: Challenges, Achievements, Best Practices and Implementation Gaps, A/HRC/RES/24/23.*

United Nations Population Fund. (2013). *Motherhood in Childhood: Facing the Challenge of Adolescent Pregnancy.* New York: UNFPA.

van Dijk, T. A. (1993). Principles of critical discourse analysis. *Discourse & Society, 4*(2), 249–283. https://doi.org/10.1177/0957926593004002006

Varadan, S. (2019). The principle of evolving capacities under the UN Convention on the rights of the child. *The International Journal of Children's Rights, 27*(2), 306–338. https://doi.org/10.1163/15718182-02702006

Vogelstein, R. (2013). *Ending Child Marriage.* Council on Foreign Relations Press. http://www.cfr.org/children/ending-child-marriage/p30734

Volpp, L. (2000). Blaming culture for bad behavior. *Yale Journal of Law & the Humanities, 12*, 89–116.

Warendorf, H. C. S., & Curry-Sumner, I. (2003). *Family Law Legislation of the Netherlands.* Antwerp; New York: Intersentia.

World Health Organization. (2011). *WHO Guidelines on Preventing Early Pregnancy and Poor Reproductive Outcomes Among Adolescents in Developing Countries.* Geneva: WHO.

World Health Organization. (2017). *Global Accelerated Action for the Health of Adolescents (AA-HA!): Guidance to Support Country Implementation.* Geneva: WHO.

Chapter 3

Compromise

With an earnest look, Siti followed the handshake between her father and her groom. She had not seen her father for ages. But here he was, as her guardian, stating that he agreed to marry off his daughter for a dower (mahr) of 2 grams of gold, her wedding ring. Wawan, her groom, replied – without stammering, she noticed – that he accepted this offer. The core of their religious marriage (ijab kabul) was over. The assistant marriage registrar (amil) led the prayer and then it was her turn, after her husband, to sign the papers. Her guardian and the two witnesses also signed, and both Wawan and her received their marriage certificates. The ring! Yes, she smiled, 17 and married …![1]

In Indonesia, the minimum age for marriage under state law at this moment is 16 for girls and 19 for boys. So in Indonesia, there is a marriage category that includes married girls aged 16 or 17, like Siti. That category is considered 'child marriage' under international conventions and a standard marriage under Indonesian law. The Indonesian government actively engages in international conventions. It has set development goals to end child marriage and comply with human rights standards. However, it also faces social resistance at every level of society. Religion plays a crucial role. In Section 1.2, I explained the reasons I chose Indonesia and Bali as the main case study. Before focusing on the Balinese contexts in Chapters 4, 5, and 6, this chapter examines the state laws and policies that are applied throughout Indonesia, including Bali. As Indonesian national policies are closely linked to Islamic power and concerns, this chapter will look into legal practices in the Muslim majority area of Indonesia, by referring mainly to research in West Java. This research consists of interviews and case analysis at religious courts that I conducted for a previous research project (Horii 2020) and ethnographic research in a village conducted by Mies Grijns (Grijns et al. 2016).

Section 3.1 portrays the Indonesian government's policies regarding this issue, in relation to the perception of child marriage in the international

1 Observation by Grijns and her research assistant, at the Office of Religious Affairs, Sukaraja, October 14, 2016.

DOI: 10.4324/9781003184546-3

development discourse. Section 3.2 examines state regulations, illustrating the dilemma the Indonesian government faces in achieving its development goals while considering Islamic power and concerns. The next two sections will explore legal practices in West Java to better understand the relationship between state law, Islam, and child marriage. Section 3.3 explains the role of institutions in registering a marriage and then describes the practice at the state court's level, focusing on marriage dispensation. Section 3.4 discusses child marriage at a village level, the various ways of practising illegal underage marriage, and the role of intermediary figures who facilitate such practices. Considering the legal and political structure and the local practice of child marriage, Section 3.5 returns to the discussion on the minimum age for marriage and the desirability of such legal reforms.

3.1. Child marriage and development in Indonesia

Indonesia ranks seventh globally in countries that have the highest absolute numbers of child marriage (UNICEF Indonesia 2016: 1). UNICEF Indonesia reports that in 2012, roughly 1,349,000 girls married before the age of 18, and some 300,000 of them married before 16 (Ibid). Surprisingly, after decades of steady decrease, the average child marriage rate plateaued at around 25% between 2010 and 2013 (Badan Pusat Statistik (BPS) 2016; UNICEF Indonesia & UNICEF 2016).

As discussed in Chapter 2, the global discourse considers child marriage to bear all kinds of negative consequences for girls. These consequences include reduced education opportunities, reproductive health hazards (difficult deliveries and a higher risk of HIV/AIDS; premature babies with disabilities), and an increased risk of mother and child mortality. Other problems associated with child marriage include domestic and sexual violence, as well as the exploitation of child brides as domestic servants or as victims of sex trafficking, either within their marriage or after, when they are left divorced or abandoned (Turner 2013: 30; Equality Now 2014: 7).

Besides the individual problems, the global discourse also mentions the societal consequences of child marriage, such as maternal mortality, low levels of education, and high divorce rates that harm people's livelihoods. According to UNICEF Indonesia (2016: 1), child marriage gives rise to intergenerational poverty. Indonesia has a large young population. The younger generations must have access to quality education, adequate nutrition, and healthcare (including sexual and reproductive health) to realize their economic potential. This is where child marriage comes in as a disturbing factor. UNICEF claims that child marriage in Indonesia caused a loss of at least 1.7 per cent of GDP in 2014 (Rabi et al. 2015). From an economic development perspective, these perceived macro consequences justify the urgency of ending child marriage.

The Indonesian government acknowledges the damaging impact of child marriage and supports the new 2015–2030 Sustainable Development Goals.

Ending child marriage is one of the targets. SDG 5.3 reads: "Eliminate all harmful practices, such as child, early and forced marriage, and female genital mutilation". The Indonesian government also actively engages in international conventions. It ratified the Convention on the Elimination of All Forms of Discrimination against Women (CEDAW) in 1984 and the Convention on the Rights of the Child (CRC) in 1990.

President Joko Widodo's government was recently praised for its national strategy to eliminate violence against children, including innovative endeavours to alleviate poverty through social protection schemes. The Smart Indonesia Card subsidizes primary and secondary students from lower socio-economic backgrounds, supporting the policy target of 12-year compulsory education instead of the present 9 years. A new national health insurance scheme has been introduced to improve health care for all. These steps could also help prevent child marriage. Behind the scenes, a programme to eliminate child marriage is already included in the Government Work Plan 2017–2018.[2] The president also requested the Ministry of Empowerment for Women and Protection of Children to prepare a proposal for a *Perppu* (Government Regulation in lieu of Law) on the elimination of child marriage. The regulation was drafted in 2016 in cooperation with civil society organizations (Kartikasari 2016). So, in principle, the government supports measures to prevent child marriage in line with the SDGs. One of the measures is the law, which the next section will discuss.

3.2. The making of state laws: Dilemmas, compromises, and contradictions

3.2.1. *The controversy over the marriageable age and Marriage Law 1974*

In the quest for legal unification in Indonesia, there have been constant struggles to accommodate diverse ideologies and norms, often resulting in dilemmas, compromises, and contradictions. Marriage Law 1974 is a good illustration of such compromises. In this section, I first discuss the history of controversy over the marriageable age, particularly over Marriage Law 1974, and introduce some state laws that define children.

Debates on the marriageable age started a century ago under the Dutch colonial government. The European standard then was that girls were allowed to marry at the age of 15, and boys at 18, and the colonial government identified marriage below those ages as a cause of poverty, hindering development, and thus attempted to prevent and forbid it by law (Van Bemmelen and

2 Interview by Grijns with Sylvana Apituley, chief expert staff at Deputy V of the Presidential Staff, March 11, 2017.

Grijns 2019: 291). But community-level enforcement continued to fail due to gaps between government and local realities, including the strong influence of local religious actors (Ibid: 294–300). At that time, the growing number of Western-educated Indonesians advocated against marrying young (Blackburn and Bessell 1997: 119). For instance, a 1912 weekly newspaper for women ("*Soenting Melajoe*"), under the heading "Undesirable customs of ours", reads: "One of these customs is parents marrying young girls to old men. [...] How bad this is!!! Abandon this bad custom, copy the Europeans!" (Ibid: 110). In contrast, the conservative groups resisted arguments voiced by a youth group that was "keen to adopt 'modern' ways that favored a larger degree of individual freedom". They argued, e.g., "It is right for parents to choose the husband. [...] If you leave it to a girl, she may be tricked into marriage by a womanizer or misled by men who deceive girls as we read about in Europe" (Ibid: 111). These stories demonstrate that, since colonial times, child marriage and marriageable age have been discussed in terms of *adat,* religion, and 'modern' or 'Western' lifestyles.

The debates and contestations continued after independence and culminated in the drafting process of the 1974 Marriage Law. This law was ultimately a compromise, following a political struggle between groups advocating progressive ideas of women's rights and those favouring more conservative ideas of marriage based on their interpretations of Islamic texts. When in 1973, the government submitted the draft bill of the Marriage Law to the parliament, one of its main intentions was to enhance women's rights in marriage (Pompe and Otto 1990: 419). However, some Muslim organizations and the Islamist party PPP (*Partai Persatuan Pembangunan,* United Development Party) strongly opposed the bill, accusing the government of hostility against Islam (Sidel 2018: 107). They staged walkouts from parliament sessions. These walkouts led the government to conclude that the potential cost of pushing through its proposal would be too high (Cammack, Young, and Heaton 1996: 62). As a result, the government changed several articles in the draft, including the article on marriageable age. The initial draft proposed that the minimum marriageable age be 18 for women and 21 for men.[3] However, after facing strong opposition from conservative Muslims, the government lowered the age to 16 for girls and 19 for boys.

In 2014, the Constitutional Court rejected a judicial review of the 1974 Marriage Law, instigated by women's and youth organizations to increase the marriageable age for girls from 16 to 18. During the hearings, all major religious organizations' opinions were presented. The judges seemed to ignore the views of moderate Islam and non-Muslim experts on the negative consequences of child marriage for girls. They referred only to the Muslim standard of *akil*

3 The Draft Marriage Law of 1973, Article 7(1): 'Marriage is permitted only if the male has reached the age of 21 years and the female has reached the age of 18 years'.

baligh, mental and physical maturity, as a measure of marriageability. The only dissenting opinion amongst nine judges, which was referring to human rights and development, came from the sole female, non-Muslim judge, Maria Farida Indrati.[4] Even after losing the case at the Constitutional Court, the campaigners continued pushing for this legislative change. With their second petition, they succeeded in winning the case in 2019. With the decision, the marriageable age for girls will be raised to 19 (Misiyah Direktur Institut Kapal Perempuan (Steering Committee Gender Watch-Program) n.d.). Section 3.5 will return to discussing the latest policies on the minimum age for marriage and their effects.

3.2.2. The Marriage Law and other laws with a definition of children

Although Article 7 (1) of the Marriage Law limits marriage to 16 for girls and 19 for boys, technically anyone can marry below that age if the court gives its consent. Article 7 (2) allows the parents of underage parties to petition for a dispensation from the court. As the article does not set any condition or requirement for judges to grant dispensations, it gives judges significant discretion.

While girls can legally marry at the age of 16 or lower (with a dispensation), the Law on Human Rights of 1999[5] defines children as all *unmarried* persons under the age of 18. So under the Law on Human Rights, married persons, regardless of age, are no longer considered children. They then fall outside that law's scope of protection, losing the right to education, information, and to rest and mix with children of their age. The UN Committee on the Rights of the Child voiced its concerns, stating that "in some State parties married children are legally considered adults, even if they are under 18, depriving them of all the special protection measures they are entitled to under the Convention" (Committee on the Rights of the Child 2007).

The exclusion of married persons from the definition of children contradicts the Child Protection Law, which defines a child as any person being less than 18 years of age. The Child Protection Law is clearly inspired by the UN Convention on the Rights of the Child. The Law's Article 2 refers to the national Pancasila[6] ideology, the 1945 Constitution, and the CRC's basic prin-

4 She stated that the original Marriage Law was a compromise 41 years ago and that Indonesian society since then had developed a much more advanced understanding of human rights. She also argued that the continuing use of the age of 16 for marriage for girls produces legal uncertainty vis-à-vis other laws that are based on the understanding of the age of 18 marking the end of childhood (CC judgment no. 30-74/PUU-XII/2014: 237, 239).

5 Law No.39 of 1999 on Human Rights.

6 The five pillars of the Indonesian state are included in the preamble of the 1945 Constitution. They are a belief in God, nationalism, humanism, democracy, and social justice. The New Order regime (1966-1998) turned these five pillars into a single ideology, which served as a means of promoting national unity amidst diversity.

ciples. The Child Protection Law includes parental responsibilities, including the responsibility to prevent underage marriages (Article 26 (1) c).

This section presented Indonesia's state laws on marriageable age and laws that define children and their rights. The overview demonstrates that religious power and liberal human rights advocates have had significant influences on law-making over the last decades. The gap between these groups results in compromises and contradictions within current family law and laws related to human rights. The next section will examine the various institutions that play roles in implementing these laws.

3.3. The role of various institutions in the state regulation of marriage

Several institutions regulate marriages in Indonesia: The civil court has jurisdiction over non-Muslim marriage and divorce disputes, while the religious court has jurisdiction over Muslim disputes (Cammack and Feener 2012: 27). Non-Muslims register their marriages at the Civil Registration Office (KCS, *Kantor Catatan Sipil*), and Muslims register theirs at the Office of Religious Affairs (KUA, *Kantor Urusan Agama*). However, only religious and civil courts may decide on dispensations for underage marriages. When granting a dispensation, the court letter allows petitioners to register their marriage even when at least one spouse is under the official minimum marital age (i.e., 16 for girls and 19 for boys).[7] Since I collected data in a Muslim majority area, this chapter in particular focuses on religious courts and KUA. Chapter 4 will deal with marriage registration for non-Muslims.

3.3.1. *Marriage registration office for Muslims*

For Muslims, Article 2 of the Regulation on Marriage Registration (issued by the Ministry of Religious Affairs[8]) clarifies the role of marriage registrars (PPN, *Pegawai Pencacat Nikah*). The registrars are employees of KUA, the Office of Religious Affairs, who examine requirements and monitor and record Muslim marriage and divorce. In Article 15, the Regulation indicates that if the marriage requirements are not fulfilled, PPN are forbidden to register such marriages.[9] The Civil Registration Law No.23 of 2006 sets various penalties for fraud or failure to register a marriage (Van Huis and Wirastri 2012: 10). Nurlaelawati (2010: 189) describes the KUA as placed at the intermediary level between

7 Article 6 of the Government Regulation No.9 of 1975 on the Implementation of the Marriage Law 1974.

8 Regulation of the Minister of Religious Affairs No. 11 of 2007 on Marriage Registration.

9 "Marriage registrars are prohibited from assisting the implementation and registration of marriages if:
1. The requirements referred to in Article 5 (2) are not met;
2. Knowing of violation of the terms or conditions of marriage". (translated by the author)

'*ulama*' (traditional religious authorities) and the religious courts. She finds that KUA officials consider themselves more as guardians of *shari'a* and interpretations of the *ulama* than as state officials. She further emphasizes KUA's insight into marital problems in practice because KUA officials themselves are firmly rooted in local society (Ibid).

Local leaders such as the village head (*kepala desa*) and *amil* play an important role in preparing marriage registrations. The *amil* is an assistant marriage registrar at the village level (P3N, *Pembantu Pegawai Pencacat Nikah*), who supports officials at the sub-district level. In practice, they register marriages at KUA in cooperation with PPN, so that people in the village rarely need to go to KUA and can leave all of the dealings to their *amil*. This practice will be explained in detail later in this chapter.

3.3.2. Legal practice of underage marriage: Judicial perspectives and justifications

As explained earlier, Article 7 (2) of Marriage Law 1974 grants courts discretion in issuing marriage dispensations. My previous research on religious courts in West Java and a report from Plan International Australia found that more than 90% of the marriage dispensation cases brought to courts are approved (Horii 2020; Evenhuis and Jennifer Burn 2014). The number of applications has increased significantly in recent years, reaching 9,632 in 2012 (Indonesian Legal Aid Association for Women 2012). According to Koalisi 18+'s report on marriage dispensation cases in three different districts in Indonesia (Tuban, Bogor and Mamuju), marriage dispensation was granted in 367 out of 377 cases (Eddyono et al. 2016). The most common reasons for applying were "*pacaran*" (dating), "*akil baligh*" (maturity to get married), and readiness to be housewife/breadwinner (Ibid: 189).

In my previous study, the court decision analysis indicated that fear of *zinah* was the most influential factor for judges to grant dispensations. They did so to protect girls from social stigma if they may have already engaged in sexual intercourse (Horii 2020). Thus, judges sought to protect girls through granting marriage to allow them to escape the emotional stress resulting from social pressure and to protect their unborn children, who might otherwise be labelled as illegitimate (Ibid). My analysis also found that judges cite Islamic laws based on the *Quran* and *Sunnah*[10] as often as state laws, while they never applied any aspect of the Indonesian Child Protection Law or referred to international human rights.

One of the Islamic principles that judges refer to as guiding their decisions is "*kemaslahatan*" (common good) (Ibid). *Kemaslahatan* stipulates that avoiding harm is more important than doing good (Ibid). This concept of avoiding

10 The sayings and deeds of the Prophet Muhammad.

"causing harm" (*madharat* or *mafsadat*) may lead judges to rule in favour of child marriage for young pregnant girls. They may do so to protect them from the social stigma they may suffer for being an unwed mother, since for them, avoiding harm (social stigma) is more important than doing good (avoiding child marriage) (Ibid).

So judges at religious courts facilitate legal underage marriages for the protection of children, namely girls and babies. However, dispensations account for roughly only 8% of underage marriage cases. This figure is calculated with the number of dispensations granted in Indonesia in 2012 (8,500), divided by the estimated number of girls that marry under the age of 15 each year (110,000) (UNICEF Indonesia 2016: 1). The number of dispensations is calculated by multiplying the approval rate of marriage dispensation in religious court (90%) by the total number of dispensations submitted to courts in 2012 (9,632 cases).

3.4. Child marriage in a rural Muslim setting

3.4.1. Heterogeneity of child marriage

If the court facilitates only 8% of underage marriages, how do 'underage' people marry in other cases? To understand why the court is not more often involved in such cases, I collaborated with Grijns, who conducted an ethnographic study at the village level in the northern part of the Sukabumi district in West Java. The roughly 8,000 inhabitants are originally migrants from other regions of West Java. They were attracted over a century ago by the large tea plantation that dominated the local economy until about twenty years ago. Most households have a modest income. Around 40% of the population is considered poor according to local standards. Sundanese culture and Islam are the shared elements in this village. Still, there is a range of Islamic orientations, from traditionalist syncretism to more puritan communities, from Islamic modernism to a *Persis* (*Persatuan Islam*) group from Bandung and a puritan Salafist community.[11]

This heterogeneity is reflected in the different types of under-18 marriages that Grijns found during her fieldwork. The two main types were love matches (i.e., young people choosing their partners) and marriages inspired by orthodox beliefs that encourage early matrimony (for the complete typology, see Section 1.3). The driving force behind most child marriage is the fear of *zinah*. Marriage is the only acceptable solution in cases of teenage pregnancy since abortion is legally forbidden and access to contraception is very limited for

11 See Shepard (2014: 235-46) for an explanation of the different doctrinal orientations. Persis is a doctrine from the 1920s that accepts only teachings from the Quran and Hadith, opposing 'un-Islamic' heresy, myth, and superstition.

unmarried couples. Marriage is also used as a defence against pernicious slander when a dating couple is considered to be getting too intimate. For example, Aulia was pushed to marry at 15. "*It took my mother a month to persuade me to get married*", Aulia says.[12] "*She kept saying: 'Don't embarrass me'*". They had just started dating and certainly did not have marriage in mind. But "*There was all this shaming*", her husband recalls, "*I hadn't actually kissed her, and everybody gossiped about her being pregnant*".

In general, village girls today have more agency than their mothers had in their *choice of a partner*. Increased mobility helps, aided by mobile phones and education outside the village.[13] However, parents still have a big say in the *timing of the marriage*. When gossip about *zinah* gets unbearable, instant marriage is arranged to secure the girl and family's honour.[14] Aulia is a good example. Conversely, some adolescents successfully use the same argument to push unwilling parents into arranging a marriage for them.

The minimum marital age is not counted in years. People refer to the Muslim concept of *akil balig* (i.e., mental and physical maturity) as a sign of marriageability. For boys '*kuat gawe*' (being able to work) is a local benchmark (Kartikasari 2016: 14). For girls, the onset of puberty means they are ready for marriage since they are destined to become mothers and (house)wives. Teenage marriage is widely accepted, although there is a trend towards later marriages.

What international institutions define as 'child marriage' is not necessarily considered bad in this local context. On the one hand, adolescents appreciate certain outcomes. These include the preservation of their honour, the right to a sexual relationship, and their increased status as adults, which gives them a say in community life. On the other hand, there is regret. Most girls are deprived of further education, they miss their old friends, and many live in social isolation with heavy domestic work and are responsible for their husband and children. In Siti's case, love evaporated faster than it took to flourish. They divorced after Wawan lost his job. Girls that have children will remain responsible for them. If they left their parental home upon marriage, they often return to live with their parents. Sundanese culture does not place a large taboo on divorce, unlike many other areas of Indonesia, including Bali (see Chapters 4, 5, and 6).

Grijns' 2014 village survey found that 35% of ever-married women aged 20–24 were first married before the age of 18 (Grijns et al. 2016). However, when analysing qualitative case studies of early marriages, Grijns discovered

12 These quotes are from the newspaper article written by Topsfield and Rosa (2017). Grijns helped these journalists interview the girls in the village and was present during the interviews.

13 See also van der Kooy (2016), who did research in the same area.

14 Honour is less of an issue for men, but in principle the impregnator must marry the girl, except in cases of incest.

that there were more hidden underage marriages. There appeared to be a whole repertoire of illegal practices, as the next section will discuss.

3.4.2. Illegal practices around underage marriage: Procedures and reasons

When people in a village need to react to unwanted situations, they look for local solutions rather than going to court for a marriage dispensation. They assume a court case would be costly (Van Huis 2015: 154) and scary, and some associate court with criminal cases. The community prefers the safest, fastest, and most affordable solution, which usually means acting outside the state's legal scheme.

Marriage for Muslims consists of a religious ceremony, an *ijab kabul*. This is sufficient for couples and families to avoid the feeling of dishonour caused by an unwanted pregnancy or overly intimate dating. But without registration, such a marriage is not legal under state law. This means that the new household has no access to state-funded welfare.[15] If the couple have children, they will only be registered under the mother's name, which brings shame on the child for being considered illegitimate and means they lose inheritance rights (detailed in Sections 3.3.2 and 4.4.3).[16]

A religious marriage must be registered at certain times in specific ways to avoid those consequences. Depending on the reasons behind an underage marriage, there are four local procedures:[17]

1. *Katrol usia* (literal translation being 'pulley of age'): This procedure involves increasing the bride or groom's age by changing their birthdate in the required documents, enabling them to receive their official marriage certificates right after the religious ceremony. The village head (or lower staff) and the *amil* facilitate the change. It is a fast solution for girls who are already pregnant and want to protect their honour and that of their unborn child. It is also used to let the bride 'jump' to 17, the minimum age for an identity and family card, which makes her eligible for factory work and welfare support. For example, when Nenen was going to get married at 15, her father went to the *amil* with Rp. 50,000 (€ 3,50). The *amil* accepted this and came to their house to marry them. In her marriage certificate, Nenen was listed as being 17 years old.[18]

15 Marriage Law 1974 Article 2 (1) (2).

16 See Van Huis (2015: 232–4) on the registration of polygamy cases and a Constitutional Court judgment about children born out of wedlock that might give them inheritance rights.

17 Interviews by Grijns and her research assistants, with the village head at his home, May 26, 2016; Interviews with the *amil* at his home, May 27 and June 26, 2016.

18 Interview by Grijns and her research assistants with Nenen and her mother, May 24, 2016 at their home. This is a poor family, her mother earning only Rp. 125,000 a month.

2. *Isbath nikah* (i.e., having a court recognize a marriage retroactively) is quite a common, pragmatic procedure (Bedner and Van Huis 2010: 188). However, parents cannot arrange *isbath nikah* in court for an underage child, because they should have first applied there for a dispensation. So they resort to a local version of *isbath nikah*. This often happens when adolescents are pressured to get married early for moral reasons. They will not register their marriage for a while, so they can easily split up if the relationship does not work out. If a pregnancy follows, the marriage can still be registered through the local *isbath nikah* route. Bedner and Van Huis observe that this "allows adolescents in rural areas more sexual liberty than they would otherwise be likely to enjoy" (Ibid).
3. Backdating a wedding date: The *amil* deals with two backdating variants, depending on whether he attends the religious ceremony. If he attends, he does not issue a marriage certificate and notes the marriage in his register without assigning an official number. When the couple reaches the proper age, they go to KUA, pretending it is a new wedding. KUA registers their marriage with an official number in the KUA archives, and they receive their backdated marriage certificate. This is a cheaper procedure because it only involves the *amil*, so fewer people need a 'gift' for their services. The second backdating option is more complicated. Only a religious leader would have attended the religious ceremony, so it takes the *amil* extra effort to register such a marriage through a backdoor route. Some young girls from orthodox families marry, divorce, and remarry quickly. They then only apply to register their second or third marriage, when the relationship seems more stable, and the couple seriously plans a family.
4. Arranging a 'secret' religious marriage (*nikah siri*) that will remain unregistered. Only certain conservative religious leaders facilitate this in a private setting, without the *amil* or any other authority. Grijns encountered cases of girls below age 15 who were handpicked by religious leaders from outside the village, who took them as second or third wives. This way the husbands avoided asking the first wife for a permission letter, a legal obligation for polygamy. The girls and their children do not have inheritance rights; neither do the girls have the right to a female-petitioned divorce.

The do-it-yourself approach at the village level helps (the parents of) couples with a pre-marital pregnancy or who are accused of overly intimate dating. However, the system offers little protection against domestic or sexual violence. Brides in unregistered marriages cannot obtain a legal divorce since they have not been married under state law. In registered marriages, women do have access to the legal divorce procedure in court. However, in unregistered marriages, women are left only with religious procedures for divorce, in which only husbands can initiate and conclude the divorce. In general, brides-to-be are not told what marriage entails, and they are usually ignorant about the consequences of underage marriage.

3.4.3. Illegal practices around underage marriage: The role of marriage registrars, Amil, and KUA

The *amil* and the village head (or lower village bureaucrats) are central actors in underage marriage practices.[19] Besides facilitating underage child marriage, they are also often involved in arranging the divorces that regularly happen afterwards, handing out divorce papers, arranging 'customized' birth certificates, and smoothing over cases of adultery. The *amil* can help people get married, even when they come to ask him for a next-day wedding, sidestepping the legally prescribed 10-day waiting period. The creative solutions for circumventing procedural rules on underage marriages are sometimes used for a forced marriage too. In a recent village case of rape, the exceptionally young victim was forced by her father to marry her abuser to prevent her loss of honour. She missed her final elementary school exam and had to move in with her husband. When her mother, who worked as a domestic helper in Jakarta, heard about this, she implored the school teachers and the *amil* to find another solution. The marriage was eventually annulled, the girl was declared 'never-married' and allowed to sit her final exams, and her mother could take her to school in Jakarta.

The local community (especially fathers, being the legal guardians of their daughters) together with the village bureaucracy, the *amil*, and KUA create their own support system to solve legal issues that resonate with local cultural and religious norms and values. It is at the KUA that marriages need to be registered. However, in most cases, KUA staff can pretend to be unaware of village-level manipulation. The government maintains some distance between KUA and the community by regularly rotating staff. *Penghulus* work as marriage registrars, with *amils* closely assisting them. They have regular monthly meetings, where *penghulus* sign the official marriage registration letters that the *amils* already prepared in their village, potentially with the village staff. When the *penghulus* are too busy to officiate all of the different district village weddings, they ask the local *amil* to officiate weddings in his village. In other words, the *penghulu*, as a KUA official, simply registers cases prepared by the *amil* and relies on him to deal with all of the village-level work. This role division between *amil* and *penghulu* allows villagers to deal with their *amil* without ever having to go to the KUA. At the KUA, all documents look 'clean', and the employees do not need to fear sanctions.

As an intermediary between the state institution and the people, the *amil* is in a difficult position. He understands why people need underage marriage as a solution for shameful situations and acknowledges societal rules. State law cannot always meet people's needs, so he must be flexible. There is great pressure

19 There is a parallel with what Lipsky (1980: 27) called street-level bureaucrats. He mentions the relatively high degrees of discretion and regular interaction with citizens as notable features of jobs at the lowest level of public services.

from the community on the *amil* to perform according to their expectations. During one interview, the *amil* told us, grinning: "*The village head is aware of this. If the community is not being served, maybe this house and the village office would be attacked*".[20] On top of that, the *amil* is an unpaid official.[21] He is not on the KUA's or village administration's payroll. Instead, he depends on his own land's proceeds, gifts from people that come for his help,[22] and his informal share of the payments that go to the *penghulu* for officiating marriages.

Penghulus are in a similar situation. They may be aware of underage marriage's negative impacts on girls. However, they feel that they cannot do much because of strong local norms and potentially serious community opposition to (attempts at) changing them. According to one of the *penghulus*, the law in the village is a combination of religious, cultural, and state values that regulate the community.[23] Religious law in villages is interpreted and explained by local religious leaders, who each teach their version of Islamic theology and laws, including the legal validity of Islam. *Penghulus*, as state representatives, are themselves religious authorities. Many of them are sensitive to local norms because they are part of the community and share the same values.

3.5. Legal reform on the minimum age for marriage

The local practice of child marriage, its motivations, consequences, and procedures, is illustrated by the case of a village in West Java. Considering such local practices, this section turns to their implications for legal reform of the minimum age for marriage. This discussion is especially relevant for today's Indonesian society, where the Constitutional Court has decided to increase the minimum age for marriage after campaigners filed a second petition (the first petition filed in 2014 has been rejected, see Section 3.2.1). After the court's decision, parliament legislated that 19 be the new minimum marital age for both women and men. There have also been some regional initiatives for similar changes. In 2015 and 2016, some provincial regulations (e.g., in Yogyakarta, West Nusa Tenggara, and South Sulawesi) were enacted to prevent child marriage. Some of them set the local marriageable age above that set by the 1974 Marriage Law. Indicating that changes are possible, these measures have fuelled activists' efforts to end child marriage through legal reforms.

The question is whether legal measures will be sufficiently effective. Even if the marriageable age is raised, there are at least four ways to get married outside

20 Interview by Grijns and her research assistants with the *amil* at his home, May 27, 2016.

21 Huis & Wirastri (2012: 15) argue that an assistant marriage registrar should be made into a civil servant and paid to avoid fraudulent marriage registrations.

22 It is a common custom to pay people like traditional midwifes, Quran teachers, and religious leaders for their services in gifts (in cash or in kind). There is no fixed tariff and people give according to their means.

23 Interview by Grijns and her research assistants with *Penghulu* A, May 30, 2016, Sukaraja.

of the state legal system, as the previous section indicated. These ways can be costly, with lots of small bribes paid to local actors throughout the process. Likewise, high costs are incurred in seeking a marriage dispensation from a court, which is another way to legalize an underage marriage. Applicants seeking such dispensations, usually the parents of the young bride or groom, have to travel to the court at least three times, in some cases hours away from their village, and then pay for the procedure. Such procedures can cause even more problems for families already facing trouble in their community, e.g., due to the social stigma attached to pregnancy out of wedlock, which is the most common reason for early marriages.

Unregistered marriages are especially problematic. They leave wives and children vulnerable, lacking legal protections such as welfare support for the new household, inheritance rights, and the right to a legal divorce procedure. Moreover, children born from unregistered marriages cannot obtain a normal birth certificate (*akta kelahiran*), necessary for access to education. A so-called 'single birth certificate' (*akta tunggal*) can be issued outside of marriage, but these 'deviant' certificates often bring with them a social stigma and bullying for the child (see Section 4.4.3). Despite the financial and social costs involved, underage marriage remains prevalent, and no quick solution is apparent. Increasing the marriageable age is likely to increase the frequency of those underground marriages, therefore increasing the number of vulnerable children and causing families to become even more vulnerable.

Another problem with the legislative measures to increase the minimum age for marriage (i.e., effectively banning child marriage) is that such measures treat *all child marriages alike*. Campaigns and legislative measures to ban child marriage are often motivated by the stereotypical image of child marriage, which is a forced one driven by poverty, typically with a big age gap between an unhappy small girl and an abusive older man. In reality, there is much diversity in the types of child marriage, as the following chapters on Bali will demonstrate.

These legislative reforms have noble intents: To uphold human rights norms, to protect children, and to empower women. However, they do not offer an effective solution to the prevalence of child marriage in Indonesia. At worst, they could aggravate the problem. Even if the law bans child marriage, children will continue to be married outside of the legal system, as long as motivation remains. A large number of child marriages will go underground, rendering the married couples legally unprotected and thus even more vulnerable. Furthermore, by failing to consider the diversity of child marriages, the proposed one-size-fits-all legal reform fails to address the broader underlying issues that spur child marriage in the first place (e.g., adolescent sexuality). I will further discuss this in Chapter 5.

The Dutch East Indies attempted a similar legal reform to forbid child marriage. Kern, an advisor for the Dutch Office for Native Affairs, concluded that such legislation was unfeasible and undesirable for several reasons. First, young marriage was a practice defended by the Indonesians. Second, legislators could not intervene in the most intimate affairs of the Native populations, except in the most urgent cases. Third, opposing the practice would create conflict with Islamic law (Blackburn and Bessell 1997: 116–117). In his view, the only answer was "to rely on the social evolution already under way in the Indies" (Ibid). In today's reform discussion, is there any other answer? Chapters 5, 6, and 7 include my proposals for alternative reforms.

3.6. Conclusions: Compromises and dilemmas

The findings presented in this chapter indicate that child marriage is sustained through conservative Muslim interpretations of how to deal with adolescent sexuality, i.e., to control immorality through marriage. Until the Constitutional Court ruled to increase the marriageable age in 2019, the conservative Islamic perspective dominated the national discourse on this issue. The 2014 judicial review was a good example of the strong political power of conservative Islamic discourse in Indonesia. This dominance of Islamic values is understandable, given that the family law rules have a firmer textual basis in the Koran than other legal topics (Cammack, Young, and Heaton 1996: 50–51).

The Indonesian government officially agrees with international goals and policies that aim to eliminate child marriage. The tension between how the Indonesian government presents itself to the international community and the influential Islamic discourse was visible in both the law-making process and existing laws. The initial drafters of Marriage Law 1974 had to compromise because of resistance from an Islamist party. Contradictions exist within existing state laws (e.g., Marriage Law 1974, the Law on Human Rights of 1999, and the Child Protection Law). Judges, within their discretion under state laws, at times reached judicial decisions to permit underage marriages. They did so by referring to both state and Islamic laws.

In 2019, the national debate on the marriageable age took a different turn. The continuous advocacy and lobbying by human rights bodies and civil society organizations have come to bear fruit, and the Constitutional Court has accepted their petition for increasing the marriageable age. The court ruled that Article 7 of the 1974 Marriage Law is a form of gender-based discrimination, hence unconstitutional (Sapiie 2019). The decision also concerns the negative impact of child marriage on children's rights to health and education.[24] Parliament subsequently has agreed to set the age at 19 for both women and men (Dewan Perwakilan Rakyat Republik Indonesia n.d.). Still, research findings at the local level suggest the challenges of implementing such state rules.

At the local level, Muslim village bureaucrats create a semi-autonomous social field, which sustains customs, rules, and symbols internally. It is also vulnerable to rules and decisions from outside the field (Moore 1973: 720).

24 Law No.16 of 2019 on the Amendement to the Marraige Law 1974.

They use their unofficial support system to solve legal issues in a way that accords with local cultural and religious norms and values. Such a system is created to meet their local community needs. Villagers usually resort to this unofficial system without any involvement from state institutions. Grijns' and my findings on these village practices are specific to our research area, but the main conclusions are relevant for other Indonesian areas as well. Using marriage to cover the shame of extra-marital sexual relations (Karolus et al. 2019), manipulating age and wedding dates (see Chapter 4), marriage dispensations (Eddyono et al. 2016; Fadhli 2019), and reacting to teenage pregnancies by arranging child marriage (I'anah 2019; Idrus 2019), these practices also occur elsewhere in Indonesia, including in non-Muslim areas. The main differences are related to kinship customs (e.g., bilineal in Java versus patri- or matrilineal in other areas) and the size of dower or bride prices (e.g., relatively modest in our research area).

The observations I made with Grijns lead me to conclude that the dilemmas and compromises seen at each level of society are the results of continuous struggles with the diversity of values on marriage, family, and adolescent sexuality. The question is whether the law is effective in supporting the government's developmental policy that aims to end child marriage. On the one hand, formal law can create an "enabling environment" (Shell-Duncan et al. 2013: 804, 812) and strengthen those who seek to eliminate child marriage. On the other hand, it is likely to stimulate underground practices of child marriage. One-size-fits-all legislative measures, such as banning child marriage, fail to address the broader underlying issues that spur child marriage in the first place, such as education and adolescent sexuality. To protect women's and children's rights, the government could instead focus more on supporting laws and policies on gender equality, education, and sexual and reproductive health rights. Chapters 5, 6, and 7 will partially discuss alternative reforms.

Bibliography

Badan Pusat Statistik (BPS). (2016). *Kemajuan yang Tertunda: Analisis Data Perkawinan Usia Anak di Indonesia*. Jakarta, Indonesia: BPS.

Bedner, A., & Van Huis, S. (2010). Plurality of marriage law and marriage registration for Muslims in Indonesia: A plea for pragmatism. *Utrecht Law Review*, *6*(2), 175–191.

Blackburn, S., & Bessell, S. (1997). Marriageable age: Political debates on early marriage in twentieth-century Indonesia. *Indonesia*, *63*, 107–141. https://doi.org/10.2307/3351513

Cammack, M., & Feener, R. M. (2012). The Islamic legal system in Indonesia. *Pacific Rim Law & Policy Journal*, *21*(1), 13–42.

Cammack, M., Young, L. A., & Heaton, T. (1996). Legislating social change in an Islamic Society-Indonesia's Marriage Law. *The American Journal of Comparative Law*, *44*(1), 45–73. https://doi.org/10.2307/840520

Committee on the Rights of the Child. (2007). *General comment No. 7 (2007), Implementing Child Rights in Early Childhood, CRC/C/GC/7/Rev.1.*

Dewan Perwakilan Rakyat Republik Indonesia. (n.d.). Paripurna DPR Sepakat 19 Tahun Jadi Batas Usia Minimal Perkawinan, http://www.dpr.go.id/berita/detail/id/25935/t/Paripurna+DPR+Sepakat+19+Tahun+Jadi+Batas+Usia+Minimal+Perkawinan (accessed on April 20, 2021).

Eddyono, S. W., Sidauruk, A. R. F., Napitupulu, E. A. T., & Kamilah, A. G. (2016). *Menyingkap Tabir Dispensasi Perkawinan: Analisis Terhadap Praktik Perkawinan Anak di Kab Tuban, Kab Bogor, dan Kab Mamuju*. Jakarta, Indonesia: Koalisi 18+.

Equality Now. (2014). *Protecting the Girl Child: Using the Law to End Child, Early and Forced Marriage and Related Human Rights Violations*. New York; Nairobi; London: Equality Now.

Evenhuis, M., & Burn, J. (2014). *Just Married, Just a Child: Child Marriage in the Indo-Pacific Region*. Melbourne: Plan International Australia.

Fadhli, A. (2019). Marriage dispensation in Tanah Datar district, West Sumatra: Problem or solution? In M. Grijns, H. Horii, S. Irianto, & P. Saptandari (Eds.), *Marrying Young in Indonesia: Voices, Laws and Practices* (pp. 147–174). Jakarta, Indonesia: Yayasan Pustaka Obor Indonesia.

Grijns, M., Limijaya, S., Restuningrum, N. H., Fathurrohman, I. H., Damayanti, V. R., & Harahap, R. A. (2016). Pernikahan Anak di Sukabumi Jawa Barat: Diri dan Agensi Anak Perempuan. *Journal Perempuan*, *21*(1), 9–33.

Horii, H. (2020). Legal reasoning for legitimation of child marriage in West Java: Accommodation of local norms at Islamic Courts and the paradox of child protection. *Journal of Human Rights Practice*, *12*(3), 501–523, https://doi.org/10.1093/jhuman/huaa041

I'anah, N. (2019). A child carrying a child: Portrait of a teenager's life after early marriage due to pregnancy in Ungaran, Semarang, Central Java. In M. Grijns, H. Horii, S. Irianto, & P. Saptandari (Eds.), *Marrying Young in Indonesia: Voices, Laws and Practices* (pp. 39–62). Jakarta, Indonesia: Yayasan Pustaka Obor Indonesia.

Idrus, N. I. (2019). "Ready or not, be prepared!": Marital status, the state and consequences of child marriage in East Tomoni, Luwu Timur, South Sulawesi. In M. Grijns, H. Horii, S. Irianto, & P. Saptandari (Eds.), *Marrying Young in Indonesia: Voices, Laws and Practices* (pp. 79–118). Jakarta, Indonesia: Yayasan Pustaka Obor Indonesia.

Indonesian Legal Aid Association for Women. (2012). *Early and Forced Marriages in Republic of Indonesia: A brief submitted to the Office of the High Commissioner for Women's Rights and Gender Section (WRGS) at the 26th session of the Human Rights Council.*

Karolus, M. L., Dewi, S. C., & Partini. (2019). "Listen, I want to tell a story": Peer group as a mean to prevent child marriage in Yogyakarta. In M. Grijns, H. Horii, S. Irianto, & P. Saptandari (Eds.), *Marrying Young in Indonesia: Voices, Laws and Practices* (pp. 263–286). Jakarta, Indonesia: Yayasan Pustaka Obor Indonesia.

Kartikasari, D. (2016). *Kearah Perppu Anti Perkawinan Anak*. Jakarta, Indonesia: Koalisi Perempuan Indonesia.

Lipsky, M. (1980). *Street-Level Bureaucracy: Dilemmas of the Individual in Public Services*. New York: Russell Sage Foundation.

Misiyah Direktur Institut Kapal Perempuan (Steering Committee Gender Watch-Program). (n.d.). Revisi Terbatas UU Perkawinan Agenda Mendesak, https://mediaindonesia.com/read/detail/260064-revisi-terbatas-uu-perkawinan-agenda-mendesak (accessed on April 20, 2021).

Moore, S. F. (1973). Law and social change: The semi-autonomous social field as an appropriate subject of study. *Law & Society Review*, 7(4), 719–746. https://doi.org/10.2307/3052967

Nurlaelawati, E. (2010). *Modernization, Tradition and Identity*. Amsterdam University Press.

Pompe, S., & Otto, J. M. (1990). Some comments on recent developments in the Indonesian marriage law with particular respect to the rights of women. *Verfassung Und Recht in Übersee / Law and Politics in Africa, Asia and Latin America, 23*(4), 415–433.

Rabi, A., Rumble, L., Irdiana, N., Hoelscher, P., & Suharti. (2015). *Cost of Inaction: Child and Adolescent Marriage in Indonesia*. Jakarta, Indonesia: United Nations Children's Fund, Bappenas (Ministry of National Development Planning).

Sapiie, M. A. (2019). Breaking: Court orders revision of minimum age for women to marry. *The Jakarta Post*. https://www.thejakartapost.com/news/2018/12/13/breaking-court-orders-revision-of-minimum-age-for-women-to-marry.html

Shell-Duncan, B., Hernlund, Y., Wander, K., & Moreau, A. (2013). Legislating change? Responses to criminalizing female genital cutting in Senegal. *Law & Society Review, 47*(4), 803–835. https://doi.org/10.1111/lasr.12044

Shepard, W. E. (2014). *Introducing Islam*. New York, NY: Routledge.

Sidel, J. T. (2018). *Riots, Pogroms, Jihad: Religious Violence in Indonesia*. New York, NY: Cornell University Press.

Topsfield, J., & Rosa, A. (2017, September 15). Child brides: Why underage girls are marrying in Indonesia. *The Sydney Morning Herald*. https://www.smh.com.au/world/child-brides-why-underage-girls-are-marrying-in-indonesia-20170913-gyg6p8.html

Turner, C. (2013). *Out of the Shadows: Child marriage and slavery*. Anti-Slavery International.

UNICEF Indonesia. (2016). *Annual Report Indonesia 2015*. Jakarta: UNICEF Indonesia.

UNICEF Indonesia, & UNICEF. (2016). *Child Marriage in Indonesia: Progress on Pause*. Jakarta, Indonesia: UNICEF Indonesia.

Van Bemmelen, S. T., & Grijns, M. (2019). Child marriage contested, from colonial to present Java: Adat, religion and the staet. Anything new under the sun? In M. Grijns, H. Horii, S. Irianto, & P. Saptandari (Eds.), *Marrying Young in Indonesia: Voices, Laws and Practices* (pp. 287–329). Jakarta, Indonesia: Yayasan Pustaka Obor Indonesia.

van der Kooy, Y. (2016). *Early Marriage in West Java: Understanding Girls' Agency in the Context of 'Traditional' and Changing Norms Regarding Gender and Sexuality* [Master Thesis]. University of Amsterdam.

Van Huis, S. (2015). *Islamic Courts and Women's Divorce Rights in Indonesia: The Cases of Cianjur and Bulukumba* [Doctoral Thesis]. Leiden University.

Van Huis, S., & Wirastri, T. D. (2012). Muslim marriage registration in Indonesia: Revised marriage registration laws cannot overcome compliance flaws. *Australian Journal of Asian Law, 13*(1), 1–17.

Chapter 4

Harmony

The previous chapter explained the state laws regarding child marriage practices. It used studies in West Java to illustrate how local actors navigate these laws to accommodate people's needs at the grassroots level. This chapter turns to legal practices in Bali. To understand the roles that the state and *adat* law systems play, I analyze two types of legal cases: Marriage dispensation and prosecution for pre-marital sexual intercourse involving a minor (hereafter 'sex crime'). I begin with Ratna's story, which illustrates how these two types of legal cases relate to each other in the context of teenage pregnancy and child marriage.

4.1. The story of Ratna

Ratna is an 18-year-old mother, living with her parents and her newborn baby in downtown Denpasar. When Ratna found out about her pregnancy, she had already been separated from the baby's father, Pranata, who is one year younger than her. Ratna's family then went to Pranata's family to urge him to "take responsibility" (i.e., to marry her), which Pranata's family refused. Ratna's family then decided to report the case to the police as a sex crime (i.e., prosecution for pre-marital sexual intercourse involving a minor), for which Pranata could be imprisoned for years. As the court hearing was approaching, tension grew between the families. Ratna became nervous. I was helping her prepare to testify in court. A few days before the first hearing, I heard from Ratna's lawyer that Pranata's family came to Ratna with a marriage proposal, which Ratna's family accepted. Around this time, Ratna also gave birth. I heard that the baby was ill and hospitalized, so I went to see them in one of Denpasar's public hospitals. When I entered the room, I saw Ratna and Pranata's families sitting around the hospital bed where the baby was sleeping. Ratna's mother, who was previously telling me how evil-minded Pratana's family was, approached me and asked shyly:

Mother: "Did you … hear? About this?" (pointing at Ratna and Pranata)
Author: "Yes, I heard".

DOI: 10.4324/9781003184546-4

Mother: *"They are back together".*
Author: *"Will they marry?"*
Mother: *"Yes, but after finishing school".*
Author: *"Is that so? But when is their adat (customary) wedding?"*
Mother: *"Maybe next month, it will just be a small wedding".*
Author: *"Will you register their marriage in the registration office?"*
Mother: *"No ... only when they are adults (dewasa). Pranata is still 16 years old".*
Author: *"I see ... but you know there is a system of dispensation. You can go to the court and ask for dispensation to register your marriage under the minimum age".*
Mother: *(Not really understanding what it is) "Yes, we will go to the court next Wednesday. Continuation of the [sex crime] case".*
Author: *"Oh, so the case is still not finished ..."*[1]

Remembering this scene still strikes me with confusion. The two families were about to confront each other in a criminal case but settled their marriage agreement. In that sense, they quickly reconciled and cared for their baby together. A few days later, they would meet in court to testify about the crime with which Ratna's family had charged Pranata. In the hospital, Ratna and Pranata were sitting side by side, holding hands and teasing each other, just like young lovers. This episode shows the complexities of extra-marital pregnancies, of interrelations between the state and *adat* marriage system, and of prosecuting pre-marital sexual intercourse involving a minor in Bali. Like Ratna's case, extra-marital pregnancy and birth cause a family two problems, arising from two different legal systems. First, there is no place for the baby in their *adat* community. Second, the baby lacks a birth certificate. In such cases, what international institutions frame as 'child marriage' becomes a solution to both of these problems. State agents such as marriage registrars, judges, and prosecutors facilitate the solution by navigating between the state and *adat* law systems.

4.2. Legal pluralism and human rights

What exactly is state law, and what is *adat* law? Debates on legal pluralism have long tried to answer this question (F. von Benda-Beckmann and Benda-Beckmann 2002; Tamanaha 2007; Twining 2010). Some argue it is hardly constructive to see the legal pluralism concept as a theory, explanation, or claim of truth and consider legal pluralism as a starting point for considering the complexity of multiple legal orders coexisting. From this view, it is useful only as a sensitizing and analytical tool (Benda-Beckmann and Benda-Beckmann 2002: 40; Macdonald 2013: 35; Tamanaha 2000). This perspective propels the use of related concepts and associated theories, such as Moore's (1973)

1 Personal communication, July 2017.

"semi-autonomous social field" and Santos' (1987) "inter-legality", which many researchers have used as a framework for their studies.

In this chapter, I discuss each legal system as a tool for social engineering, designed to achieve ideas of justice, rights, and process (Merry 2014, 120). More specifically, I discuss the state law system as an institution of liberal legalism and the *adat* law system as an institution of locality. This approach allows me to examine the tension between different ideas stemming within and from these two institutions and how these ideas interact and transform in the application of both legal systems. I pay particular attention to judges, as they are on the front line of the interaction and tension between liberal legalism and locality.

Dossa (1999: 76, 79) describes liberal legalism as a "rational machine" under the name of judicial formalism, recognizing only the individual interests while scanting the ideals of communal harmony and collective good. Nader (1991) suggests that the "harmony ideology", the perception that harmonious behaviour is more desirable than disputing behaviour, has roots in colonialism. In Weber's view, modern law was driven by logic and rational calculation (Calavita 2010: 12). By contrast, customary law "is local knowledge; local not just as to place, time, class, and variety of issue, but as to accent-vernacular characterizations of what happens connected to vernacular imaginings of what can" (Geertz 1985: 215).

Engle (2016), who studied injury cases in Thailand, argues that state tort law has liberal legalism at its core. Therefore, it is not compatible with how a traditional Thai community works, which is based on the "relational self", shaped by belonging to traditional kin and community (Merry 2009: 404). This conceptualization of the relational self explains why individualistic views of rights and autonomy (rooted in the European tradition of liberal legalism) often fail to explain the grounded research data from Southeast Asian societies (Chua and Engel 2015: 213). These studies suggest a possible blind spot in human rights mechanisms: The protection of individual rights does not necessarily protect the rights of the relational self. These two kinds of rights co-exist and occasionally conflict.

The tension between rights-based liberal legalism and community-based customary law is illuminated by the debate over legal pluralism and human rights. From one perspective, the existence of legal pluralism is in tension with the universalism of human rights: A legally pluralistic society, containing a variety of fragmented sources of legal orders, may conflict with the universal standards prescribed by human rights norms (Sheppard 2013: 142). International bodies acknowledge such challenges. The Committee on the Elimination of Discrimination against Women (2004) stated that the co-existence of legal orders, where customary and religious legal orders prevail over the state legal order, remains a source of great concern for the defence of women's rights. Regarding child marriage, the report by international human rights organization Equality Now (2014) sees child marriage tolerated by governments and permitted in law because they are defined as cultural norms or traditions or are viewed as religious practices (ibid: 15). Therefore, "[s]tates must conduct a full review of customary and religious laws and traditional practices and evaluate how these laws and practices affect girls and women and perpetuate child marriage" (ibid: 16). However, some scholars argue that human rights standards may spread more effectively and with greater legitimacy if they are adapted to local cultural contexts and customary laws (Sheppard 2013; An-Na'im 1992; Macdonald 2013; Merry 1997).

How should we address legal pluralism for the realization of human rights? Unifying multiple legal orders by completely abolishing the informal justice systems has proven unrealistic and perhaps undesirable: Customary law, or informal justice, is prevalent and resilient (see, e.g., Ubink 2011; Kerrigan et al. 2012; Bruce et al. 1994). This chapter thus begins by exploring an alternative, examining what the existence of multiple legal orders means for realizing human rights. Is legal pluralism an obstacle to achieving this goal? The analysis of legal cases regarding child marriage practices offers an excellent opportunity to investigate how a pluralistic legal system affects the process of human rights law implementation and enforcement.

4.3. Legal pluralism in Indonesia

An extensive volume of existing literature about the pluralistic nature of the Indonesian legal system discusses the friction that liberal values cause amidst other values. Lubis (1999: 171) explains that liberalism in the Indonesian state law system (i.e., the *rechtsstaat* or the state based on law) is the government officials' commitment (in principle) in modern Indonesia. The *rechtsstaat* guarantees human rights protection, an independent and impartial judiciary, and strict adherence to the principle of legality (Lubis 1999: 172). Fitzpatrick (2008: 502) explains Indonesian criminal law as a Western-style law, which is centralized, inflexible, hierarchical, and of a secular nature. The 1974 Marriage Law specifically commits to liberal values such as establishing the legal equality of Indonesian women (Butt 2008: 282), although these values have also been compromised (see Chapter 3). Liberal ideals of *reformasi* have also influenced Islamic family law (Cammack et al. 2015). The Child Protection Law is a typical example of aspired liberalism in the state law system, basing its principles of basic rights on the 1945 Constitution and the Convention on the Rights of the Child.[2]

Despite these liberal principles and influential Islamic values in state lawmaking (Grijns and Horii 2018), collectivism is also politically strong and practically persistent in Indonesian ideology (Bourchier 2015; Reeve 1987). Such collectivist ideology is often expressed as "harmony". The importance of the

2 Elucidation of Law No.23 of 2002 on Child Protection.

"spirit of harmony as a prevailing social value" (Lubis 1999: 179) or the "cultural obsession for harmony" (Fitzpatrick 2008: 503) is at times in tension with the principle of legality. Community interests outweigh those of the individual (Hooker 1978: 55), and the application of the *rechtsstaat* principle remains doubtful because of the prevailing notions of *asas kekeluargaan* (communal principles) and harmony (Lubis 1999: 183–184). This ideology is also reflected in Indonesian state law. The 1945 Constitution is an example of the tension and compromise between different ideologies. It commits to *rechtsstaat* principles while granting space for collective ideologies in implementation, e.g., through the loose phrasing of the original text (Bourchier 2008: 100). This somewhat forced integration of two ideologies explains Indonesian state law's minor influence in practice, described as "law without law" (Katz and Katz 1975) or as only having some normative influence as a principle (Fitzpatrick 2008: 512). The more recent constitutional amendments from 1999-2002 reflect the transition of Indonesian legal ideologies from integralism to liberalism, at least in principle (Bedner 2017).

Legal pluralism in Indonesian family law has been explored through various issues: Divorce (Van Huis 2015; O'Shaughnessy 2009), polygamy and mixed marriage (Butt 2008), and inheritance (Von Benda-Beckmann 1984; Bowen 2003). In comparison, child marriage in Indonesia remains an underexplored area of study in relation to Indonesia's pluralistic legal system. While child marriage in Indonesia has attracted social and scholarly attention, including rich anthropological accounts, few reports mention studies on marriage dispensations (Eddyono et al. 2016), and scholarly contributions are still limited. Furthermore, studies have not yet connected sex crimes to the study of child marriage, although both primarily result from adolescents' sexual relations outside of marriage. This chapter combines the analysis of the two case types, namely marriage dispensation cases and sex crime cases, to gain a nuanced and accurate understanding of the different legal systems around the issue of child marriage and sexual morality.

In this chapter, I focus on understanding how the state institutions and authorities try to manage their rules and norms in practice when confronted with pre-marital sexual intercourse and teenage pregnancy. While Bali is a multicultural area with tourists and migrants, I mainly focus on the practice of Balinese Hindus to identify the role of their *adat* law. I investigated the cases and functions at *Pengadilan Negeri* (hereafter PN, civil court), which adjudicates marriage-related legal issues among non-Muslims and criminal cases for all citizens. I collected about 30 court decisions, issued between 2013 and 2016 from three different civil courts (PN Bangli, Semarapura, and Denpasar). I analyzed these court decisions in light of interviews I conducted with judges and clerks who worked at these three courts (Appendixes 2 and 3). Some were ethnic Balinese and others were non-Balinese. The following sections clarify that the ethnicity of judges has an influence on their views and decision-making process.

For this chapter's analysis, I also use other interviews I conducted with various informants, including judges, Civil Marriage Registration Office (KCS) marriage registrars, *adat* law scholars, and families involved in legal cases. Family members included 1) a couple's parents applying for marriage dispensations, 2) a couple who had civil marriage registration by manipulating their age, 3) a girl with an extra-marital pregnancy whose parents reported the case to the police as a sex crime. I also relied partly on observations and remarks at Focus Group Discussions with local activists and Balinese adolescents.

Section 4.4 discusses the Marriage Law, including both the 1974 Marriage Law and the Balinese *adat* law on marriage. An analysis of the civil marriage registration practice and marriage dispensation cases demonstrates how state law is used in court practices to accommodate the demands of *adat* law. Section 4.5 investigates sex crime cases, which punish boys for extra-marital sexual intercourse. These two sections provide an analysis of civil and criminal cases, focusing on the use of the Child Protection Law, among others, to examine the roles that state legal agents play in reacting to extra-marital pregnancies. The conclusion returns to the question of what legal pluralism means for the realization of human rights.

4.4. Marriage laws: The minimum age for marriage, marriage registration, and dispensation

4.4.1. Social norms and adat law on marriage and pregnancy

In Bali, marrying young is generally not a preferred option. Today's ideal age for marriage for both men and women is in the early 20s. Most prefer to at least finish high school *(SMA*, until the age of 18) and start working before they marry. According to a paralegal I interviewed, people should ideally finish university education before marrying, i.e., after they are 21. In a Focus Group Discussion with adolescent girls in the Denpasar area, one of the participants said, "*I want to continue school, rather than to marry because nowadays it is difficult to find a job. People who only have a bachelor's degree find it difficult to become employed*".[3] The *Niti Sastra* text, a summary of ancient wisdom and a standard of courtesy and good manners (Gonda 1976: 244), writes *"semara ruang puluhing yusa"*, that the ideal age for falling in love is 20 years old.[4]

Concern for reproductive health is also a popular discourse in determining the general ideal age for marriage. An official from BKKBN (*Badan Kependudukan dan Keluarga Berencana Nasional*), the national family planning institute, stated that the ideal age to marry is 23 for women and 25 for men,

3 FGD with adolescent girls in a *banjar* in Denpasar, July 19, 2017.

4 Interview with a professor of *adat* law in Bali, May 25, 2017, Denpasar.

because "The mortality rate of teenage mothers and their babies is high".[5] In an FDG with a group of adolescent girls in Denpasar, most girls expressed that the ideal age for marriage is 25 for girls and 27 for boys. One of the participants said that was because "Reproductive organs are not ready below the age of 20". These remarks indicate that marriage is closely linked with pregnancy in Balinese society.

Despite the public perception that the ideal marital age is rising, people also feel they have to marry before these ideal ages if they become pregnant. Girls who become pregnant and their boyfriends are expected to marry. This expectation relates to the Balinese patrilineal kinship system. In Bali, a marriage regulates the transfer of women from one lineage to another (Jennaway 2002: 60), and babies 'belong' to the father's lineage. So in extra-marital pregnancies, marriage under the Balinese *adat* system is a practical necessity to identify the father of the babies (Ibid: 69). A child is considered to 'belong' ("*darah kami*", our blood) to the family of his biological father, so there is strong pressure on and motivation from the paternal family to marry when a woman is pregnant with his child (Van Bemmelen 2015). All of these lineages and marriages are organized around the Balinese *adat* community, i.e., *banjar* (commonly translated as 'hamlet'). This organization is present in both rural and urban parts of Bali. In cases of unwanted teenage pregnancies, the teenagers' parents and the *local banjar* decide on the marriage. In one case, a marriage decision between a pregnant girl and her boyfriend resulted from a mediation process with the *banjar*'s leader. Although these youngsters did not want to marry, their parents and the head decided otherwise.[6]

To deviate from *adat* rules is not easy. For instance, consider Article 80 of *Awig-awig banjar Pekandelan Klod, Lingkungan Pekandelan, Kelurahan Semarapura Klod, Kecamatan Klungkung, Kabupatan Klungkung*[7]:

1. *Village/Hamlet has an authority to impose sanctions upon residents who commit wrongdoings.*
2. *The imposition is carried out by the Adat Village Head or Chief of Hamlet according to the procedures.*
3. *The degree of sanctions is based on the degree of the wrongdoings by considering the sense of humanity.*
4. *The forms of sanctions are:*
    a. *Fines (money or goods).*
    b. *Asking for an apology.*
    c. *Panyangaskaran ceremony.*
5. *The Village/Banjar owns fines or goods derived from sanctions.*

5 Interview with an officer at BKKBN, June 15, 2017, Denpasar.

6 Interview with the head of a local NGO, May 2019.

7 Translated from Balinese by a local research assistant.

The family is expected to perform a ceremony in their *banjar* when a baby is born outside of wedlock. This performance can combine different ceremonies: *Mecaru* or the simpler *prascita* (to purify the 'polluted' (*kotor, cuntake*) environment) and *meperas* (to adopt the baby born out of wedlock). These ceremonies can be costly and sometimes involve several people from the community, so they function as both economic and social sanctions. The price of *mecaru* in a village can be up to 13 million rupiah (€770), according to an applicant for marriage dispensation I interviewed. He added: "*For me who works as a sculpture artisan, 13 million rupiah is a huge amount of money*".[8]

The ritual regarding pollution (*cuntake*) refers to the sense of communality that is built on genealogy or ancestry. Warren (1993: 4) explains that *adat* law in Bali involves *tata krama* (local practice), *sima* (rules and norms), and *dresta* (*adat*/custom) as "a field of meanings covering ritual obligation, social institution, legal regulation and ancestral evocation". Accordingly, *adat* law governs not only the bodily aspect of its *adat* members but also the territory's supernatural aspects. *Adat* law defines the boundary between the sacred and the profane and maintains the positive spiritual influences within the community so that members can live in harmony among each other and with the environment. For example, when a murder occurs in an *adat* territory, it implies that someone has died and the perpetrator shall be sanctioned. It also has the spiritual implication that the killing has "polluted" the village's positive aura. This may bring a bad spirit to the territory and may influence others to do bad things. Similarly, extra-marital births are believed to bring negative spirituality to both the family and the community as a whole. Present-day human beings are believed to be reincarnated ancestors in their patrilineal family, so the question of fatherhood is social, cosmological, and existential.

Heavy sanctions are imposed on families who fail to perform *mecaru*. The whole family is denied access to the local cemetery and temples or is ostracized by the entire village community (Ramstedt 2013: 121). A lawyer at KPPAD (*Komisi Pemberdayaan Perempuan dan Anak Daerah*, Regional Commission for Development of Women and Children) explained that for the Balinese, *adat* law is of a greater significance than state law. This is because *adat* is part of Balinese life through the *banjar* (customary hamlet) and *desa adat* (customary village), so its sanctions are imposed collectively on members through *sangkepan* or *paruman* (customary assembly of the *banjar* members).[9] In Bali, *adat* law at the *banjar* level is also codified as *awig-awig*, which includes provisions about *adat* marriage. For instance, Article 63 of *Awig-awig banjar Pekandelan Klod, Lingkungan Pekandelan, Kelurahan Semarapura Klod, Kecamatan Klungkung, Kabupatan Klungkung* regulates *adat* marriage as follows:

8 Interview with parents of children intending to marry in a marriage dispensation case in a district court, June 2017.

9 Interview with a lawyer at KPPAD, April 10, 2017, Denpasar.

(1) *Marriage is an engagement between a male (purusa) and a female (pradana) based on an agreement to live together through love to pursue happiness sekala niskala (materially and spiritually) through a sekala (physical) and niskala (spiritual) witnessing ceremony.*
(2) *The two types of marriage ceremony are:*
   a. *Pepadikan: A marriage that begins when the man and woman's families meet and consent to the marriage.*
   b. *Ngerorod: A marriage without parental consent, for those who already love each other but for some reasons their families disagree about them getting married.*
(3) *The conditions to get married are:*
   a. *The parties are adults.*
   b. *It should be based on love.*
   c. *It is conducted based on religious rules.*
   d. *In the case of inter-religious marriage, there should be a letter from the non-Hindu party mentioning that he/she converts to Hinduism and has conducted sudi widani (a religious conversion ritual).*
(4) *Marriage should also be conducted following the existing [state] laws and regulations.*

The case study of Evi demonstrates the difficulties in not adhering to the *adat* rules on marriage. In her case, she gave birth outside of wedlock, but she could obtain an *akta tunggal*, a state certificate of birth without the father's name (see Chapter 3). With it, her child will be able to go to school, although they may experience certain stigmas. However, her situation was problematic for her and her family primarily because of the *adat* system. Her baby boy could not belong to any family temple, so there was no place to pray or perform any *adat* ceremonies for him. In Ratna's case, these *adat* hurdles were also the main motivation for accepting the apology and marriage proposal from Pranata's family.

Previous research on Bali has recorded diverse *adat* marriage practices and rules. Korn (1932, 469–516) documented several types of *adat* marriage in Bali, including *ontmoetingshuwelijk* (an arranged marriage), *schenkhuwelijk* (donation marriage[10]), *vluchthuwelijk* (elopement), *schaakhuwelijk* (marriage by kidnap), and *dienhuwelijk* (serving marriage[11]). Boon (1977) has categorized Balinese *adat* marriage into three types: Marriage by (mock) capture, arranged marriage for an alliance, and endogamy. *Adat* law is still diverse and differs from one customary village to another. Disputes within the *adat* domain are resolved through an assembly at the *banjar* level.[12]

10 A marriage where wealthy people let their servants marry their daughters to show appreciation for their work and loyalty (Korn 1932, 476).

11 A marriage where the husband agrees to work for his wife's father instead of paying the bride price (Korn 1932, 491).

12 Interview with a lawyer at KPPAD, April 10, 2017, Denpasar.

The philosophy at the foundation of these *adat* rules, sanctions, and systems is that every family in a village will need other families in the community, so they should maintain a good relationship with each other. *Adat* in Bali has "always been embodied in what is essentially community praxis" (Warren 1993: 296). Therefore, rituals are conducted to guarantee the continuation of social order. The infringement of any *adat* rules is believed to endanger the well-being of the collective rather than the individual (Ramstedt 2014a: 62). Furthermore, according to Ramstedt, the Balinese *adat* law constitutes "feeling rules" that require cognitive bodily emotion work to release what the social environment deems inappropriate feelings (Ramstedt 2014b). More specifically, a "calm" feeling in oneself indicates one's world is in balance (Wikan 1990: 272).

4.4.2. Relationship between adat and state law

Although *adat* law is central to people's lives in Bali, it does not exist in a vacuum but is closely interwoven with state law. For instance, as part of a recent decentralizing process, the Indonesian government has enacted a series of laws on provincial governance, which provided the Balinese provincial parliament with new legislative autonomy. The provincial parliament accordingly codified Balinese *adat* law so that it is now the major source of law at the village level (Ramstedt 2014a: 61). These changes also indicate an increased tension between state and *adat* law, since lower-level legislation challenges state law norms (Ramstedt 2014a: 61).

Today's civil administration in Bali has two parallel systems. *Desa adat* deals with cultural, social, and spiritual affairs. *Desa dinas* deals with civil registration, such as issuing identity cards and certificates (Putra and Creese 2016: 106–107). Accordingly, *adat* and civil marriage registrations have different procedures, consequences, motivations, and meanings. While *adat* marriage is to be accepted by the community,[13] people engage in civil marriage registrations to have official documentation, mainly marriage and birth certificates. While *adat* marriage is a prerequisite to civil marriage registration, civil marriage registration is a separate step to be completed after *adat* marriage. In this sense, they are two different systems. The civil marriage registrars emphasize that they do not interfere with the *adat* marriage rules and focus on executing state regulation. One civil registrar explained:

13 To be legitimate under *adat* law, the Balinese marriage requires three witnesses (*Tri Upasaksi*), namely (1) *Dewa Saksi*, God's witness through a religious ritual, (2) *Manusa Saksi*, the people's witness by *Bendesa* or *Kelian Adat* or other *adat* officials and families of both parties, and (3) *Bhuta Saksi*, the holy spirit's witness through a religious ritual.

> *Marriage based on religious ceremony alone is not enough and we regard this as not yet being married in our database. If you want to have religious marriage, well, please go ahead, but these marriages will be blocked (will not be valid) at the Civil Registration Office (Silahkan menikah agama, tapi tutup di KCS).*[14]

Judges also seem to emphasize this clear functional division between the *adat* and state law system. One judge explained that he does not use *adat* law in court decisions. He only uses *adat* law to reduce the penalty, using it for "balancing" (*mempertimbangkan*). By using *adat* law, he does not mean citing written *adat* law such as *awig-awig*, which are different in each area and so are difficult to apply in courts. Instead, he means considering "*adat law process*", i.e., reconciliation or a negotiation process between families, sometimes also with *kelian adat* (a local leader).[15]

One judge I interviewed said that in principle, in criminal cases, state law is above *adat* law. Still, *adat* law is important for balancing. In reality, state law is the solution if *adat* law cannot solve the dispute among people.[16] In civil cases, judges claim that *adat* law is as valid as state law, and they "*mix (campur)*" the use of these two laws depending on cases.[17]

Judges, marriage registrars, and *adat* law professors all accept *adat* marriage as "*sah*" (valid) in Balinese society. Judges are authorized to use *adat* law,[18] although not all judges use it.[19] A judge who is originally from the other province told me that when she needs to apply *adat* law in her judgement, she asks her Balinese colleagues for advice.[20] A good judgement, according to judges, is one that does not neglect social aspects and *adat* law while complying with state law and due process.[21]

In an interview, an *adat* law professor in Bali referred to Article 1 (2) of the Marriage Law that stipulates the validity of a marriage when it is conducted based on the couple's religious law and faith. They explained that in Bali, such religious law is found in *adat* law that derives its rules and principles from the *hukum asli* (living law) and Hindu law. There is no difference between *adat* and religious law in Bali: They are deeply intertwined and indistinguishable. He says that due to marriage's inherently private nature, it is difficult for the

14 Interview with a marriage registrar at the Civil Marriage Registration Office, July 3, 2017, Denpasar.
15 Interview with a judge (A) at the Denpasar District Court, June 16, 2017.
16 Interview with a judge (A) at the Denpasar District Court, June 16, 2017.
17 Interview with a judge at the Semarapura District Court, July 13, 2017.
18 The Second Amendment to the 1945 Constitution is seen to have acknowledged *adat* law as a legal source (Priambodo, 2018), and Article 27 of Law No.15 of 1970 on the Basic Principles of Judicial Powers states that a judge must identify, follow, and understand the values of the living law of the community.
19 Interview with a judge at Bangli District Court, May 31, 2017.
20 Interview with a judge at Semarapura District Court, July 13, 2017.
21 Interview with a judge at Semarapura District Court, July 13, 2017.

state to control it in practice, even when state law regulates it. "*State law cannot intervene in culture or adat. Laws need to be in harmony with culture, and social norms and they come from society*".[22]

4.4.3. Civil marriage registration

Interaction between *adat* law and state law is observed in civil marriage registration practices. Civil marriage registration is becoming increasingly important for people's lives due to increased educational opportunities because it is required for obtaining a birth certificate, which is needed for school attendance. There are two types of birth certificates in the Indonesian civil system: A 'normal' birth certificate (*akta kelahiran*) with the name of two parents and 'deviant' single birth certificate (*akta tunggal*) with only the mother's name.[23] What enables a child to obtain the normal birth certificate is his or her parents' civil marriage registration before birth.

To obtain the 'normal' birth certificate, what matters is the date of the *adat* marriage ceremony, as the civil marriage at KCS is registered retrospectively at the date of the *adat* marriage ceremony. A civil marriage registrar explains:

> *To have the father's name on a birth certificate, a child needs to be born after the adat marriage ceremony. Otherwise, the father can be anybody and we can't know. Even if the baby is born only one day before the adat marriage date, the birth certificate cannot be issued, but only the akta tunggal.*[24]

A child with *akta tunggal* is considered an 'illegitimate child' (*anak luar kawin*). One of the difficulties for children with *akta tunggal* is the absence of inheritance rights. As Bali is a patrilineal society, those who do not have a father's name on their birth certificate have no inheritance rights. Another difficulty is the social stigma attached to unmarried mothers and *akta tunggal*. A judge explained the consequences of having *akta tunggal* in one of the hearings:

> *If the marriage is not recorded in KCS, the baby cannot have a status as an "anak bapak" (father's child), he/she will still be an "anak ibu" (single mother's child). Please do not give another burden to the baby just because his parents were being irresponsible. This baby must have a birth certificate with both names of his parents so that in the future he can go to school without problem or minimize the possibility to be bullied.*[25]

22 Interview with a professor of *adat* law in Bali, May 25, 2017, Denpasar.
23 Law No.24 of 2013 on Population Administration.
24 Interview with a marriage registrar at the Denpasar Civil Marriage Registration Office, July 3, 2017.
25 Court hearing, July 2017.

The mother's birth certificate and her ID card (KTP) or family card (*kartu keluarga*, a document that contains information such as residency and family members) are required for an *akta tunggal*. As the KTP is available only for those who are above 17 years old, if the mother is under 17 years old, she has to wait until she reaches that age.[26]

These certificates' functions and roles explain why people try to obtain civil marriage registrations even though an *adat* marriage is sufficient to avoid sanctions against extra-marital pregnancies. Chapter 3 explained the legal and illegal methods for registering marriages below the legal marriageable age. One of my case studies involves age manipulation, which is illegal, called *katrol usia*. When Novi and Angga married according to *adat*, Novi (a girl) was 17 years old, and Angga (a boy) was 15. A few months after their *adat* marriage ceremony, Angga's father asked the head of his community to issue Angga's KTP, listing his age as 19 (4 years older than his actual age). "*If I am not mistaken, we paid 300,000 Rp (€18) to issue the marriage certificate*", said Novi, but it seemed that this was all arranged by Angga's father.[27]

In their case, they married because Novi's family from North Bali pressured them when the family found out that they were living together in Denpasar. "*My family wanted me to get married because their friends and families knew about our relationship. This was to avoid embarrassment (malu) in the village*", said Novi. To avoid the feeling of *malu*, it is enough to marry according to *adat*. The young bride and groom did not even know the minimum age for marriage under state law until Angga's father told them. However, the marriage registration was important to Angga's father because it allowed them to obtain a birth certificate, which will allow their children to go to school. In another case of extra-marital pregnancy and underage marriage in Bangli (a regency in the east part of Bali), the girl's family wanted to ensure the birth certificate was available for the baby. The girl's uncle, who worked at the KCS in Bangli, arranged a KCS marriage registration by changing the boy's age from 18 to 19.

While such age manipulation operates outside of the state legal system, marriage dispensation is the only legal way to obtain civil marriage registration in the case of underage marriages. Although the 1974 Marriage Law does not specify when judges should grant dispensations, judges do usually grant them, understanding the importance of the certificates. One of the judges added:

> *It is also because people are not comfortable and afraid of the stigma attached to pregnancy outside of marriage. There is this idea that if a couple already lives together*

26 Interview with a marriage registrar at the Denpasar Civil Marriage Registration Office Denpasar, July 3, 2017.

27 Interview with a couple that had a civil marriage registration by manipulating their age, May 2017.

without being married, the area becomes dirty (cuntake). So as a judge, I consider and balance all the factors (mempertimbankan).[28]

Another judge explained that people mostly apply for marriage dispensations because of extra-marital pregnancies and mutual love relationships (*suka-sama-suka*). She granted a dispensation to conform to social norms (*norma sosial*) and the community's law (*hukum dari masyarakat*). She said:

> *I have to think about the effect on and pressure from society – they will keep thinking, "who is the husband, who is the father?", unless the pregnant girl gets married. So, there is the need to clarify the status. If the father's status is not clear, it is painful (sakit) for the baby when he/she grows up. So I feel pity (kasihan) for such situations.*[29]

4.4.4. Marriage dispensation cases

To investigate the reasons and justifications for marriage dispensation, I analyzed eight cases of marriage dispensation from two District Courts (*PN Bangli* and *PN Semarapura*), judged between 2016 and 2017 (see Appendix 2). The applicants were all parent(s) of either the candidate wife or husband, sometimes of both of them. The couples were all young adolescents (14-20 years old). Perhaps surprisingly, in 75% of the cases, the underage party was a boy (i.e., a husband candidate). In the other two cases, the underage parties were girls as young as 14 years old. In three out of eight cases (Cases A, B, and C), the girl was pregnant at the time of the hearing. In the other five cases (Cases D, E, F, G, and H), the couple already had a child who was born after their *adat* marriage, conducted two to five years before the hearings. In these five cases, the couple conducted the *adat* marriage following the pregnancy.

In principle, a couple must obtain a marriage dispensation before an *adat* wedding,[30] but all of the cases were heard after such a wedding. One applicant I interviewed, the father of the wife candidate in a dispensation case, explained the urgency for an *adat* wedding: "*We needed to hurry because there are not many 'good days' (hari baik) – and we were afraid that the baby would be born before the adat marriage*".[31] In Bali, an *adat* marriage is to be planned on auspicious days called '*hari baik*', which can make the planning of such a wedding complicated and pressing.

28 Interview with a judge at Bangli District Court, May 31, 2017.

29 Interview with a judge at Semarapura District Court, July 13, 2017.

30 Interview with a judge at Semarapura District Court, July 13, 2017.

31 Interview with an applicant for marriage dispensation in a district court (parents of the children who were to marry), June 2017.

According to a civil marriage registrar, marriage dispensation has been increasingly difficult to obtain, as judges and courts do not want to be seen as legalizing underage marriages.[32] Indeed, some judges sympathize with the liberal values and clarify their point that underage marriages are "strongly discouraged", as "they risk reproductive health of women who are unprepared and still psychologically unstable". They emphasize that "it should not be too easy to grant dispensations to underage marriages if there are no logical reasons for the children's interest" (Cases D, F, and G).

The court decisions also explicitly denounce certain young sexual relationships. The court decisions often use phrases such as "the relationship over the limit (*hubungan tersebut melewati batas*)" (Case C), "such a free relationship (*pergaulannya yang begitu bebas*)" (Cases D, F, and G), "a relationship as if between husband and wife (*hubungan layaknya suami istri)*" (Case E), to describe the relationship between the couples. They claim such a sexual relationship is caused by "their social freedom and lack of supervision from parents" (Cases D, F, and G).

In spite of such moral condemnation of adolescent relationships and liberal ideals to prevent child marriages, judges granted dispensations in all eight cases. The judges justify their decisions in several ways. First, they rely on the Child Protection Law:

> *Their marriage (pregnancy) was caused by their social freedom and lack of supervision from parents, so the future of the newborn baby requires a complete family consisting of father and mother to provide care and devoted love for the baby's growth. Child protection aims to guarantee the fulfilment of children's rights in order to live, grow, develop and participate optimally in accordance with human dignity and values, and to be protected from violence and discrimination (Article 3 of the Child Protection Law)* (Case D, F, and G).

A second justification notes the negative consequences of not granting a dispensation. "If the marriage dispensation is not granted, there will be an unfavourable negative impact for both parties, so the judge believes that the best legal solution is to provide marriage dispensation" (Case B). This vague use of 'negative impact' resonates with the use of the Islamic concept '*kemaslahatan*' (common good) in the marriage dispensation cases in West Java (Horii 2020; see also Chapter 3). This comparison also illuminates that judges in West Java and Bali use different means (religious law, customary law, and state law) to arrive at the same conclusion (to grant the dispensation). While Bali judges did use the Child Protection Law, the outcome did not differ from the West Java court decisions, where judges relied instead on Islamic and state laws.

32 Interview with a marriage registrar at the Denpasar Civil Marriage Registration Office, July 3, 2017.

Judges also strengthen their reasoning by proving that their decisions do not conflict with state law. Case B writes: "Granting marriage dispensation has been reasoned and is not against state law". Case A emphasizes that the decision does not contradict with Article 7(1) of the Marriage Law, as "the minimum age limit in the provision means that married persons are expected to have maturity, mental maturity, and adequate physical strength". Another judge uses Article 2(1) of the Marriage Law, which recognizes the validity of a marriage that took place in accordance with the religious laws of the parties. That judge stated: "Their marriage was a lawful marriage carried out by a Hindu religion, so it has fulfilled the provision" (Cases D, F, and G).

While the judges use various arguments to discourage and justify underage marriage simultaneously, other judges grant dispensations more straightforwardly. For instance, Case E reads, without elaborating: "They were married in October 2014, when they were both 17 years old. As they obtained their parents' permission for the marriage, and as their marriage was based on mutual love and no-coercion, the marriage was lawful". This contrast shows the difference in judges' attitudes and opinions towards underage 'child' marriage.

Three out of eight cases mention *adat*/religious law. Some cases discuss the concept of *cuntake/leteh*: "As the girl is pregnant, if she is not immediately married, there will be a *cuntake/leteh* situation according to *adat* and religion" (Cases A and B). They also stated that *adat* law does not prohibit underage marriage: "*Adat* law does not set a certain age limitation on performing marriage" (Case A), "The decision also does not conflict with the rules and legislation in force and *adat* law in the applicants' residence" (Case A), and "There was no barrier to conducting the marriage either in terms of kinship and *adat* relationships, no prohibition to conduct marriage according to Balinese *Adat* Law and Hinduism" (Case B). Case H lists the elements that validate a Hindu marriage[33] to demonstrate that the underage marriage was religiously valid.

Judges emphasize the relational aspect of marriage in association with *adat* law, to justify the marriage of a child. Case A reads:

> *Adat law allows the marriage of children to be executed. This is because in adat law, marriage is not merely the union of both individuals, but also the union of two relatives (keluarge kerabat). An underage marriages or a marriage of children is not a problem in adat law because the wife and husband will be guided by their family, so adat law does not prohibit a marriage of children.*

33 "Their marriage was conducted according to Hinduism and *adat* so it is legal (*sah*). According to the Decisions (*Keputusan-keputusan dan Ketetapan-ketetapan*) of the Parisada Hindu Dharma (PHDI Kabupaten Badung, 1986): The validity of a Hindu marriage is determined by the presence of *panyangaskara* with *bhuta* witnesses and witnesses as well as *penyaksi* (witness) from *prajuru adat* (*adat* leader) as elements from *manusa saksi*. This is what is often referred to as *tri upasaksi* in a marriage ceremony (*samskara wiwaha*)" (Case H).

This communal nature of *adat* marriage was also explained by an *adat* law professor in Bali:

> *The structure of adat law starts from the family and goes up to the banjar (hamlet) and the desa (village) levels. Each part of this structure has an equal position. (...) This is why in Bali, marriage is not only marriage among the couple, but also among their extended family, banjar and village, as a marriage involves a number of parties representing these structures and the witnesses at the wedding ceremony.*[34]

The analysis of dispensation cases demonstrates that judges use both state and *adat* law to justify and strengthen the legal grounds for their decisions to grant marriage dispensation to underage couples. They emphasize the importance of marriage in reaction to extra-marital pregnancies. Marriage practically facilitates participation in the welfare state and education system through civil marriage registration. Meanwhile, it is also of moral importance because it preserves the moral equilibrium of the community.

The Child Protection Law is used in a counter-intuitive way to serve both moral and practical goals. On the one hand, the law is inspired by modern values and liberal principles, inspired by the UN Convention on the Rights of the Child. Article 26(1) stipulates the parental obligation to prevent child marriages. On the other hand, it is used in practice to legalize underage marriages and thus, to protect babies from societal harm. This reasoning highlights that babies are also children, so 'child brides' are not the only 'children' on which international advocacy should focus.

4.5. Criminal law: Sex crimes

Another way to understand how judges (as state representatives) deal with young people's extra-marital pregnancies is cases of 'sex crimes' involving minors. As discussed, extra-marital pregnancies are the main motivation for marriage dispensations. This section will demonstrate that sex crimes are sometimes used in cases where marriage dispensation fails as a solution to such pregnancies. Therefore, these two types of cases are closely interlinked. Under the current Indonesian Penal Code and the Child Protection Law, it is a criminal offence to "play tricks, tell a series of lies, or persuade" children under age 18 to have sexual intercourse. Pompe's (1994) study on criminal cases of extra-marital sex in Indonesia is illuminating. He observed that in the 1990s, "the judiciary was drawing *adat* more and more into the sphere of state criminal law" (Ibid: 112). For instance, the Supreme Court based its judgements in several Balinese cases on an old Balinese code of law, which specifies that if a man induces a woman to have sexual intercourse with him by making false

34 Interview with a professor of *adat* law in Bali, May 25, 2017, Denpasar.

promises of marriage, he is liable to punishment (Ibid: 116). He concluded that "*adat* is the instrument, the legitimation, and the pretext in the effectuation" of a kind of moral reform by the judiciary "to fight the social reality of extra-marital sexual relations, and, more in particular, the practice of men inducing women by means of a false promise of marriage to have sexual intercourse with them" (Ibid: 118).

Today, the media report sex crime cases sensationally, and people in Bali are well aware that pre-marital sexual intercourse by minors can be a criminal offence. The fear of prosecution and imprisonment has become an incentive for the boy and his family to agree on marrying the girl. The girls' families also use the state legal system to take revenge, to disagree with their daughters' relationship, or to negotiate with the boy's family.

In Ratna's case, her family reported the case to the police when her ex-boyfriend and his family were not willing to marry her. This reporting was her family's way of negotiating. In other cases, however, girls' families report the case even when the boy is willing to marry. A judge explained:

> *It is always parents of the girl who bring such cases to the police. Parents who do not agree to marry their daughters. Even though the boy's (defendant's) family often offer to marry the girl. But the girls' family members are angry at the situation of their daughter's pregnancy, and refuse the offer, as they want their daughters to continue school and start working (instead of marrying).*[35]

I documented seven cases of sex crimes regarding sexual intercourse between a boy (16–18 years old) and a girl (13–18 years old), decided between 2013 and 2016 in the District Court Denpasar (see Appendix 3). In six out of seven cases, the boy (defendant) and the girl (victim) were in a romantic relationship (*pacaran*).

The primary source of state law used in these cases is the Child Protection Law, sometimes accompanied by some provisions from the Penal Code (KUHP). Article 82 of the Child Protection Law states:

(1) *Everyone who deliberately commits violence or threats of violence, forcing a child to commit sexual intercourse with him or with others, is subject to a maximum penalty of 15 (fifteen) years of imprisonment and 3 (three) years and a fine of Rp. 300,000,000 (three hundred million) at most and Rp. 60,000,000 (sixty million) at least.*

(2) *The provision of crimes as meant in verse (1) also apply to every man who deliberately plays tricks, tells a series of lies, or persuades a child to commit sexual intercourse with him or others.*

35 Interview with a judge (B) at Denpasar District Court, June 16, 2017.

The law does not specify the gender of the defendants ("Everyone who deliberately commits ..."). Still, the analyzed cases always involved male defendants, including when the girl was older than the boy, such as in Ratna and Pranata's case. A judge explained in an interview:

> *It is because girls are often younger and manipulated. For instance, they are in pacaran, but the boy promises the girl that he will marry. This is an act of lying, and this can be the ground of the charge. [...] Because there is a feeling. At the beginning, they are both happy, but later it is the girl who gets hurt. Girls often say, "I was forced", or "he said he would marry me". This is considered as seduction (bujuk rayu). [...] If the boy reported to the police for being cheated, the police would ask: What did he lose from the sexual intercourse? Male virginity (keperjakaan)?*[36]

The first observation is that, as Pompe (1994) also noted, the boys' promises to marry weigh heavily. Making these promises is considered "playing tricks, telling a series of lies, or persuading a child to commit sexual intercourse" (Child Protection Law, Article 82(2)). Case D's court decision emphasized that when the victim was hesitant to begin sexual intercourse, the defendant convinced her by promising to 'take responsibility' (i.e., to marry her) and by saying that he wants to have sex as a proof of her love towards him. In Case G, the court decision wrote: "[W]hen the victim refused to have sex because of the fear of pregnancy, the defendant insisted and promised her to take responsibility and marry her if she would become pregnant".

Notably, this promise itself falls under 'tricks, lies, or persuasion', and the intention and the outcome did not matter. For instance, in Case A, the defendant was sentenced to imprisonment, although he clearly was willing to marry the victim after she became pregnant. The court decision notes what the defendant said: "I came inside. I will marry you". "If you fail to have [a] miscarriage,[37] we will just marry. I have a house in Buleleng, we [will] just live there". In the end, the victim did not want to marry the defendant. She already had another boyfriend, whom she married by the time of the hearing.

So why did the judge find him guilty? The judgment writes, "Because of the pregnancy, the girl had to marry and become a housewife, ... [so] she cannot enjoy the childhood period with her peers". This "damage to the future of the victim" is an important factor in other cases as well. Cases A, D, E, C, F, and G mention this as an aggravating factor.

It should be noted that this 'damage to the future' is caused not necessarily by a pregnancy, but merely by the act of sexual intercourse. Judges place weight on the 'tainted' reputation of the girl and her family. The court decisions emphasize the shame of losing one's virginity, which causes long-term

36 Interview with a judge (B) at Denpasar District Court, June 16, 2017.

37 As abortion is illegal in Indonesia, people often use 'miscarriage' in place of 'abortion'.

damage to the girl's future. These factors are mentioned in the indictments' reasons, especially in cases of mutual love (*suka-sama-suka*), such as Case E. In these cases, judges justify their decisions with societal factors. Case E reads:

> *Even though intercourse was based on mutual willingness, and there was no compulsion, the defendant's action negatively impacted the victim amid her community. The victim's reputation got tainted. The surrounding community scorns her if she is not a virgin, resulting in prolonged shame for both the victim and her extended family. The defendant's act is not a good example for other children. His act has caused the victim trauma and shame among her community and her school. His act damaged the victim's future. His act disturbed society (masyarakat).*

In addition to basing the indictment on state laws, in Cases A, B, and E, judges also relied on the society's moral code. The court decisions write: "The religious norm that is not to have sexual intercourse outside of husband/wife relationship is violated"; "according to 'religious norms' and 'norms in community', the act is only for legally (*sah*) married adults"; and "sexual intercourse without *adat* marriage is against 'norms of decency' and 'legal norms' that damage the reputation of the girl even if it was a case of mutual love".

The moral codes are also emphasized in hearings. Judges ask questions about the nature of the relationship between the girl as a victim and the boy as a defendant. For example, they ask about the length of their relationship, and how often and where they had sexual intercourse. When the girl would answer, the judge would clearly condemn their actions. "*So you were already in a relationship when you were in SMP? What kind of decision is that?*" "*7 times (you had sexual intercourse)? What did you say to your parents? [...] You told your parents you were 'going out' but in reality you were 'going in'!*"[38]

The judge also preached *adat*/religious norms to the youngsters:

> *How did you score on the religious subject? I learnt this subject when I was in elementary school, and I still remember it today. It is called "Brahmacari", meaning the phase to study for your future when you are entering the next level, "Grehasta" (marriage life). [...] Have you heard the Balinese word "Luh Luih (perempuan baik-baik, i.e., a good girl)"? But if you can't protect yourself, you just become a "Luh Luhu" (Luhu means rubbish. So Luh Luhu means naughty girl or bitch).*[39]

Such moral and societal elements are fundamental factors for the judges. According to a judge, "*It is a matter for the two families. If there is no conflict, there is no problem*".[40] I asked him why such defendants could be exempted from the

38 Court hearing, July 2017.
39 Court hearing, July 2017.
40 Interview with a judge (A) at Denpasar District Court, June 16, 2017.

indictment through a settlement since it is technically a fixed criminal charge once reported. Police also turn a blind eye if no one reports the case. He explained the answer was "*restorative justice*". He said, "*That is because it's about two families, and about community. If they get married, the problem is already over. This is because society thinks it's acceptable. It's about the environment and the societal connection (lingkungan), and the community (masyarakat)*".[41] In Ratna and Pranata's case, after they agreed to marry, while they could no longer withdraw the case, the judge eventually decided not to indict Pranata. The judicial outcome would have been different, however, if they had continued to be hostile to each other without the marriage plan that reconciled them.

Mediation (*diversi*) plays an important role in this regard. Judges explained: "*If the boy and the girl are still in love, they can try mediation. She would decide that the boy does not need to go to jail, and only needs probation (hukuman percobaan)*".[42] "*If the boy's family offers to marry the girl and if the girl's family also accepts it at mediation, the boy will not be charged*".[43]

Judges consider a good judgment to note the environment's spiritual balance:

> *We have to look at children and their environment. [...] Balancing the feelings of both families is also important. Feelings of justice (rasa keadilaan) for the community should also be considered, as a judgment needs to set a good example for the society.*[44]

The analysis of the court decisions and interviews indicates that those judgements aim to calm down familial and communal unrest, rather than being technical judicial decisions. Such decisions, according to judges, are to "restore harmony and peace in the community". In this sense, my findings indicate a slightly different perspective than Pompe's (1994) account on how judges handle sex crime cases. While he suggests that judges take a moral approach in using *adat* law to condemn extra-marital sexual relations, my cases show that it is also a pragmatic approach to restoring harmony, choosing solutions that maximize benefits for all parties.

However, imprisoning boys as a solution for 'harmony' can unfairly damage their future, a sacrifice for the community's moral equilibrium. It is an undesirable outcome of over-criminalization (Hermawan 2018) that disproportionally affects boys. In both sex crime and dispensation cases, courts use state laws somewhat differently than how they were designed to be used. The Child Protection Law is meant to protect children regardless of gender, and the specific clause about criminalization of sexual intercourse with a minor is made

41 Interview with a judge (A) at Denpasar District Court, June 16, 2017.
42 Interview with a judge (B) at Denpasar District Court, June 16, 2017.
43 Interview with a judge (A) at Denpasar District Court, June 16, 2017.
44 Interview with a judge (B) at Denpasar District Court, June 16, 2017.

to protect children from sexual violence (particularly paedophilia). However, in practice, it specifically penalizes boys who had sexual relations with their girlfriends.

4.6. Conclusion: Realizing human rights in pluralistic legal systems

In this chapter, I presented two types of legal cases: Marriage dispensations and sex crimes. These cases illuminated how state agents in Bali navigate state law through local concerns and *adat* law when dealing with extra-marital teenage pregnancies. When the community's morality is at stake in such 'emergencies', families, *adat* authorities, and state agents collaborate to find a way to solve the situation through a locally accepted normative system.

Marriage dispensation, as part of the state law system, is a solution facilitated by judges, reconciling the state system with local solutions according to *adat*. Judges emphasize both the moral and practical importance of granting dispensations. To be able to grant them, the Child Protection Law is used in a counter-intuitive way. The law is inspired by modern values and is liberal in principle. However, when applied with *adat* law in local courts, it serves communitarian values, mainly maintaining social equilibrium by legalizing underage marriages. When marriage does not work as a solution to the 'emergency', parties sometimes begin a sex crime prosecution to quell the familial and communal unrest. The possibility of prosecution is occasionally used to pressure boys to marry. The two types of legal cases illuminate that state laws, designed to achieve the goals of liberal legalism, are in practice used by judges to serve the goals of collectivism, to maintain the community's harmony and morality.

What does the existence of multiple legal orders mean for the realization of human rights? In most of the examined cases, judges allowed the legalization of child marriages by navigating different kinds of legal systems. Thus, it might seem that legal pluralism *hinders* the realization of human rights. In other words, it did not contribute to the substantive goals of *eliminating child marriage*, towards which human rights institutions aspire. However, judges' decisions to maintain or restore harmony also seem to help children (at least girls and babies), their families, and their community by saving them from 'emergency'. If Indonesia indeed shares the "harmony ideology" then "a bad compromise is better than a good fight" (Nader 1991: 1), whereas we should also acknowledge that harmony occasionally comes at a cost to individuals (Ibid: 309). Communitarianism is not inconsistent with the idea of human rights unless the community begins to "impinge unduly" on the individual (Henkin 1989: 16).

Even if the compromise for the sake of harmony means hindering the realization of human rights, it seems wrong to blame legal pluralism, since judges used both *adat*/religious law and state law to maintain the harmony. When comparing the marriage dispensation cases in West Java and Bali, it also becomes apparent that even if means are different (e.g., the types of laws the judgements are based on), the outcome is the same (i.e., granting the dispensation). That means allowing the legalization of child marriages did not stem from legal pluralism. Could it then be that legal pluralism *leads* to the realization of human rights? That depends on how one defines the nature of human rights.

In light of liberal values, the protection of autonomy and individual rights is well embedded in principle but is out of reach in practice. This may be irrelevant. As the analysis has shown, laws in practice in Bali (i.e., judicial decisions) are in favour of social equilibrium and the protection of rights of the 'relational self'. The difficulties Ratna's family faced with Ratna remaining an unmarried mother indicate that compliance with *adat* law is essential to protect relational self-rights, both for Ratna and for her baby. This weight on relational rights also has to do with the communal nature of Indonesian marriage (see, e.g., Platt 2017). For those convinced that child marriage is intrinsically harmful, it might be hard to conceive of the practice as serving a protective function. However, there are clearly local logics of child protection, focusing on consolidating family interests and securing the social place (Boyden et al. 2012).

Considering people's needs for marriage arise from both *adat* and state laws, it is understandable that marriage is the best possible solution to teenage pregnancies. This is the conclusion that all local activists agreed on during a Focus Group Discussion I organized.[45] These activists included a local legal aid association, a government agency for the protection of women and children, and a women's section of a Hindu organization in Bali. They suggested that the two families make a legal agreement that the children will marry but will continue their education and live in separate households. This is precisely what Ratna and Pranata did. It secures a desirable future for the children within the existing *adat* framework. *Adat* rules are thus somewhat dynamic and flexible. For instance, the Majelis Utama Desa Pakraman Bali (MUDP, Supreme Assembly of the Village Council) has changed the Balinese *adat* law on inheritance so that husbands and wives have the same status and property rights within marriage (Westendorp 2015: 441–442). Given the possibilities for such changes, another solution to child marriage is to adapt the *adat* rules. At the FGD, a female member of the Hindu organization (*Peran Wanita Hindu Dharma Indonesia*, WHDI) suggested changing the Balinese *adat* law regarding divorce, so that child brides and grooms have easier legal means of exiting the marriage.[46]

As this chapter has shown, marriage's communal aspects are extremely important for Balinese people. Marriage impacts their sense of belonging to the local community and the community's moral equilibrium. Therefore, the rights of the relational self should be as protected as modern individual rights. Depending on how one defines the nature of rights, as Chua and Engle (2015:

45 FGD with local activists, August 7, 2017, Denpasar.
46 FGD with local activists, August 7, 2017, Denpasar.

225) write, both state law and customary/traditional law can be both empowering and disempowering, both liberating and constraining. In this sense, it would not be helpful to identify legal pluralism or *adat*/religious law as an obstacle to the realization of human rights. On the contrary, if their realization means it occurs from the perspectives of rights-holders themselves, *adat* law is an essential tool for both understanding what rights mean for them and supporting them in claiming *their* rights.

Bibliography

An-Na'im, A. A. (1992). Introduction. In A. A. An-Na'im (Ed.), *Human Rights in Cross-Cultural Perspectives: A Quest for Consensus* (pp. 1–15). Philadelphia: University of Pennsylvania Press.

Bedner, A. (2017). The need for Realism: Ideals and practice in Indonesia's Constitutional history. In M. Adams, A. Meuwese, & E. H. Ballin (Eds.), *Constitutionalism and the Rule of Law: Bridging Idealism and Realism* (pp. 159–194). Cambridge, UK: Cambridge University Press. https://doi.org/10.1017/9781316585221.006

Benda-Beckmann, F. von, & Benda-Beckmann, K. von. (2002). Who's afraid of legal pluralism? *The Journal of Legal Pluralism and Unofficial Law, 34*(47), 37–82. https://doi.org/10.1080/07329113.2002.10756563

Benda-Beckmann, K. von. (1984). *The Broken Stairways to Consensus: Village Justice and State Courts in Minangkabau*. Dordrecht: Foris Publications.

Boon, J. A. (1977). *The Anthropological Romance of Bali 1597–1972: Dynamic Perspectives in Marriage and Caste, Politics and Religion*. Cambridge; New York: Cambridge University Press.

Bourchier, D. (2008). Positivism and romanticism in Indonesian legal thought. In T. Lindsey (Ed.), *Indonesia: Law and Society* (pp. 94–104). Leichhardt, N.S.W.: The Federation Press.

Bourchier, D. (2015). *Illiberal Democracy in Indonesia: The Ideology of the Family State*. London; New York: Routledge.

Bowen, J. R. (2003). *Islam, Law, and Equality in Indonesia: An Anthropology of Public Reasoning*. Cambridge, UK; New York, NY: Cambridge University Press.

Boyden, J., Pankhurst, A., & Tafere, Y. (2012). Child protection and harmful traditional practices: Female early marriage and genital modification in Ethiopia. *Development in Practice, 22*(4), 510–522. https://doi.org/10.1080/09614524.2012.672957

Bruce, J. W., Migot-Adholla, S. E. [editors, Place, F., Roth, M., Hazell, P., Matlon, P., Blarel, B., Benneh, G., Atsu, S., Oluoch-Kosura, W., Carter, M. R., Wiebe, K. D., Roth, M., Cochrane, J., Kisamba-Mugerwa, W., Unruh, J., Barrows, R., Golan, E. H., Bruce, J. W., & Atherton, J.](1994). *Searching for land tenure security in Africa* (p. 1). The World Bank. http://documents.worldbank.org/curated/en/630121468742824113/Searching-for-land-tenure-security-in-Africa

Butt, S. (2008). Polygamy and mixed marriage in Indonesia: Islam and the Marriage Law in the courts. In T. Lindsey (Ed.), *Indonesia: Law and Society* (pp. 266–287). Leichhardt, N.S.W.: The Federation Press.

Calavita, K. (2010). *Invitation to Law and Society: An Introduction to the Study of Real Law*. Chicago: University of Chicago Press.

Cammack, M., Bedner, A., & Huis, S. van (2015). Democracy, human rights, and Islamic family law in post-soeharto Indonesia. *New Middle Eastern Studies, 5*, 1–24.

Chua, L. J., & Engel, D. M. (2015). State and personhood in Southeast Asia: The promise and potential for law and society research. *Asian Journal of Law and Society*, *2*(2), 211–228. https://doi.org/10.1017/als.2015.10

Committee on the Elimination of Discrimination against Women. (2004). *Statement to Commemorate the Twenty-Fifth Anniversary of the Adoption of the Convention on the Elimination of All Forms of Discrimination against Women.*

Dossa, S. (1999). Liberal legalism: Law, culture and identity. *The European Legacy*, *4*(3), 73–87. https://doi.org/10.1080/10848779908579973

Eddyono, S. W., Sidauruk, A. R. F., Napitupulu, E. A. T., & Kamilah, A. G. (2016). *Menyingkap Tabir Dispensasi Perkawinan: Analisis Terhadap Praktik Perkawinan Anak di Kab Tuban, Kab Bogor, dan Kab Mamuju.* Jakarta: Koalisi 18+.

Engel, D. M. (2016). Blood curse and belonging in Thailand: Law, Buddhism, and legal consciousness. *Asian Journal of Law and Society*, *3*(1), 71–83. https://doi.org/10.1017/als.2016.2

Equality Now. (2014). *Protecting the Girl Child: Using the Law to End Child, Early and Forced Marriage and Related Human Rights Violations.* New York; Nairobi; London: Equality Now.

Fitzpatrick, D. (2008). Culture, ideology and human rights: The case of Indonesia's code of criminal procedure. In T. Lindsey (Ed.), *Indonesia: Law and Society* (pp. 499–514). Leichhardt, N.S.W.: The Federation Press.

Geertz, C. (1985). *Local Knowledge: Further Essays in Interpretive Anthropology.* New York, NY: Basic Books.

Gonda, J. (1976). Old Javanese literature. In H. Kähler (Ed.), *Handbuch der Orientalistik: Literaturen* (pp. 187–245). Leiden: E.J.Brill.

Grijns, M., & Horii, H. (2018). Child marriage in a village in West Java (Indonesia): Compromises between legal obligations and religious concerns. *Asian Journal of Law and Society*, 5(2), 453–466. https://doi.org/10.1017/als.2018.9

Henkin, L. (1989). The Universality of the concept of human rights. *The Annals of the American Academy of Political and Social Science*, *506*(1), 10–16.

Hermawan, A. (2018). Commentary: How morality-obsessed Indonesia fails its children. *The Jakarta Post.* http://www.thejakartapost.com/news/2018/07/24/commentary-how-morality-obsessed-indonesia-fails-its-children.html

Hooker, M. B. (1978). *Adat Law in Modern Indonesia.* Kuala Lumpur: Oxford University Press.

Horii, H. (2020). Legal reasoning for legitimation of child marriage in West Java: Accommodation of local norms at Islamic courts and the paradox of child protection. *Journal of Human Rights Practice*, *12*(3), 501–523. https://doi.org/10.1093/jhuman/huaa041.

Jennaway, M. (2002). *Sisters and Lovers: Women and Desire in Bali.* Lanham: Rowman & Littlefield Publishers.

Katz, J. S., & Katz, R. S. (1975). The new Indonesian Marriage Law: A mirror of Indonesia's political, cultural, and legal systems. *The American Journal of Comparative Law*, *23*(4), 653–681. https://doi.org/10.2307/839240

Kerrigan, F., McKay, A. L., Kristiansen, A., Kyed, H., Dahl, L., Dalton, P., Roesdahl, M., & Vehils, N. (2012). *Informal Justice Systems: Charting a Course for Human Rights-Based Engagement.* New York, NY: United Nations Development Programme, UN Women, UNICEF.

Korn, V. E. (1932). *Het adatrecht van Bali.* The Hague: Naeff, 's-Gravenhage.

Lubis, M. (1999). The Rechsstaat and human rights. In T. Lindsey (Ed.), *Indonesia: Law and Society* (pp. 171–185). Leichhardt, N.S.W.: The Federation Press.

Macdonald, R. (2013). Pluralistic human rights? Universal human wrongs? In R. Provost & C. Sheppard (Eds.), *Dialogues on Human Rights and Legal Pluralism* (pp. 15–36). Dordrecht; Heidelberg; New York; London: Springer.

Merry, S. E. (1997). Global human rights and local social movements in a legally plural world. *Canadian Journal of Law and Society, 12*, 247–272.

Merry, S. E. (2009). Relating to the subjects of human rights: The culture of agency in human rights discourse. In M. Freeman & D. Napier (Eds.), *Law and Anthropology: Current Legal Issues Volume 12* (pp. 385–407). London; Oxford: Oxford University Press.

Merry, S. E. (2014). Global legal pluralism and the temporality of soft law. *The Journal of Legal Pluralism and Unofficial Law, 46*(1), 108–122. https://doi.org/10.1080/07329113.2014.882103

Moore, S. F. (1973). Law and social change: The semi-autonomous social field as an appropriate subject of study. *Law & Society Review*, 7(4), 719–746. https://doi.org/10.2307/3052967

Nader, L. (1991). *Harmony Ideology: Justice and Control in a Zapotec Mountain Village*. Stanford, Calif: Stanford University Press.

O'Shaughnessy, K. (2009). *Gender, State and Social Power in Contemporary Indonesia: Divorce and Marriage Law*. Oxon; New York: Routledge.

Platt, M. (2017). *Marriage, Gender and Islam in Indonesia: Women Negotiating Informal Marriage, Divorce and Desire*. New York: Routledge.

Pompe, S. (1994). Between crime and custom: Extra-marital sex in modern Indonesian law. *Bijdragen Tot de Taal-, Land- En Volkenkunde, 150*(1), 110–122.

Priambodo, B. B. (2018). Positioning Adat Law in the Indonesia's legal system: Historical discourse and current development on customary law. *Udayana Journal of Law and Culture, 2*(2), 140–164. https://doi.org/10.24843/UJLC.2018.v02.i02.p02

Putra, I. N. D., & Creese, H. (2016). Negotiating cultural constraints: Strategic decision-making by widows and divorcees (janda) in contemporary Bali. *Indonesia and the Malay World, 44*(128), 104–122. https://doi.org/10.1080/13639811.2015.1100869

Ramstedt, M. (2013). Religion and disputes in Bali's new village Jurisdictions. In F. von Benda-Beckmann, M. Ramstedt, B. Turner, & K. von Benda-Beckmann (Eds.), *Religion in Disputes—Pervasiveness of Religious Normativity in Disputing Processes* (pp. 111–128). Basingstoke: Palgrave Macmillan.

Ramstedt, M. (2014a). Discordant temporalities in Bali's new village jurisdictions. *The Journal of Legal Pluralism and Unofficial Law, 46*(1), 60–78. https://doi.org/10.1080/07329113.2014.893722

Ramstedt, M. (2014b). Converging ontologies, flattening of time—Discordant temporalities and feeling rules in Bali's new village Jurisdictions. In T. Stodulka & B. Röttger-Rössler (Eds.), *Feelings at the Margins: Dealing with Violence, Stigma and Isolation in Indonesia* (pp. 53–80). Frankfurt; New York: Campus.

Reeve, D. (1987). *Golkar of Indonesia: An Alternative to the Party System*. Singapore; New York: Oxford University Press.

Santos, B. de S. (1987). Law: A map of misreading. Toward a postmodern conception of law. *Journal of Law and Society, 14*(3), 279–302. https://doi.org/10.2307/1410186

Sheppard, C. (2013). Equality through the prism of legal pluralism. In R. Provost & C. Sheppard (Eds.), *Dialogues on Human Rights and Legal Pluralism* (pp. 129–144). Dordrecht; Heidelberg; New York; London: Springer.

Tamanaha, B. Z. (2000). A non-essentialist version of legal pluralism. *Journal of Law and Society*, *27*(2), 296–321. https://doi.org/10.1111/1467-6478.00155

Tamanaha, B. Z. (2007). Understanding legal pluralism: Past to present, local to global. *Sydney Law Review*, *29*, 1–63.

Twining, W. (2010). Normative and legal pluralism: A global perspective. *Duke Journal of Comparative & International Law*, *20*, 473–518.

Ubink, J. (2011). *Customary Justice: Perspectives on Legal Empowerment* (M. Thomas, Ed.). Rome: International Development Law Organisation (IDLO); Van Vollenhoven Institute.

Van Bemmelen, S. T. (2015). *Sekilas Perkawinan Dini di Bali*. Child Marriage, Sexual Moralities, and the Politics of Decentralization in Indonesia, Jakarta.

Van Huis, S. (2015). *Islamic Courts and Women's Divorce Rights in Indonesia: The Cases of Cianjur and Bulukumba* [Doctoral Thesis]. Leiden University.

Warren, C. (1993). *Adat and Dinas: Balinese Communities in the Indonesian State*. Kuala Lumpur; New York: Oxford University Press.

Westendorp, I. (2015). Personal status law and women's right to equality in law and in Practice: The case of land rights of Balinese hindu women. *Journal of Human Rights Practice*, 7(3), 430–450. https://doi.org/10.1093/jhuman/huv013

Wikan, U. (1990). *Managing Turbulent Hearts: A Balinese Formula for Living*. Chicago: University of Chicago Press.

Chapter 5

Modernity

The previous chapter demonstrated how pre-marital sexual intercourse could be risky for boys: They can be sent to jail since judges are concerned about girls' now-tainted reputations. This is the judicial argument for resolving conflicts between families based on the official moral discourse. However, such discourse can differ from young people's moral perspectives. This chapter turns to young people's experiences and views on sex and marriage. It examines the socio-cultural conditions whereby young people in Bali are marrying today. Swasti's story indicates some of the underlying factors for so-called 'child marriage' in present-day Bali.

5.1. The story of Swasti

Swasti, aged 29, lives in a rural village in Bali and runs her own beauty salon. She proudly showed me some photos of Balinese style weddings she had arranged for her customers. She seemed reluctant to talk to us when her daughter was present, so we arranged to conduct our interview when she was alone. She was afraid that her 13-year-old daughter might "*do the same (takut dia ikut)*" (i.e., "*marrying young (kawin muda)*") if she hears the story of her mother's teenage marriage. Swasti does not want her daughter to marry young since she wants her to continue her education.

Swasti became pregnant when she was 15 years old and had a customary (*adat*) marriage before giving birth at the age of 16. She had then been courting (*pacaran*) her boyfriend for over a year, who was six years older than her. When her boyfriend asked to have sex as *"proof of love"*, she agreed, although she admitted she was scared. She found out that she was pregnant when she was three months along. *"Maybe I was too free at that time (Mungkin terlalu bebas saat itu)"*, she said. Her parents were busy working away from home, so she was free ("*makanya bebas*"). She repeated the word '*bebas*'.

When she told her boyfriend that she was pregnant, he first denied that it was his child and refused to marry her. After a week, he eventually agreed to get married since he was *"ashamed" (malu)* because their relationship was known in their small village. The news about her pregnancy upset her parents.

DOI: 10.4324/9781003184546-5

Her mother told her to have an abortion, as they were still too young. She wanted her to continue studying, and that was not possible while pregnant. However, Swasti decided not to have an abortion because she was *"scared"*.

Although she does not regret having a child, she regrets marrying her husband. *"If I could go back to the time when I became pregnant, I would choose to be a single mother"*. However, at that time, it was not an option. People in the village did not accept single mothers. If she gave birth without getting married, her and her family would have been ostracized from the local community (*banjar*).[1]

5.2. The danger of the 'rights discourse'

Swasti's story is one case of a so-called 'child marriage'. International development organizations tend to frame child marriage as a human rights violation and an obstacle to global development, perpetuating poverty, inequality, and insecurity (Girls Not Brides n.d.b). These organizations seem to be oblivious to the diversity of child marriage practices (Horii and Grijns 2019).

This generalizing definition of child marriage risks encouraging a "rights discourse" (Grugel 2013: 20), which focuses on individuals who have been deprived of their "rights". Grugel argues that the rights discourse risks detracting attention from underlying structures that shape inequalities and their reproduction (Ibid). I have argued that aiming to 'end child marriage' altogether is not an effective approach (Horii 2018; see also Chapter 3), because of the diverse types of and motivations for child marriage (Horii and Grijns 2019; see also Chapter 3). Boyden et al. (2012: 520) also pointed out the risk of the abolitionist approach, which could neglect the most critical social and economic problems. What then are the motivating factors for child marriage to which we need to redirect our attention? I rely on empirical data to answer this question, demonstrating real-life cases of child marriage in Bali.

5.3. Modernity and tradition

To analyze the structural reasons why children are marrying, I use the concept of modernity. On the one hand, modernity's ideals are the basis of the current international advocacy to end (all) child marriage (i.e., marriage below the age of 18), as demonstrated in Chapter 2. Human rights advocates consider child marriage as a problem, a 'harmful traditional practice', and tend to view those who practice it as 'traditional', i.e., insufficiently modern. In this chapter, I challenge this viewpoint by discussing data that shows that these young people use under-age marriage to navigate the modern world in which they live.

As a concept, modernity requires careful distinction. Modernity in Bali has been discussed extensively. Vicker's (1996) presentation of modernity as

1 Interview, July 2017.

a continuous condition in Bali and his use of plural "modernities" show the varied meanings of the word. Modernity created "tradition" as a by-product, sometimes as institutions and attitudes which were left behind by those who were engaged in "progress", and sometimes as collective values that were perceived as "lost" (Schulte Nordholt 2000: 102). In the Indonesian context, 'modernity' and 'globalization' are often used in popular discourse to denounce any foreign influences. Words such as '*terbuka*' (open) and '*bebas*' (free) are both often used to describe young people's lives in Bali. When they are used in association with the perceived image of a Western liberal lifestyle, primarily liberal sexual morality (in their words, *"promiscuity"*[2]), they carry a negative connotation. Swasti said, *"I was too free"* in a regretful tone, referring to her pre-marital sexual intercourse, a moral transgression.

This is the kind of discourse about 'modernity' that is often used in contrast to 'tradition'. Distinguishing from modernity as a discourse, here I use modernity as a changing social condition, borrowing Giddens' idea that the modern world is where social life is "open" with multiple lifestyle choices (Giddens 1991: 6). Consider the educational opportunities that are increasingly available to young generations in Bali. *"Children are already open (terbuka). They want to continue with school, and they want to continue until university"*, a lawyer working for social programmes told me.[3] The wide variety of life-choices now open to these individuals emancipates them but can also threaten traditional communities and creates a normative gap between generations. Parents and children today have different perspectives on the world, lifestyles, courtship, and marriage. The "relational self", which is shaped by ties to traditional kin and community (Merry 2009: 404), becomes conflicted with one's desire for the 'new world'.

In this chapter, I use two additional concepts that are relevant to changing social conditions ('modernity'). One is the idea of a reference network, which I use to unpack the 'openness' of modern society. The other is the idea of relational autonomy, which I use to explain the youth's decision-making process (see also Section 1.5.3). In the following sections, I will further discuss all three concepts, use them to interpret data, and explain how they are related and support this chapter's main argument.

5.4. Adolescents' communities and child marriage cases in Bali

This chapter's analysis builds on interviews and Focus Group Discussions I conducted during my fieldwork. I interviewed two groups of Balinese Hindu adolescents whose class and lifestyles differed significantly. I called one of

2 Interview with a girl from a local community in Denpasar, August 2017.

3 Interview, June 2017, Denpasar.

the groups the 'Pasar Community', as most of them work in the *pasar* (traditional market) as carriers. They were all from a specific remote rural area in East Bali. They live with limited life resources (housing, food, educational and work opportunities), and most have never had any formal schooling experience. The second adolescents' group is called the 'Teruna Teruni Group'. This is one of the *adat* (customary) communities for youth '*teruna teruni*' in Denpasar. In this group, adolescents gather for community *adat* ceremonies or perform Balinese dancing for hamlet ceremonies. They are from upper-middle-class families, tend to be followers of Balinese customs, and are knowledgeable about local practices. To understand the link between child marriage and adolescents' sexuality in Bali, I also interviewed legal practitioners, CSO staff members, government officials, health care personnel, and teachers.

Among the 20 child marriage cases that I refer to in this chapter, the 11 cases first involved teenage pregnancy and then child marriage. Five cases involved child marriage without pregnancy, while four cases involved teenage pregnancy without marriage. I specifically use these cases to examine the causality between teenage pregnancy and child marriage and to illustrate how adolescents decide to marry in pluralized normative systems. To study these cases, I interviewed the young women and men involved and their parents and family members. I interviewed most of these people in Denpasar, the capital city of Bali, though some of the informants were only working there and were originally from other areas of Bali.

5.5. Sexual morality for adolescents in today's Indonesia

5.5.1. Child marriage and sexual morality

From the 16 cases of child marriage that I studied during my fieldwork in Bali, at least 11 were caused directly by an unplanned teenage pregnancy, including Swasti's. Two of the other cases were caused by a fear of pregnancy, as this case illustrates:

> Krisna and Sri had been in a relationship for two years. They lived together in an apartment in Denpasar for three months when they decided to marry. Krisna was fifteen and Sri was seventeen when they married through the *adat* ceremony. Their cohabitation was unsettling to Sri's family, who worried she might become pregnant. To ensure that Krisna would be responsible for the consequences of a possible pregnancy, Sri's family insisted that they marry. Sri also said, *"My family wanted me to marry to avoid shame (malu) in the village as the neighbours and relatives already knew about our relationship"*. Krisna's father initially disagreed with the marriage, arguing that Krisna was still too young. However, Sri's family insisted.

A (fear of) pregnancy outside of marriage significantly motivates child marriages in both Bali and other areas of Indonesia, including West Java (see Chapter 3). The stigma of *zinah* is not limited to the girl involved but extends to her family, especially her parents, who are considered to have failed in raising their daughter properly (Utomo and McDonald 2009). A 2015 study by Rumah Kita Bersama also showed that in 36 out of the 52 studied cases of child marriage, the marriage was motivated by a pregnancy (Marcoes and Putri 2016).

The link between child marriages and adolescent sexual behaviour becomes clearer when explained in the broader context of modernity. Factors such as increased educational opportunities and mobility and an expansion of choices and social networks for youngsters distinguish today's young generation from their elders' generation. In Indonesia, like many other countries of the Global South, the young generation today is better educated than the previous generation (Naafs and White 2012: 10). They also have wider physical and digital mobility, and this extends to all social classes and genders (Ibid: 12). These expansions mean increasing freedoms in dating patterns. ECPAT International, a CSO network, released a report mentioning a growing number of children's "love marriages" as a result of increasing educational opportunity and mobility (Chaudhuri 2015).

Statistics show the recent marriage patterns of young people: The rise of female (mid- to late-) teenage marriage in urban areas. First, Jones's research analyzed the difference in 2005 marriage patterns between a 20–24 and 50–54-year-old female cohort (Jones and Gubhaju 2008). The younger cohort had almost half the number of teenage marriages, but more marriages in their late teenage years (i.e., 18 and 19) (Ibid). UNICEF Indonesia (2016) also finds that marriages increased among girls aged 16–17 between 2008 and 2012. Second, the 2013 National Household Survey shows a slight increase in child marriage rates in Indonesia between 2010 and 2012, associated with an increase in urban child marriage rates since 2008 (Badan Pusat Statistik (BPS) 2016). Between 2008 and 2012, the child marriage rate steadily decreased in rural areas (33.5% to 29.2%) while increasing in urban areas (18.8% to 19.0%) (Ibid). A comparison of 2008 and 2012 census data revealed child marriage rate increases in nine provinces, including DKI Jakarta (12.8% to 14.9%) and Bali (15.9% to 16.5%) (Ibid).

One of the possible explanations for the puzzling rise in urban female teenage marriages is the changing lifestyle and consequent anxiety about moral decay. A judge at the religious court in West Java stated, *"Child marriage is increasing because of globalization"*. Harding (2008) helps us to understand this remark: Indonesian youth now interact more with the outside world and 'Western' cultures, which are regarded as a threat to traditional Indonesian cultural and religious values. In relation to this, the social anxiety associated with adolescents' sexual behaviour pressures girls to marry early. Some data support the changes underlying the anxiety: Utomo (2001) demonstrated a recent rise in pre-marital sexual intercourse, particularly in large cities in Indonesia.

Human rights advocates demanding a rise in the legal marriageable age adds to the tension between the conservative and progressive groups. This tension is observed in the divided opinions about the proper marriageable age, expressed during the 2014 hearings at the Constitutional Court judicial review (see Chapter 3). Moderate Islam and non-Muslim experts supported the proposal due to the negative consequences of child marriage on girls. However, representatives from major Islamic organizations in Indonesia argued that maintaining the current marriageable age is a solution to prevent 'free sex', a word commonly used in Indonesia to criticize any sexual relationship outside of (and particularly before) marriage. According to Marcoes (2018), child marriage has become part of the political identity of Islamic fundamentalists in Indonesia. This controversy around the issue indicates that, for conservative religious groups, early marriage is a way to control youths' sexual behaviour without directly engaging with the discussions on teenage sexuality and safe sex.

5.5.2. An accepted taboo: Sex before marriage in Bali

In Muslim-majority rural West Java, pre-marital sexual intercourse is a sin and taboo. By contrast, pre-marital sex is somewhat more socially accepted in Muslim-minority Bali, generally described as the 'permissiveness' of sexual behaviours among young people (Van Bemmelen 2006; Lewis and Lewis 2009). It is also not uncommon for a prospective groom and his family to try to determine whether the prospective bride is "*berisi*" (fertile), because it is important that she can give birth to a son as the successor to the father's lineage (Van Bemmelen 2015). Singarimbun's research (1991) comparing adolescents' sexual behaviour in urban/rural Yogyakarta and urban/rural Bali concluded that Bali respondents had engaged in more sexual experiences than those in Yogyakarta. Utomo (1997) also found that adolescents who live in Muslim-minority provinces in Indonesia show more permissive attitudes concerning sexual relationships than those living elsewhere. Notably, the 'permissiveness' discussed in the 1990s and 2000s was referring to sexual *behaviour*, not sexual *norms*, although the two are interlinked.

The ambiguous relation between sexual norms and behaviour is demonstrated in Jennaway's (2002) ethnographic fieldwork in a rural village of North Bali in 1992. It showed general societal disapproval of young girls' promiscuity: When a girl lost her virginity without a guarantee of marriage, it implied 'moral laxity' (Ibid: 163). The girls involved in the study spoke of being torn between upholding norms of chastity and their romantic and sexual desires (Jennaway 2001: 93). Jennaway (2002: 144) also suggested the generalized image of love had a creeping influence, shared via mass media outlets such as village televisions. Bellow's study also documented anxieties among the Balinese about the influences of Western modes of dating and marriage for love, introduced through tourism, social interaction, and television or imported pornographic videos (Bellows 2003: 8, 16).

Today, when I asked adults in Bali across classes and from various positions, *"Is it okay to have sex before marriage?"* they avoided answering 'yes' or 'no'. Instead, they said, *"It's already common"*. This answer seemingly indicates that adults generally still consider pre-marital sexual intercourse as a taboo that is prohibited by their religious/customary norms. Therefore, they do not explicitly say 'Yes, pre-marital sex is okay', but acknowledge that it is happening. In the following paragraphs, I will demonstrate the normative gap regarding pre-marital sexual intercourse that exists between today's young people and the older generation.

In an interview with the head of PHDI (*Parisada Hindu Dharma Indonesia*), he explained that the concept of *zinah* exists in Balinese *adat* as '*mitra ngalang*'. The idea prohibits sexual intercourse without an *adat* marriage.[4] The court decisions analyzed in Section 4.4.4 regarding marriage dispensations show that pre-marital sexual intercourse is officially condemned. A marriage registrar at the Civil Marriage Registration Office (KCS) explained that young people's marriage is mostly due to "Marriage By Accident" (marriage because of pregnancy), stating: *"We always tell them that it is not correct. We tell them, if you want to have sex, please wait until marriage"*.[5] This is the official discourse on pre-marital sexual intercourse.

According to Gajah Mada University researchers (Arida et al. 2005), *adat* leaders or old generations still maintain these official *adat* norms. However, adolescents' behaviour and their perspectives on pre-marital sexual intercourse differ from the old *adat* norms. In one of my FGDs, participants from both the Pasar Community and Teruna Teruni Group expressed their opinion about pre-marital sexual intercourse as being an "*aib*" (disgrace) and a "*dosa*" (sin). They said, *"it is salah (wrong) according to Hindu"*. However, a participant later told me individually, *"That's what our parents say. We are the generation of millennials, globalization, and such. For us, it is ok to have sex (sex boleh aja). We know about those things"*.[6] This shows the normative gap between parents and children. What this girl said around peers and in private also emphasizes the moral ambivalence that exists surrounding pre-marital sex.

5.5.3. *Kehamilan Tak Diinginkan ('unwanted' pregnancy)*

Kehamilan Tak Diinginkan ('unwanted' pregnancy), known as KTD, is often discussed as a problem in Bali. Since pre-marital sex is not permitted in principle, in-school sex education is very poor, and any communication about the topic is difficult. In most cases, teenagers acquire knowledge about contraception

4 Interview, June 2017, Denpasar.

5 Interview with a marriage registrar at the Denpasar Civil Marriage Registration Office, March 20, 2017.

6 Interview, August 2017.

only through the Internet or social media (including pornographic videos), where the shared information is often incorrect. Many of the teenage informants told me their incorrect understandings about 'safe sex'. They sometimes do not know that sex can cause a pregnancy, and often believe that pregnancies do not happen if sexual intercourse occurs only once, or if they take a shower after intercourse. Teenagers often express their difficulties in purchasing contraception. They feel *'embarrassed' (malu)* buying condoms, although they are available in shops. The practice itself is not strictly stigmatized ('permissiveness'), and so teenagers engage in sexual relationships without the proper tools and knowledge. This explains the frequency of 'unwanted' teenage pregnancies.

In Bali, it has been a popular discourse to blame *"modernization"* or *"globalization"* for teenage pregnancies, associated with the widespread use of mobile phones and pornographic content. A government official told me *"Teenage pregnancy in Bali has been increasing because of technology that entered into Bali and pornography"*.[7] A medical doctor said to me, *"The Internet makes children want to try or practice what they see on it, such as YouTube or social media"*.[8] Others blame *"parents' lack of control over their children's behaviour"* for the increase in teenage pregnancy.[9] *"Normally, parents have to monitor children's behaviour, but nowadays, parents are too busy. They do not have a good relationship and communication with their child"*, said a judge.[10] In an interview, a CSO head expressed how globalization affects youngsters' ideas of sexuality: *"Because of the globalization, Balinese people 'maju' – became progressive. They became more 'bebas' – free, and they use gadgets (holding her smartphone)"*.[11]

People blame the above factors for both teenage pregnancies and child marriage. *"Gadgets (mobile phone) are a cause of underage marriage. Both in urban and rural areas, most of the children use mobile phones from elementary school (SD). This makes it easier to interact with their boyfriend/girlfriend. Family cannot control the children"*. These were the causes of child marriage according to a CSO's legal assistant.[12] Many other interviewees also identified mobile phones as a cause of child marriage, referring to the accessibility of videos that make children *"curious"*. In a CSO's workshop about reproductive health, when teachers were asked what causes unwanted pregnancies among teenagers, they named three factors: (1) Technology and pornography, (2) non-educative media, and (3) broken homes and lack of parental control. For them, there is no distinction between the causes of child marriage and teenage pregnancy since 'safe sex' does not officially exist and pregnancy almost always leads to marriage.

7 Interview, April 2017.
8 Interview, April 2017.
9 Interview, April 2017. Interview, March 2017. Interview, June 2017.
10 Interview, June 2017.
11 Interview, May 2017.
12 Interview, June 2017.

National policies and regulations significantly explain why safe sex is not a common practice. First, contraceptive tools are only officially available to married people. BKKBN is in charge of distributing contraceptives. However, it distributes its supplies exclusively to married people. *Perkumpulan Keluarga Berencana Indonesia* (PKBI), a CSO for family planning in Indonesia, is slightly more liberal with its distribution of contraception and with abortion practices. Still, it must handle these sensitive issues very carefully. Second, according to Article 75 of Law No.36 of 2009, abortion is illegal except, e.g., when rape has occurred or where pregnancy could cause health problems to the mother or the baby. Even legal abortions that meet these conditions carry negative connotations, so PKBI call them "*medical abortions*" or "*menstrual regulations*".[13] The director said, "*We call this abortion a 'menstrual regulation' or to make menstruation flow. This term is chosen to make abortion not too vulgar because in the society the term 'abortion' has a very negative connotation*".[14] The general inaccessibility of abortions obviously affects the rate of teenage pregnancies. Young pregnant girls perceive they must choose between having the baby and protecting themselves from 'shame' by marrying young or having an illegal abortion.

PKBI has to refuse most teenage requests for abortions since they do not meet the conditions established in Article 75. The high refusal rate of PKBI is dangerous since young girls or women might then look elsewhere for an abortion. Unofficial forms of abortion are available, such as a medicine (*cytotec*) available at *jamu* (traditional medicine) sellers or private medical practitioners. According to the head of PKBI, many midwives and doctors practice abortion illegally.

In four out of 15 cases of extra-marital pregnancies I studied, the girls had an abortion or miscarriage. One of the informants told me that she intentionally had an abortion by taking medicine. For the rest, it remained unclear whether they intended to have an abortion. The informants told me that they had a 'miscarriage', but they did not prevent it, and some even promoted it to occur. One kept working as a carrier, carrying heavy bags every day. Another kept eating young pineapples, a method the couple found when they searched online for 'how to have a miscarriage'. The other 11 cases of pregnancy led to marriage. When I asked the couples if they considered having an abortion, one of them told me that she and her boyfriend married because they had failed to have an abortion with the unofficial medicine. Many others replied that they did not consider this because they were *'ashamed' (malu)* or *'afraid' (takut) 'of the risks'* or *'of karma'*. These remarks show that abortion is not a safe or legal option for adolescents in Bali.

While dating and pre-marital sexual intercourse are somewhat accepted in Bali, strong stigmas and severe consequences are attached to birth outside of

13 Interview with staff at PKBI, May 2017, Denpasar.

14 Ibid.

wedlock. Krisna discussed his school friends who married because of pregnancy and said, "*If you get pregnant, the only way is to get married (jalan satu-satu nya kawin)*".[15] In the Balinese patrilineal kinship system, babies are supposed to belong to the father's lineage, and the only way to identify the father is through marriage, according to the Balinese *adat* system. When an unmarried woman gives birth, *adat* sanctions are imposed on the family involved, as Chapter 4 explained.

Thus, when teenagers become pregnant, their options are limited. They can have a legal abortion if they fulfil the requirements or attempt an illegal abortion. They can give birth without marrying and face the consequences or marry young. It is understandable why many choose to marry, considering the difficulties associated with having an abortion or giving birth outside of marriage. When I discussed these options at the workshop I organized with LBH Apik Bali (a legal aid association), all of the participants agreed that the best possible reaction to a teenage pregnancy was marriage. A participant from Wanita Hindu Dharma Indonesia (WHDI, the female division of PHDI) also suggested making divorces easier for women under Balinese *adat* law (see Section 4.6). This would add another dimension to the options available to pregnant teenagers, an option to end a marriage if it does not work out. However, in Bali, divorce is extremely difficult and has been disadvantageous for women (Jennaway 2002: 87–88). Swasti, having divorced her husband, legally does not have custody over her children or the right to their shared property (e.g., their house). Additionally, divorce carries such a negative stigma that Swasti still wears a ring on her finger to pretend that she is married. *"I just bought it myself. (Pause) Well … if I wear this, people think I am married"*.[16]

5.6. Current pluralized normative systems for adolescents

5.6.1. Opportunities and restrictions in modern social conditions

Modernity in Bali affects adolescents' lives in various ways. Both boys and girls are now seeking higher educational opportunities and engaging in career planning. These adolescents find it increasingly difficult to spend time and money participating in communal village rituals. They are being pulled between traditional temporality and the tempo of modern life (Ramstedt 2014: 74). Adolescents also have more mobility, with both girls and boys having more opportunities and locations to meet and mingle with the opposite gender. An increased prevalence of mobile phone usage gives youngsters access to people

15 Interview, May 2017.
16 Interview, July 2017.

outside of their communities and provides chances to text their love interests. As Naafs and White (2012: 16) highlighted, young people who have access to cell phones and the Internet can connect themselves to a wider world. Since this new lifestyle is often incomprehensible to parents, it regularly becomes subject to moral panic and is criticized by the older generation for embodying excessive materialism, individualism, and a loss of important cultural and religious values (Ibid: 13–14).

Such emancipation and increasing individual autonomy are at modernity's core, which implies individual detachment from the traditional identity, which is externally shaped by custom, religion, and family. Giddens (1991: 6) describes this as the "openness" of social life in modernity, which consequently forces individuals to navigate a diversity of options and contexts of actions. Interestingly, such changes are also dangerous, in that feelings associated with sexual and marital life become more mobile, unsettled, and open (Ibid: 13). In a modernizing world where the power of the traditional structures is arguably undermined, individuals have to guide themselves across fragile ground.

To unpack this phenomenon, I use the socio-psychological concept of 'reference network'. A reference network is defined as a set of individuals whose actions and opinions we care about when we make our choices (Bicchieri 2016: xiii). We constantly observe what others do, and from these observations, we get clues about appropriate behaviour, other's preferences, beliefs, and so forth. Accordingly, individuals prefer to conform to the socials norms of their reference network. They prefer this on the condition that (1) they believe that most people in their reference network conform to it (empirical expectation) or (2) that most people in their reference network believe they ought to conform to it (normative expectation) (Bicchieri 2016: 41–51). What Giddens (1991: 6) calls the "diversity of authorities" can be explained as the multiplication of an individual's reference networks.

Utomo and McDonald (2009) have described the conflicting moral values among young Indonesians. Liberal values are promoted through Westernized education, media marketing propaganda, and peer pressure. Meanwhile, traditional Indonesian Islamic teachings are promoted through religious schools and groups, families, and the state. Although Bali has a majority Hindu population, they also have a similar structure of conflicting values. Novi, a girl from the Pasar Community, said at the FGD that *"I have three boyfriends!"* but when we asked about what she does with her boyfriends, she said, *"it's private, it's not your business!"* She stated that *"sex before marriage is sin"*, but was eager to know the functions of condoms when we explained them to her while remarking, *"but we are ashamed to buy condoms, they are only for adults"*. These conflicting remarks and behaviours reflect the different reference networks with which she lived. Novi wanted to look 'cool' in front of her peers. However, she also disliked appearing immoral or promiscuous in front of older people, such as those interviewing her. In other words, these young people have several reference networks, which sometimes have conflicting social norms.

The multiplication of an individual's reference networks is consistent with Gidden's theory of modernity. However, this also shows that there is a certain illusion in the modern idea of freedom and openness. Children or adolescents specifically are not as 'free' and 'open' as they might think because they are always constrained by different normative frameworks. A remark by one of the girls from Teruna Teruni Community clearly illustrates what it is like to live in this gap: *"This friend of mine who got pregnant used to go home early morning, drunk, and in open clothes. Even more open than people in the West. [...] In the West they can be open about relationships between boys and girls, but here rumour can spread and taint a good name of the family"*.[17] Bellow (2003: 8–9, 442) has also pointed out the continuous implication for Balinese cosmologies in sexual norms (i.e., sex is intended for procreation rather than pleasure), albeit on the surface, sexual practices appear to have gone "global".

5.6.2. The exercise of agency in pluralized normative system

How then do adolescents make choices in co-existing and often conflicting reference networks? Gidden's notion of agency considers persons as reflexive beings and agency as a capacity to observe one's experience and give reasons for one's actions (Tucker 1999: 80). Individuals can then both resist 'structures' (i.e., rules and patterns of social relationships) and consciously follow the rules of different reference networks. This is consistent with Mahmood's (2004: 15) concept of "agentival capacity" that is entailed not only in acts that resist norms but also in the multiple ways one inhabits norms. Some adolescents are in between modern and customary ideas of sexual morality and marriage. Such adolescents' marital decisions should be considered in light of "relational autonomy" and how much their autonomy is limited by corrosive disadvantage (e.g., social, political, economic, and educational) or coercive, abusive, or violent social relationships (Mackenzie 2013: 43).

In the pluralized normative system in which modern youth in Bali live, their decision to marry is not only about their autonomy, choice, and bodily integrity but also about a sense of community, religious faith, and family. Swasti's case is one of the many cases I studied that demonstrates the customary and communitarian normative system that affects autonomous decisions. Particularly in rural areas where the community is so central and strict in their rule enforcement, pregnant teenagers are left with no choice but to marry (at least from Swasti's perspective). In Evi's case, when she became pregnant at the age of 17, her mother expressed her concern:

> *I am afraid if we don't accept the apology and marriage proposal from the family of the boy (Evi's boyfriend), Evi's baby will have problems in the future. As an*

17 Interview, August 2017.

> *adult he must have his ancestral temple and at any kinds of life events (e.g., when he wants to marry) he must ask permission from his father's family. And the baby cannot enter our family's temple according to religion and adat.*

The examples of Evi and Swasti indicate the significance of the 'relational self'. Belonging to their community is crucial for them. Within this framework of their life, marriage was the only 'solution' to the more urgent problem of an extra-marital pregnancy.

Despite the fear and social pressure, Krisna and Sri's case also illustrates the exercise of relational autonomy. Although it was Sri's parents who initiated and insisted on the marriage plan, Krisna said that they were '*very keen to get married*', as they did not want to be separated. The thin line between their motivations (to marry) and the underlying social factors (e.g., customary rules, shame, peer norms, and parental pressure) accurately shows the conflicting normative systems that adolescents deal with when making both daily and momentous decisions.

Wikan (1990: xvii, 137, 139) suggests a seemingly peculiar aspect of Balinese decision-making: From a Balinese point of view, there is no difference between feeling and thought, and "*keneh*" ("feeling-thoughts") is the person's choice and responsibility. Therefore, "*Ngabe keneh*" ("bringing the feeling-thought") and "managing the hearts" is at the root of a Balinese design for living (Ibid: xvii, 95). Today in Bali, adolescents manage 'their heart' (the feeling-thoughts in their romantic and sexual relationship) by balancing the demands of the modern era within the customary and communitarian normative system.

Swasti wants her daughter to marry after 20: '*She should finish school and work first*'. When I asked her if she had spoken with her daughter about how to prevent unwanted pregnancies, she said, *'I talk about sex and such a little bit, but not much, because I do not want to confuse her. It's hard to communicate about it'*. While Swasti's parents forbid her from dating a boy and engaging in sexual activity before marriage, she allows her daughter to have *pacaran*, but *'with limits' ('dengan batas')*. Swasti herself 'managed her heart' by secretly dating a man with whom she was in love. She agreed to have sexual intercourse with him before marriage and married him when she became pregnant. So how will her daughter manage her heart 'with limits' when she is in love?

5.7. Paradox of modernity

I now have elaborated on the three concepts that are central to this chapter's arguments. So how do these three concepts (modernity, reference networks, and relational autonomy) relate to one another, and what do they tell us about the socio-cultural conditions in which Balinese adolescents marry? The framework of reference networks illuminates the multiple normative frameworks and social connections in which Balinese youth live. In the modern social conditions with increased mobility and education, individual choices have diversified and expanded, and so norms have pluralized. Krisna and Sri, for instance, moved to the city from North Bali. Their marriage was a compromise between their living situation and the rural village's customary rules and sentiments. Consequently, modern Balinese youth's reference networks are rather fragile and erodible since their generation is in an ambiguous relationship with their elders' generation. Navigating their modern world thus means trying to make the best of their lives within their context of family and community relations. This process of decision-making in multiplied normative frameworks is the essence of relational autonomy, the way such autonomy can be maximized.

By this logic, what international institutions call 'child marriage' is a way that teenagers can manage their romantic and sexual relationships within the pluralized normative framework. It is a way to fill the normative gap between generations. International actors advocate eliminating child marriage, aiming to achieve modernity's ideals of emancipation and self-determination. However, child marriage is actually a response or solution to modern social conditions. This paradox of modernity and child marriage can be explained in two ways. First, child marriage is a way for youngsters to manage their romantic relationships within the modern structure. Second, child marriage becomes a 'problem' through the demands of modern times (see Chapter 2). Let me emphasize this point by quoting a local activist:

> *You know, I was thinking about the early marriage problem. I said earlier that you need to be 30 to be ready to marry. But actually, if girls get menstruation at age 12 or 13, it means the God created us to be reproductively ready at that age. There is nothing wrong with having a child or marrying at that age. People used to marry immediately after starting menstruation. When I said people should be 30 to marry, it is because of the modern system. In the modern system, before 30 women have lots of learning opportunities. So, it is because of the changing world.*[18]

So, in a sense, child marriage is simultaneously a problem *created* by modernity and a *solution* to modernity's problems in a "changing world".

5.8. Conclusion: Child marriage as a 'solution'

Love or romance is a notion that has been developed throughout history and "it is an ethnocentric error to expect Balinese ideals of love and sexuality to conform with Western constructions of romantic love" (Jennaway 2002: 143). The cases I presented in this chapter have shown that for modern youth in Bali, 'child marriage' is a way to manage their romantic and sexual relationships within the customary normative system. In the modern era, increased educational opportunities provide them with more possibilities and spaces to mingle

18 Interview, June 2017.

with the other gender. Mobile phones give them access to people outside their community and provide chances to communicate with their love interests via text. Such emancipation is at modernity's core, resulting in an individual's detachment from traditional identity, which is shaped by custom, religion, and family. Individuals' normative systems become pluralized, and feelings associated with romantic life become more open and unsettled.

For adolescents who are in between different ideas of sexuality and marriage, the decision to marry should be understood in light of relational autonomy. International advocacy surrounding child marriage is based on modernity's ideals of libertarian agency and the normative principle that we all (especially women) should be able to decide how to live our lives instead of submitting to the traditional order. Relational autonomy suggests that such a conceptualization of agency is an illusion, as our 'selves' are all embedded in social interactions and relationships.

This understanding of autonomy or agency is useful towards overcoming the well-known challenge of development: Not to dismiss the agency of women in the Third World (Mohanty 1984). Alongside respecting non-Western women's agency, there is also an increasing need to respect children's agency (Bourdillon 2004). The common protectionist approach of 'saving' children is increasingly considered unproductive, as it deprives those under 18 of agency and choice (Grugel 2013: 23; Hart 2006). In this sense, the agency of girls in the Third World is the most precarious in international development discourse. Recognizing the relational aspects of agency is a way to 'open up space for the agency of non-western peoples' in development discourse (McEwan 2001: 95) and to challenge the paternalistic notions of development that rely on 'assumptions of superiority, linear progress and Western women's freedom' (MacDonald 2016: 6).

In the case of child marriage, by acknowledging that some children can exercise their agency to marry, the hidden core problem comes to the surface. Although the frequency of KTD ('unwanted' pregnancies) is a problem in Bali, the problem is not sexual relationships before marriage itself. In a society where teenage pre-marital sexual activity is allowed and accepted, they can safely participate in these activities by being well informed about sex and contraception, resulting in lower rates of unwanted pregnancies. However, this is not the case in Bali, and in Indonesia more broadly. Teenage pregnancy is caused by a gap between reality and morality. Child marriage is not per se a problem. On the contrary, it is the present solution to a core developmental problem: Lack of access to reproductive health tools.

In fact, in Indonesia, it currently seems that early marriage is a way to control youth sexual behaviour without directly discussing it and safe sex. Thus, policies and programmes for reducing child marriage will be more effective if they address this core problem directly. Swasti wants to prevent her 13-year-old daughter from following the same path as her but feels it is too early to teach her about pregnancy. The head of PKBI stated: *"Parents become anxious when children want to go out and do their own stuff. It is like children riding motorbikes. It is parents who are afraid, not the children themselves. Children are 'setengat sadar', not completely aware of their behaviour"*. If a child wants to ride a motorbike, one can teach them how to ride it safely instead of forbidding it out of fear of injuries. If it is 'too early' to teach them, when will the time come?

Bibliography

Arida, I. N. S., Widiana, I. G. P. G., Wulanyani, N. M. S., Wijaya, N. K. A., & Meydianawati, L. G. (2005). *Seks Dan Kehamilan Pranikah: Remaja Bali di Dua Dunia* (P. M. Kutanegara & B. D. Putranti, Eds.). Yogyakarta, Indonesia: Universitas Gadjah Mada.

Badan Pusat Statistik (BPS). (2016). *Kemajuan yang Tertunda: Analisis Data Perkawinan Usia Anak di Indonesia*. Jakarta, Indonesia: BPS.

Bellows, L. J. (2003). *Traditional Sex/Modern Meaning: Desire and Foreign Influence in Bali* [Doctoral Thesis]. University of Virginia.

Bicchieri, C. (2016). *Norms in the Wild: How to Diagnose, Measure, and Change Social Norms*. New York, NY: Oxford University Press.

Bourdillon, M. F. C. (2004). Children in development. *Progress in Development Studies, 4*(2), 99–113. https://doi.org/10.1191/1464993404ps079oa

Boyden, J., Pankhurst, A., & Tafere, Y. (2012). Child protection and harmful traditional practices: Female early marriage and genital modification in Ethiopia. *Development in Practice, 22*(4), 510–522. https://doi.org/10.1080/09614524.2012.672957

Chaudhuri, E. R. (2015). *Thematic Report: Unrecognised Sexual Abuse and Exploitation of Children in Child, Early and Forced Marriage*. Bangkok, Thailand: ECPAT International.

Giddens, A. (1991). *Modernity and Self-Identity: Self and Society in the Late Modern Age*. Stanford, CA: Stanford University Press.

Girls Not Brides. (n.d.). *About Child Marriage*. Girls Not Brides. https://www.girlsnotbrides.org/about-child-marriage/ (accessed on April 20, 2021).

Grugel, J. (2013). Children's rights and children's welfare after the Convention on the rights of the child. *Progress in Development Studies, 13*(1), 19–30. https://doi.org/10.1177/146499341201300102

Harding, C. (2008). The influence of the "decadent west": discourses of the mass media on youth sexuality in Indonesia. *Intersections: Gender and Sexuality in Asia and the Pacific, 18*, 4-41.

Hart, J. (2006). Saving children: What role for anthropology? *Anthropology Today, 22*(1), 5–8. https://doi.org/10.1111/j.1467-8322.2006.00410.x

Horii, H. (2018). Child marriage, not all alike. *Inside Indonesia*, 134. https://www.insideindonesia.org/child-marriage-not-all-alike

Horii, H., & Grijns, M. (2019). Introduction. In M. Grijns, H. Horii, S. Irianto, & P. Saptandari (Eds.), *Marrying Young in Indonesia: Voices, Laws and Practices* (pp. 1–36). Jakarta, Indonesia: Yayasan Pustaka Obor Indonesia.

Jennaway, M. (2001). Inflatable bodies and the breath of life: Courtship and desire among young women in rural Bali. In L. Manderson & P. Liamputtong (Eds.), *Coming of Age in South and Southeast Asia: Youth, Courtship and Sexuality* (pp. 75–95). Richmond, Surrey: Routledge.

Jennaway, M. (2002). *Sisters and Lovers: Women and Desire in Bali*. Lanham: Rowman & Littlefield Publishers.

Jones, G., & Gubhaju, B. (2008). Trends in age at marriage in the Provinces of Indonesia. *Asia Research Working Paper*, 105.

Lewis, J., & Lewis, B. (2009). *Bali's Silent Crisis: Desire, Tragedy, and Transition*. Lanham, MD: Lexington Books.

MacDonald, K. (2016). Calls for educating girls in the third world: Futurity, girls and the 'Third World Woman'. *Gender, Place & Culture, 23*(1), 1–17. https://doi.org/10.1080/0966369X.2014.991699

Mackenzie, C. (2013). The importance of relational autonomy and capabilities for an ethics of vulnerability. In C. Mackenzie, W. Rogers, & S. Dodds (Eds.), *Vulnerability: New Essays in Ethics and Feminist Philosophy* (pp. 33–59). New York, NY: Oxford University Press.

Mahmood, S. (2004). *Politics of Piety: The Islamic Revival and the Feminist Subject*. Princeton, NJ: Princeton University Press.

Marcoes, L. (2018, November 16). A religious/cultural approach in prevention of child marriage: case study of the experiences of Rumah Kita Bersama and KUPI. In *Criminalizing and Emancipatory Trends in Family Law in Indonesia and Other Muslim Majority Countries*. Leiden, The Netherlands.

Marcoes, L., & Putri, F. D. (2016). *Kesaksian pengantin bocah*. Rumah KitaB.

McEwan, C. (2001). Postcolonialism, feminism and development: Intersections and dilemmas. *Progress in Development Studies, 1*(2), 93–111. https://doi.org/10.1177/146499340100100201

Merry, S. E. (2009). Relating to the subjects of human rights: the culture of agency in human rights discourse. In M. Freeman & D. Napier (Eds.), *Law and Anthropology: Current Legal Issues Volume 12* (pp. 385–407). London; Oxford: Oxford University Press.

Mohanty, C. T. (1984). Under western eyes: Feminist scholarship and colonial discourses. *Boundary 2, 12/13*, 333–358. https://doi.org/10.2307/302821

Naafs, S., & White, B. (2012). Intermediate generations: Reflections on Indonesian youth studies. *The Asia Pacific Journal of Anthropology, 13*(1), 3–20. https://doi.org/10.1080/14442213.2012.645796

Ramstedt, M. (2014). Discordant temporalities in Bali's new village jurisdictions. *The Journal of Legal Pluralism and Unofficial Law, 46*(1), 60–78. https://doi.org/10.1080/07329113.2014.893722

Schulte Nordholt, H. (2000). Localizing modernity in Colonial Bali during the 1930s. *Journal of Southeast Asian Studies, 31*(1), 101–114. https://doi.org/10.1017/S0022463400015897

Singarimbun, M. (1991). Norma-Norma Dan Perilaku Seks Remaja. *Populasi, 2*(1), 11–23.

Tucker, K. (1999). *Anthony Giddens and Modern Social Theory* (1st edition). London; Thousand Oaks, CA: SAGE Publications Ltd.

UNICEF Indonesia, & UNICEF. (2016). *Child Marriage in Indonesia: Progress on Pause*. Jakarta, Indonesia: UNICEF Indonesia.

Utomo, I. D. (1997). *Sexual Attitudes and Behaviour of Middle-Class Young People in Jakarta* [Doctoral Thesis]. The Australian National University.

Utomo, I. D. (2001). Sexual values and early experiences among young people in Jakarta. In L. Manderson & P. Liamputtong (Eds.), *Coming of Age in South and Southeast Asia: Youth, Courtship and Sexuality* (pp. 207–227). Richmond, Surrey: Routledge.

Utomo, I. D., & McDonald, P. (2009). Adolescent reproductive health in Indonesia: Contested values and policy inaction. *Studies in Family Planning, 40*(2), 133–146.

Van Bemmelen, S. T. (2006). Apakah Msyarakat Bali Memang Permisif? *Bali Sruti, 2*, 29.

Van Bemmelen, S. T. (2015). *Sekilas Perkawinan Dini di Bali.* Child Marriage, Sexual Moralities, and the Politics of Decentralization in Indonesia, Jakarta.
Vickers, A. (1996). *Being modern in Bali: Image and Change.* New Haven, CT: Yale University Southeast Asia Studies.
Wikan, U. (1990). *Managing Turbulent Hearts: A Balinese Formula for Living.* Chicago, IL: University of Chicago Press.

Chapter 6

Agency

For me, 15 years old is good enough to marry, because girls do not go to school, and I was bored of being a child (bosan menjadi anak-anak). [...] I am more free when I am married – I do not have to work and raise money so I can be lazy at home.[1]

This is what Ayu, who lives in a poor Denpasar community told me during one of our several interviews. When I first met Ayu, she was 14 years old, married, and holding her two-week-old newborn daughter. Her marriage to a boy from the same community had occurred only recently, despite her mother's disagreement. She went through a *kawin lari* (run-away marriage). She ran away from home with her boyfriend and stayed in his family's place outside of Denpasar for a few months. When the couple returned to Ayu's parents, they were already married under customary law. Engaged in household chores, holding her baby in her arms, she looked like a young mother in her late teens. Yet when she was explaining that she was happy she had had a baby and that she wanted another child, her shy and innocent smile reminded me that she was still only 14.

Readers will probably respond differently to this story. People might feel moral condemnation for marrying at such a young age. Others might feel empathy for her poor living conditions. Some may regard it as the happy story of young lovers. If we take her word literally; she wanted to marry. It was her choice to do so at the age of 14. Though if we look at her situation through the international human rights framework, such a marriage is a human rights violation. On the other hand, scholars and policymakers recognize the growing demand for children's rights policies and frameworks to consider children's perspectives. If we consider this changing paradigm, there is an increasing need to take Ayu's decision seriously.

As this chapter will demonstrate, the child marriage framework still relies on a traditional protective approach. Most human rights advocates argue that child

1 Interview, May 2017.

DOI: 10.4324/9781003184546-6

marriages are by definition 'forced marriages', even when the child appears to have given his or her consent (see, e.g., Equality Now 2014: 53; United Nations Children's Fund Innocenti Research Centre 2001; UN Committee on the Elimination of Discrimination against Women 1994: para 36; Irdiana 2015). Campaigns against child marriage never suggest accommodating children's decisions to marry, even though Articles 5 and 12 of the CRC recognize children's evolving capacities and their right to be heard. These campaigns discuss girls' agency, but only their agency *not* to marry (see for instance United Nations Population Fund 2018; Reiss 2018; Child Helpline International n.d.).

Like Ayu, children decide to marry in many cases, especially those in their mid to late teens. The question is whether such a decision is really the child's decision, considering the surrounding social pressures, power dynamics, extended family, and local leaders. Even when it is the child's autonomous decision, to what extent should policymakers take their voices seriously? This chapter provides empirical evidence about children's agency and capacity in deciding to marry. It thus establishes that the current binary child marriage framework overlooks agency's complexity.

The next section will explain the changing paradigm in children's rights through the literature on the diversity of childhood and children's agency. I then examine the influence of the new paradigm on the CRC principles and provide a legal analysis of the extent to which the child marriage framework is in line with the principles. Later, I try to understand to what extent, and how, children exercise agency, based on my empirical findings. For my analysis, I rely on 16 cases of 'child marriage' among the Balinese Hindu populations across different social classes. These case studies involved interviewing girls, boys, and their parents and family members. In the analysis, I pay particular attention to two aspects:

1) Relational: The power dynamics among children, their parents, their extended family, and local leaders.
2) Situational: The options the children had at the time of the decision-making.

The conclusion builds on the findings to discuss an alternative approach to the current binary framework of child marriage.

6.1. A paradigm shift?

Since the 1990s, the sociology of childhood has discussed a paradigm shift, moving from the protective approach to one that regards children as active agents (James and Prout 1997; Leonard 2015). In his book, *The Invention of Childhood*, Cunningham (2006: 45) argues that the modern outlook on children overlooks their capabilities and that the protective approach "downplays their abilities and resilience". When it comes to children's rights, the protective approach is reflected in what Tobin (2015) calls the "vulnerability approach", which leads to the objectification and silencing of children. He thus calls for a broader conceptualization of children as being both vulnerable and resilient, to recognize their evolving capacities and right to participation in decision-making processes that involve them (Ibid). Tisdall (2017: 64) also problematizes vulnerability as a "controlling and stigmatizing label" that can be used to constrain people's rights to make decisions. One alternative to the vulnerability approach would be a "capabilities approach", which takes into account what children need from their perspectives (Domínguez-Serrano et al. 2019; Peleg 2013).

This shift away from the protective approach closely relates to the deconstruction of the dominant view on childhood. Over a decade, childhood scholarship has tried to incorporate the diversity of childhood at the theoretical level. James, Jenks, and Prout (1998: 9) have tried to "explain and deconstruct those very discourses that have established taken-for-granted 'truths' about childhood", fuelled by child developmental psychology from the early twentieth century (James and Prout 1997: 9–10). According to Liebel (2012: 206), the long-standing western concept of childhood has perished and "children's protagonism" is on the rise, with an increasing awareness of young people's capabilities and their influential role in society. The concept of protagonism is an alternative to "paternalists" and "developmentalists", who see the poor and ethnic minorities as underdeveloped people who are uncivilized and culturally backward (Ibid). Bunting (2005) criticizes the assumed uniformity of concepts such as childhood and marriage and calls for wider and more careful recognition of their diversity. Jenks (2004: 5–6) proposes discussing "the proliferation of childhood*s*", saying that "the idea of childhood as a universal category does not meet the real experiences of children across the globe".

These changing views have prompted children's rights and childhood scholarship to take an increasing interest in the voices of children. The "living rights" concept considers children's rights as a "'living practice' shaped by children's everyday concerns" (Hanson and Nieuwenhuys 2012: 8). Some scholars have designed research with children as co-researchers (Spyrou 2016; Warming 2016). Others use photographs to capture a sense of children's perspectives on their everyday environment (Mizen and Ofosu-Kusi 2012).

Despite the shift in childhood studies, a protectionist view continues to influence policies concerning children. A good example is child labour. Nieuwenhuys (1996: 237) demonstrates that children are denied their agency in the creation and negotiation of value by the modern idea of removing children from their economic activities. Saadi (2012: 160) has documented the continuous tension between the movements of working children and core international actors committed to the eradication of child labour. While international organizations present former child labourers whose life stories fit well into their human rights agenda, they tend to mute the voice of the working children's group who advocate for their rights to work (Ibid: 158, 161). Van Daalen and Mabillard (2018) have documented the unequal power relation where global actors in Geneva ignore working children's voices. Boyden (1997: 205) points out the danger of such global power relations: West-centric measures that intend to resolve children's problems can be harmful in the South. As child labour studies show, documenting and verifying the effects of children's rights' policies in real-life contexts is one way to incorporate childhood diversity into policies that are based on a homogenous protectionist view of childhood (Reynolds, Nieuwenhuys, and Hanson 2006). This emphasizes anthropology's role in the study of children's rights (Hart 2006).

6.2. Child marriage framework within the CRC

6.2.1. Evolving capacity and rights to be heard

The Committee on the Rights of the Child (2007: para 5) encourages the above-mentioned paradigm shift, stating that "a shift away from traditional beliefs that regard early childhood mainly as a period for the socialization of the immature human being towards mature adult status is required". Article 5 of the CRC incorporates the concept of "evolving capacity": The more the child knows, experiences, and understands, the more direction and guidance should be transformed into advice and finally should eventuate an exchange on equal footing (Committee on the Rights of the Child 2009: para 84). This concept seems to have been accorded an increasingly important role by the Committee on the Rights of the Child since the CRC's adoption in 1989 (Varadan 2019). Article 12 of the CRC stipulates the "right to be heard", requiring that State Parties ensure that children have the right to express their views freely and that due weight is given to those views in accordance with the age and maturity of the child.

Despite these principles, when it comes to child marriage, international institutions are still reluctant to recognize children's capacities and seem to fall back on the protective approach. A joint general recommendation by the CEDAW and CRC committees suggests "respecting the child's evolving capacities and autonomy in making decisions that affect her or his life" and allows "a marriage of a mature, capable child below 18 years of age". However, the committees stipulate that this type of marriage may only occur when the following two conditions are met:

1) The child is at least 16 years old, and
2) "Such decisions are made by a judge based on legitimate exceptional ground defined by law and on the evidence of maturity, without deference to culture and tradition" (Committee on the Elimination of Discrimination against Women & Committee on the Rights of the Child 2014).

The conditions are strict, and it is unrealistic to expect the majority of child marriage cases to meet them. For instance, in most child marriage cases in

Indonesia, people have limited access and motivation to go to court (Grijns and Horii 2018; see also Chapter 3). Consequently, in practice, these conditions still make it difficult for children to exercise their marital agency in an internationally accepted manner. Thus, even this committee recommendation seems tokenistic rather than an actual effort to recognize children's capacities.

6.2.2. The best interest of the child

This joint recommendation, as stated above, indicates the committees' strong position against any 'deference to culture and tradition'. This inflexibility seems hard to reconcile with the CRC's 'best interest of the child' principle, which is supposed to accommodate socio-cultural considerations. The principle may vary depending on each context's socio-cultural conditions. For instance, in highly industrialized countries, the best interests of the child are served by policies that emphasize autonomy, but in more traditional societies, the links to family and the local community might be of paramount importance (Alston 1994: 5). The principle is stipulated as "a primary consideration" (A3 of the CRC), meaning that the child's interests have high priority and are not just one of several considerations (Committee on the Rights of the Child 2013).

The Committee on the Rights of the Child (Ibid: para 32) considers that Article 3 (the best interest of the child) and Article 12 (the right to be heard) have complementary roles, in that the latter provides the methodology for hearing the child's view on matters affecting them. The child's voice is one of the elements that can be used to determine the child's best interests. However, it must be weighed against other factors, such as the preservation of family relations, the child's identity, and the protection of the child (Ibid: para 52–84). The best-interests assessment requires balancing various elements, often walking a thin line between the child's protection and empowerment.

Compared to the CRC Committee's careful considerations, the child marriage framework is rather single-minded. The CRC Committee (2017) embraces the "child rights approach" where children participate in the decision-making process. However, the "welfare approach" involving the "rescue" of children seems to overrule it in the global child marriage framework, resulting in the current abolitionist approach towards the practice. The reason for this gap can be attributed to a normative standpoint: When children don't do "the right thing", the emphasis tends to be put on the protection of children, rather than looking at their capacities (Hanson 2016). In other words, children's views are only heard when adults consider them as "rational, consistent, and on their own" (Tisdall 2016: 374). When children work, marry, or get involved in violent political struggles, the children's actions are considered 'wrong', and the concept of agency loses its significance (Ibid: 474).

This liberal paternalism partially derives from policymakers' or activists' specific assumptions. When children's behaviour does not fit the adult actors' conception of childhood, the adult tends to overlook the child's agency. As a result, the child marriage framework and international policies on children still rely on the protective approach and tend to view children, especially the ones in the Global South, as passive victims.

6.3. Children's agency and participation

The previous sections have shown that children's agency plays a significant role in recent discussions about children's rights. To understand how and to what degree children exercise their agency, children's rights scholarship has introduced 'children's participation' into the process of decision-making. Hart's (1992: 9) "Ladder of Participation" has served as a basic typology for thinking about children's participation. He classifies the first three steps of the ladder (i.e., (1) manipulation, (2) decoration, and (3) tokenism) as "non-participation" and the next five steps (i.e., (4) assigned but informed, (5) consulted and informed, (6) adult-initiated shared decisions with children, (7) child-initiated and directed, and (8) child-initiated shared decisions with adults) as "degrees of participation" (Ibid).

This model, however, is not a definitive tool. It is a "beginning typology" and should not be used as "a simple measuring stick" (Ibid: 7, 11). Lundy (2007) proposes a "new model" by conceptualizing Article 12 of the CRC with four key elements: Space (children must be given the opportunity to express a view), Voice (children must be facilitated to express their views), Audience (the view must be listened to), and Influence (the view must be appropriately acted upon, as appropriate). Tisdall (2016: 374) critically evaluates Article 12, noting it involves adults' discretionary decisions regarding children's capacity and maturity.

While children's participation is theoretically supported, understanding of children's capacities is still limited (Collins 2017: 34). Both Hart's and Lundy's models are useful in examining participation or the 'output' of children's voices. However, understanding agency must include exploring the nature of voice. For instance, Komulainen (2007) points out that those who aim at 'listening to a child's voice' have to also consider social dynamics. Anthropological and sociological scholarship has long tried to understand what constitutes 'agency' and how the surrounding relationships, structures, and norms influence one's agency (e.g., Giddens; Mahmood; see also Section 1.5). According to these understandings of agency, it is an ability to choose by internally reconciling structure, i.e., patterned arrangements that influence or limit available choices. Children's acts of marrying (following the structure) and their act of not marrying (resisting the structure) can then equally be an outcome of exercising agency.

When it comes to children's agency, their inevitable dependence on others is particularly important. Legally, socially, and materially, parents have power and influence over their children (Fineman 2017: 145), and this shall not be neglected when 'listening to children's voices'. But it is also possible to see parental influence from another perspective. If children want to act for their parents, given the particular significance of family relationships, it is difficult to consider their action as forced. Children in Thailand working as prostitutes are an extreme example. Their jobs allow them to support their parents and fulfil their duties, and accordingly, they view themselves as good children (Montgomery 2007: 419). Of course, one can argue that such behaviour is situated in a fundamentally oppressive societal structure, but this does not reduce that there is a degree of agency within the structure.

This signifies a relational aspect of their agency. Some working children, for instance, regard their economic activities as an important element in their social life (Saadi 2012: 152). This social connection creates the "relational self" shaped by obligations to traditional kin and community (Merry 2009: 404). The "right of the relational self" (Engel 2018) occasionally conflicts with the liberal understanding of an 'individual right'. The case of a Thai child prostitute also demonstrates the significance of relationality: "[I]n Baan Nua, ensuring a child's rights to be free from sexual exploitation would mean violating their rights to live with their families and in their communities. Enforcing one right would mean infringing others that the children claim to value more" (Montgomery 2001: 94). According to Hanson (2016: 474), in the discourse about children's rights advocacy, the denial of children's right to marry, work, or participate politically ignores both children's relational selves and their agentic selves.

In evaluating children's capacity to exercise agency, the situational aspect of their capacity is important. Ansell (2009: 204) discusses children's limited "capacity to effect deliberate change" when they are in highly constrained contexts. Intense relationships with people and places, for instance, create difficulty for children to exercise agency. Hart (1992: 24) also distinguishes "children in especially difficult circumstances", describing children with no family, or who are affected by a disaster, poverty, or armed conflict as a group with a greater challenge to participation.

In sum, assessing children's participation is not enough to examine their agency in decision-making processes. In examining to what extent children are exercising agency, the relational aspect (power relationship, dependency) and the situational aspect (options, environment) are factors to be considered carefully. To discuss the boundary between "consent" and "coercion", social, economic, gendered, and cultural constraints should be considered, and possibilities for the refusal of consent is a necessary condition for "real autonomy and meaningful consent" (Bunting et al. 2016). Children may be participating in the decision-making process and be meeting the participation model criteria. However, even then, they might not be exercising their agency in the strict sense if their 'voices' stem from the particular power relationships they are in or from highly constraining contexts. Only with this 'strict' understanding of agency that considers relational and situational aspects can we explore if we are taking their voices seriously, walking the thin line between empowerment and protection. The next section will explore this through case studies.

6.4. How and to what extent do they exercise agency?

This section presents an analysis of the process of children's (in particular mid- to late teenagers') involvement in decision-making about their own marriage by using a 'strict' understanding of agency. Considering the situational and relational aspects of the decisions, each case demonstrates how and to what extent these teenagers exercise agency.

6.4.1. Case of Risky: Exercising agency that inhabits norms

When Risky married his wife Widi, he was 18 and Widi was 16 or 17 years old. They had been in a courtship (*pacaran*) since junior high school, and after four years of *pacaran*, Widi became pregnant. Widi did not tell Risky about the pregnancy at first, but he eventually found out through her parents, who came to tell him to take "responsibility". He said he was "little scared" at that time, but his father told him that he would "just have to accept it".

Risky and Widi began having sex when Risky was in his first year of high school. They used a condom the first time, but afterwards, they continued without it; "just trying" as Risky said. When I asked Risky if he was ready to marry Widi, he said yes. He was not only ready, but he *wanted* to marry her. I then asked if they were trying to become pregnant so they could marry, to which he answered, "maybe not … but just trying".

For him, the ideal age of marriage is 23. He thinks it is better to first graduate from university. When I asked him if he thought about not marrying Widi after finding out about the pregnancy, he said "no, I have to marry (*harus nikah*)". I further asked who said "*harus nikah*" and he said "myself". When I asked him if he has ever regretted that Widi became pregnant at that time, he said no. They want another baby next year.

It was Widi's parents who initiated the discussion about marriage, and Risky's father who pushed for it. It seems that the marriage decision was imposed on him at that time as something that he would "just have to accept". However, it is also evident that he understood why he had to accept it, as he understood and agreed with the norm that one has to marry when one's girlfriend becomes pregnant. He also described that it was he ("myself") who considered it necessary to marry when his girlfriend became pregnant. This is internalization, i.e., *inhabitation of the norms (*see Section 1.5*).* Therefore, although his parents initiated this marriage decision, it can also be considered Risky's act of agency.

6.4.2. Case of Agus and Mawar: Parental involvement and different types of decisions

For the first interview with Agus and Mawar, I was invited to their house, where Agus' mother was present. I explained my research and clarified that I came to talk about the marriage of Agus and Mawar. On that day, Agus' mother dominated the conversation, even when I directed my questions to Agus and Mawar. She repeated several times during the interview that they married because of mutual love ("*sama cinta*" and "*suka-sama-suka*"). If children like somebody, marriage is "up to the children", she said. I felt that Agus' mother wanted to take control of their story. I also wanted to hear the story from Agus and Mawar, so for the second and the third interview, I met them outside of their house, without Agus' mother. They then expressed the motivations behind their marriage in more detail and somewhat more freely.

Mawar married at the age of 16. Since she was young, she has lived in Denpasar with her parents, who were vendors and were often away from home, working on other islands. After finishing junior high school (SMP), she started working at the age of 15 at a tailor store. She met Agus at the store, and they started dating. Mawar first wanted to hide this from her parents, as she was afraid that her father would get angry with her for dating at such a young age. However, when they went to see her father after one year of dating, he was just startled (*kaget*). And at the second meeting, he told them to get married. Agus jokingly said that they married because Mawar's family was afraid of a "hit-and-run", that he was dating without commitment and would run away before marriage. If Mawar's father had not asked them to marry, they would not have considered marrying at that point. In fact, they never planned to have a baby or to marry, and just wanted to "follow the flow". For Agus, it did not matter whether they married sooner or later.

In Bali, parents are heavily involved in marital decisions, including decisions about the partner, the type of marriage ceremony, post-marital arrangements, and so on. Parents sometimes even decide whether their children should marry and when, especially when an extra-marital pregnancy occurs. This type of decision-making sometimes also involves a *banjar* head (see Section 4.4.1). In Agus and Mawar's case, the trigger for their marriage was the pressure from Mawar's father, but it did not seem to have disrupted their lives or plans. Both Mawar and Agus were already working, and according to Agus, they would have still married sooner or later. Thus her father influenced the timing of their marriage but not her choice of partner and other arrangements. This case shows *parental involvement in marriage decisions* and the *different types of decisions* in which agency was exercised. Although Agus and Mawar exercised little agency in deciding when to marry, they decided who to marry and about their life after marriage.

6.4.3. *Case of Ayu: Genuine agency of her own and limited life options*

Let me now detail the case of Ayu, whom I introduced at the beginning of this chapter. Ayu lives in the poorest community in Denpasar (i.e., the *Pasar Community*, as explained in Section 5.4). This community has lived in Denpasar for two or three generations, with women and children working as carriers (*tukang suun*) at a traditional market or men working as parking guards or construction workers. They are all from a village from one of Bali's most remote and poorest areas, living in a small residential complex (*kost*). They seem to have little interaction with the rest of the world. They also only marry within their circle. Most of them have never had any schooling experience and are illiterate. For generations, it has been normal for girls in this community to marry before 18, and some people consider marrying early as evidence of attractiveness.

I visited Ayu in her community several times, and I would often find her peeling a bucket of garlic or onions while holding her baby girl in a sling. She would sell a bucket of peeled garlic for Rp. 40,000 (€2.5) and 10kg of peeled onions for Rp. 20,000 (€1.2). Ayu started working as a market carrier as soon as she could, earning around Rp. 50,000 (€3.1) per day. She has never been through formal education. She said that she did not like going to school because "the teachers were very strange" and because she had a slight speech impediment; she could not pronounce the 'R' sound clearly (in Balinese, this is called the *badil*).

I talked with Ayu's mother, who herself married at the age of 16. She did not want Ayu to get married so early because to her "she was still a baby, not a teenager". She said:

> *When she marries, she is not my child anymore. She belongs to her husband. Now she will work for his family and not for me.*[2]

This remark shows the expected duties and roles of children in the community. When girls marry in the Balinese kinship system, they 'marry out', so poor families are not content when their daughters marry at a young age. As explained, she had a run-away marriage, which did not involve her mother's opinion.

Despite the *limited life options* Ayu seems to have, she was surprisingly proactive, and her marriage decision displayed *genuine agency*: She set up the plans for marriage and only later informed the adults of the decision. Ayu seemed to be aware of the limited options available to her and chose what she felt was her best option. However, proactive decisions do not necessarily lead to expected

2 Interview, May 2017.

outcomes. Her expectation of married life ("I do not have to work and can be lazy at home") was wrong, and she realized that she still has to work to earn a living in her new household. It is likely that in her situation, she was not fully aware of the consequences of her decision.

6.4.4. Case of Swasti: Social pressure

Swasti, which I introduced in the previous chapter (Chapter 5), is also relevant for the analysis here. She lived in a rural village in East Bali and became pregnant when she was 15 years old, in her last year of junior high school. She and her boyfriend lived in the same village, met in one of the neighbour's ceremonies (*upacara*), and have been in *pacaran* for over a year. When I asked her what she liked about him, she just said "I was still young and unstable". At the time of the interview, they had already divorced.

Swasti's boyfriend first denied that she was pregnant with his child and refused to marry her. However, after a week, he eventually agreed, since he was "ashamed" *(malu)* because their relationship was known in their small village. Although her mother told her to have an abortion since they were so young, Swasti decided not to have one because she was "scared". Instead, she stopped going to school. After giving birth, while being married, she managed to return to education and finished *kejar paket* B (the junior high school equivalent).

Although she does not regret having a child, she regrets marrying her husband. Looking back, she said:

> *If I could return to the time when I became pregnant, I would choose to be a single mother.*[3]

However, at that time, it was not an option. People in the village did not accept single mothers. If she gave birth out of wedlock, she and her family would have been ostracized from the local community (*banjar*). She mentioned that her parents eventually let her marry because Swasti and her boyfriend loved each other (*suka-sama-suka)*. I asked her if she *wanted* to marry him at that time, to which she replied:

How can I say … (pause) I guess, yes.[4]

Like Ayu, Swasti pushed her way through marriage because of 'mutual love'. She was highly involved in the marriage decision. However, this case also demonstrates the *social pressure* that strongly affected her decision. Especially in rural areas, community is so central to their lives that pregnant teenagers are left with no choice but to marry. The social structure Swasti lived with severely

3 Interview, July 2017.
4 Interview, July 2017.

limited her capacity to exercise agency. Although retrospectively, she would rather have been a single mother, she also acknowledged that not marrying was not an option at that time.

Notably, this social pressure also exists in urban areas. My research assistants, educated and urban Balinese young adults, explained the difficulties with the norms:

A: *People in Bali run around in circles of adat, and it is very difficult to break them.*
B: *And if you are different, while everyone believes in all those adat ceremonies and rules, you can't do anything. You just have no choice but to follow the others in those rules. It's very difficult to be different.*
A: *Exactly. If you don't do upacara, your identity will be questioned. People say to you, "Are you Balinese?"*[5]

In Denpasar, Riska's case and her remarks also suggest the strong influence of social norms. She became pregnant while still in school and outside of marriage, and she eventually had a miscarriage:

> *After I had this miscarriage, everybody said "it's going to be okay". Everybody took care of me, but I wanted them to leave me alone. They looked at me as if I was sick. They said "it's going to be okay", but I knew that it was not okay for them. I blamed myself for not being a perfect daughter. My mother always told me what she wanted me to do. To meet her expectation, I studied hard to be at the top. But I failed when I got pregnant before marriage.*[6]

These stories of expectations are not unique to Indonesia. Social pressure is omnipresent and influences our behaviour everywhere: In rural and urban areas, in the 'Global South' and 'Global North'. The reference network framework, which I explained and used in Chapter 5, indicates the inevitable correlation between social norms and individual behaviour and decision-making.

6.4.5. Child marriage by a choice?

I chose these four cases because they are especially rich in information, and therefore valuable for a qualitative analysis of the 'strict' understanding of agency. These four cases represent all 16 cases in the childrens' degrees of participation. The overall analysis of the 16 cases shows that none of those who married young expressed themselves as having been forced to marry. In Hart's Ladder diagram, the 16 cases are also mostly categorized as high-level participation. Half of the cases are in Step 8 (Child-initiated, shared decisions

5 Personal Communication, August 2017.
6 Personal Communication, May 2017.

with adults), while the other half ranges from Step 4 (Assigned but informed) to Step 7 (Child-initiated and directed).

However, as I have argued earlier, assessing children's participation is not enough to examine their agency in decision-making processes. Are those decisions an outcome of children's acts of agency, even under the 'strict' understanding of agency? Power imbalances are also evident in child-parent relationships, which influence children's voices. According to UNICEF Indonesia, "child marriage is an outcome of prevailing social norms" (Irdiana 2015). The case studies have proved that strong social pressure does exist, especially in the context of pre-marital pregnancy. For example, Swasti's choice to marry seems to have been out of necessity. In fact, 90% of the studied cases of child marriage were caused by unplanned pregnancies, to which child marriage is a 'solution' (see Chapter 5). In other words, a lack of access to reproductive health tools and the existing social structures severely limit the pregnant teen's possibilities. Various social networks build the structure: The parents and peers (see Chapter 5), their extended family members, and the larger community in which they live.

However, considering all child marriage as an outcome of prevailing social norms denies the possibility of exercising relational autonomy. Swasti's case presents a kind of 'submission' since she chose marriage because she did not see any other options. By contrast, Risky's case shows the possibility of exercising agency in a way that inhabits norms. Agency is not only about resisting social norms (i.e., the norm that 'one has to marry in cases of pregnancy') but also about following them. Ayu's case also illustrates the possibility of exercising agency in a situation with limited possibilities. She lives in a 'difficult situation', in poverty and without education. This economic condition is relevant when examining whether she really exercised her agency. Was refusing marriage a possibility for her? While advocates against child marriage describe poverty as a factor driving children into marriage (see, e.g., Vogelstein 2013), Ayu was very proactive in her decision to marry. While a 'difficult situation' requires special attention, it does not mean that people cannot exercise agency in such situations. In fact, Ayu was aware of her life choices and exercised her agency within the limited possibilities that she had. She was, in Maithreyi's (2019) words, a "strategically opportunising actor" who sought to make her life more meaningful despite the structural constraints placed on her.

The next question is 'to what extent should policymakers take children's voices seriously?' To what extent should policymakers decide what is and is not good for children? For instance, although Ayu did exercise her agency to marry, it became clear that she was either unaware of the consequences of such a decision or had wrong assumptions about it. Does it mean that she was 'too young' or 'not mature enough' to make decisions? Theoretically, children's views must be given due weight when they are capable of forming them (Article 12 of the CRC), namely when they have "sufficient understanding to be capable of appropriately forming his or her views on the matter"

(Committee on the Rights of the Child 2009). However as Lundy et al. (2019: 403–406) have indicated, 'appropriately' risks adults imposing subjective assessments on the *quality* of the children's views and "the best interests principle cannot be automatically invoked by an adult to trump the views of a child".

It is tempting to intervene in children's seemingly 'wrong' decisions. However, there is a need to step back and reconsider our assumptions. In doing so, the key question should not be whether the decision is wrong. Instead, it should be whether policymakers should attempt to withdraw the decision from the child (e.g., by imposing a general ban on child marriage), keeping in mind the problems children are experiencing. These problems may differ greatly depending on the society in which the children live. As explained in Section 6.1, childhood varies in its forms and meanings, in each society and time. This diversity of childhood*s* (Jenks 2004: 5–6; see Section 1.1) makes it extremely difficult, if not impossible, to make a moral standard universally applicable.

Chapter 2 has demonstrated that child marriage is currently described as 'a harmful tradition' (The Fourth World Conference on Women 1995; United Nations Children's Fund 2005). However, this framing is problematic as "the notion that non-Western people are governed by culture suggests they have a limited capacity for agency, will, or rational thought" (Volpp 2000: 96). Hopgood (2016), with an example of female genital mutilation (FGM) of girls, describes such intervention as "international paternalism". In the case of FGM (as well as child marriage), parental paternalism (parental authority to decide what is right and wrong for their children) competes with international paternalism (international human rights activism). Children are almost absent from the discourse (Ibid). The international paternalism "overrules" parental paternalism, presuming that cutting one's daughter is wrong (Ibid: 257). Hopgood (Ibid: 290) also raises an important point about responsibilities: While the international anti-FGM movement's gaze moves on and activists eventually get back on the plane, parents remain responsible for the long-term life prospects of their daughters. While child marriage and FGM are two considerably different issues, the types of paternalism and the responsibilities of interventions are also relevant for the discussions on agency in the child marriage framework.

The discussions about agency in 'harmful traditional practices' are highly racialized. Human rights activists tend to assume that girls in the Global South need liberation through induction into the metropolitan West's progressive social norms. Consequently, they describe 'other' girls as 'always or already victims', to be rescued from cultural norms. It is a legal fiction that children are incapable of making decisions. They are capable of both self-agency and active collaboration with adults (Tobin 2015: 178). However, taking a child who wants to marry seriously requires liberating ourselves from such discriminative notions.

Taking children's voices seriously should occur alongside saturating their world with accurate and realistic information and creating an enabling environment. That 90% of the child marriage cases in Bali arise from unplanned teenage pregnancies indicates the urgency and necessity of providing reproductive health information. Another important task is correctly informing children about the possible consequences of marriage. This knowledge, alongside better access to reproductive health tools, a way out of poverty, and equal access to basic education, can prevent adolescents from unwillingly limiting their own choices and opportunities. Children are also resilient. The case studies demonstrate that they can craft their life after marriage in the most desirable way, given the possibilities. For example, Swasti found a way to continue her education after marriage. By focusing on stimulating their resilience, policies should be designed to help already-married children continue their education and build the life they wish to lead. For the child marriage framework to be truly emancipatory, it needs to provide increasing and differentiated options instead of a general ban.

6.5. Conclusion: Walking the thin line between empowerment and protection

This chapter demonstrated that despite the changing paradigm in the children's rights discussions and policies, the child marriage framework still relies on a traditional protective approach. It first established that the child marriage framework is inconsistent with the CRC in two ways:

1) It fails to consider children's evolving capacity and the right to be heard.
2) It fails to ensure that a margin of appreciation is incorporated into the 'best interests of the child' principle.

By not considering these two principles, the rigid child marriage framework limits itself in its capacity to meet the CRC's goal.

The practice of 'listening to children's voices' is more challenging than the theories may suggest. Both academics and practitioners in the children's rights field have tried to apply the theories by assessing and enhancing children's participation in the decision-making process. However, the known participation models are not sufficient to fully explore children's 'voices' or to examine their agency in the decision-making process. In examining the extent to which children are exercising agency, both relational and situational aspects should be carefully considered.

The case studies from Bali were analyzed based on the 'strict' understanding of agency and enable us to explore whether or not we should take their voices seriously. None of those who married young expressed themselves as having been forced to marry nor did they describe their marriage as a child marriage or an arranged marriage. Although the social pressure and parental influence were evident, some children were able to reason their marriage decisions based on the norms that they inhabit. Some demonstrated their agency within the limited possibilities they had. When listening to children's perspectives, it becomes clear that they decide to marry out of love, to belong to the community, and for new opportunities.

Based on these points, I maintain that the current measures against child marriage fail to walk the thin line between children's empowerment and protection. Setting the marriageable age at 18 essentially bans child marriages, which takes this decision away from teenagers who have proved themselves autonomous enough to act with agency. The shift from protection towards empowerment requires a more holistic and inclusive approach (see Chapter 2), since taking any married children's voice seriously requires our own liberation from a fixated image of children being passive victims, especially in the Global South.

The danger of an incomplete or inaccurate framework is that it deviates reform efforts away from problems experienced by local communities. As demonstrated in Chapter 5, the problem that Balinese adolescents face is not marriage itself but unplanned teenage pregnancy. A lack of knowledge about adolescent reproductive health limits their choices and opportunities, so actors should invest in an enabling environment, including better access to reproductive health tools, poverty reduction, and equal access to a basic education system. For the international child marriage framework to focus on empowerment rather than bans, policy priorities should be designed to encourage children's participation in and collaboration with adults in decision-making, where they are informed of the consequences of marriage and their love relationships. Government policies and CSO programmes could also be improved to stimulate children's resilience, improve their life after marriage (e.g., supporting married children in continuing their education), and enable them to live the life they wish to lead.

Bibliography

Alston, P. (1994). The best interests principle: Towards a reconciliation of culture and human rights. *International Journal of Law, Policy and the Family*, *8*(1), 1–25. https://doi.org/10.1093/lawfam/8.1.1

Ansell, N. (2009). Childhood and the politics of scale: Descaling children's geographies? *Progress in Human Geography*, *33*(2), 190–209. https://doi.org/10.1177/0309132508090980

Boyden, J. (1997). Childhood and the policymakers. In A. James & A. Prout (Eds.), *Constructing and Reconstructing Childhood: Contemporary Issues in the Sociological Study of Childhood* (pp. 184–215). London, UK: Falmer Press.

Bunting, A. (2005). Stages of development: Marriage of girls and teens as an international human rights issue. *Social & Legal Studies*, *14*(1), 17–38. https://doi.org/10.1177/0964663905049524

Bunting, A., Lawrance, B. N., & Roberts, R. L. (2016). Something old, something new? In A. Bunting, B. N. Lawrance, & R. L. Roberts (Eds.), *Marriage by Force?: Contestation Over Consent and Coercion in Africa* (pp. 1–40). Athens, OH: Ohio University Press.

Child Helpline International. (n.d.). *A Story from Malawi: Escaping Child Marriage to Find Empowerment in Education*. Child Helpline International. https://www.childhelplineinternational.org/youth/blog-youth/escaping-child-marriage-education-malawi/ (accessed on April 20, 2021).

Collins, T. M. (2017). A child's right to participate: Implications for international child protection. *The International Journal of Human Rights, 21*(1), 14–46. https://doi.org/10.1080/13642987.2016.1248122

Committee on the Elimination of Discrimination against Women & Committee on the Rights of the Child. (2014). *Joint General Recommendation No. 31/General Comment No. 18 on Harmful Practices*, CEDAW/C/GC/31–CRC/C/GC/18.

Committee on the Rights of the Child. (2007). *General Comment No. 7 (2007), Implementing Child Rights in Early Childhood, CRC/C/GC/7/Rev.1.*

Committee on the Rights of the Child. (2009). *General Comment No.12 (2009), The Right of the Child to be Heard, CRC/C/GC/12.*

Committee on the Rights of the Child. (2013). General Comment no. 14 (2013) on the Right of the Child to Have His *or Her Best Interests Taken As A Primary Consideration, CRC/C/GC/14.* http://www2.ohchr.org/English/bodies/crc/docs/GC/CRC_C_GC_14_ENG.pdf)

Committee on the Rights of the Child. (2017). *General Comment No.21 on Children in Street Situations, CRC/C/GC/21.*

Cunningham, H. (2006). *The Invention of Childhood*. London, UK: BBC Books.

Domínguez-Serrano, M., del Moral-Espín, L., & Gálvez Muñoz, L. (2019). A well-being of their own: Children's perspectives of well-being from the capabilities approach. *Childhood, 26*(1), 22–38. https://doi.org/10.1177/0907568218804872

Engel, D. M. (2018, May 17). *Rights of the Relational Self: Law, Culture, and Injury in the Global North and South* [Lecture]. Van Vollenhoven Lecture 2018, Leiden, The Netherlands.

Equality Now. (2014). *Protecting the Girl Child: Using the Law to End Child, Early and Forced Marriage and Related Human Rights Violations*. New York; Nairobi; London: Equality Now.

Fineman, M. A. (2017). Vulnerability and inevitable inequality. *Oslo Law Review, 4*, 133–149.

Grijns, M., & Horii, H. (2018). Child marriage in a village in West Java (Indonesia): Compromises between legal obligations and religious concerns. *Asian Journal of Law and Society*, 1–14. https://doi.org/10.1017/als.2018.9

Hanson, K. (2016). Children's participation and agency when they don't 'do the right thing.' *Childhood, 23*(4), 471–475.

Hanson, K., & Nieuwenhuys, O. (2012). Living rights, social justice, translations. In K. Hanson & O. Nieuwenhuys (Eds.), *Reconceptualizing Children's Rights in International Development* (pp. 3–25). Cambridge, UK: Cambridge University Press.

Hart, A. R. (1992). *Children's Participation: From Tokenism to Citizenship*. New York, NY: United Nations Children's Fund.

Hart, J. (2006). Saving children: What role for anthropology? *Anthropology Today, 22*(1), 5–8. https://doi.org/10.1111/j.1467-8322.2006.00410.x

Hopgood, S. (2016). Modernity at the cutting edge: Human rights meets FGM. In *Paternalism beyond Borders* (pp. 256–291). Cambridge: Cambridge University Press.

Irdiana, N. (2015, June 9). *Ending Child Marriage: The Art (Challenge!) of Asking Difficult Questions*. Child Marriage, Sexual Moralities, and The Politics of Decentralization in Indonesia, Jakarta.

James, A., Jenks, C., & Prout, A. (1998). *Theorizing Childhood*. Cambridge, UK: Polity Press.

James, A., & Prout, A. (1997). A new paradigm for the sociology of childhood? Provenance, promise and problems. In A. James & A. Prout (Eds.), *Constructing and Reconstructing Childhood: Contemporary Issues in the Sociological Study of Childhood* (pp. 7–33). London, UK: Falmer Press.

Jenks, C. (2004). Editorial: Many childhoods? *Childhood, 11*(1), 5–8. https://doi.org/10.1177/0907568204040179

Komulainen, S. (2007). The ambiguity of the child's 'voice' in social research. *Childhood, 14*(1), 11–28. https://doi.org/10.1177/0907568207068561

Leonard, M. (2015). *The Sociology of Children, Childhood and Generation*. Los Angeles, CA: SAGE Publications.

Liebel, M. (2012). The role of children in shaping new contexts of children's rights. In M. Liebel (Ed.), *Children's Rights from Below: Cross-Cultural Perspectives* (pp. 199–225). Basingstoke, UK: Palgrave Macmillan.

Lundy, L. (2007). 'Voice' is not enough: Conceptualising Article 12 of the United Nations Convention on the rights of the child. *British Educational Research Journal, 33*(6), 927–942. https://doi.org/10.1080/01411920701657033

Lundy, L., Tobin, J., & Parkes, A. (2019). Article 12. The right to respect for the views of the child. In J. Tobin (Ed.), *The UN Convention on the Rights of the Child: A Commentary* (pp. 397–434). Oxford; New York: Oxford University Press.

Maithreyi, R. (2019). Children's reconstruction of psychological knowledge: An ethnographic study of life skills education programmes in India. *Childhood, 26*(1), 68–82. https://doi.org/10.1177/0907568218798014

Merry, S. E. (2009). Relating to the subjects of human rights: The culture of agency in human rights discourse. In M. Freeman & D. Napier (Eds.), *Law and Anthropology: Current Legal Issues Volume 12* (pp. 385–407). London; Oxford: Oxford University Press.

Mizen, P., & Ofosu-Kusi, Y. (2012). Seeing and knowing? Street children's lifeworlds through the camera's lens. In K. Hanson & O. Nieuwenhuys (Eds.), *Reconceptualizing Children's Rights in International Development* (pp. 48–70). Cambridge, UK: Cambridge University Press.

Montgomery, H. (2001). Imposing rights? A case study of child prostitution in Thailand. In J. K. Cowan, M.-B. Dembour, & R. A. Wilson (Eds.), *Culture and Rights: Anthropological Perspectives*. Cambridge; New York: Cambridge University Press.

Montgomery, H. (2007). Working with child prostitutes in Thailand: Problems of practice and interpretation. *Childhood, 14*(4), 415–430.

Nieuwenhuys, O. (1996). The paradox of child labor and anthropology. *Annual Review of Anthropology, 25*(1), 237–251. https://doi.org/10.1146/annurev.anthro.25.1.237

Peleg, N. (2013). Reconceptualising the child's right to development: Children and the capability approach. *International Journal of Children's Rights, 21*, 523–542.

Reiss, F. (2018). *I Escaped Forced Marriage—Now Is the Time to Outlaw Child Marriage in Florida*. Global Citizen. https://www.globalcitizen.org/en/content/child-marriage-florida/

Reynolds, P., Nieuwenhuys, O., & Hanson, K. (2006). Refractions of children's rights in development practice. *Childhood, 13*(3), 291–302.

Saadi, I. (2012). Children's rights as "work in progress": The conceptual and practical contributions of working children's movements. In M. Liebel (Ed.), *Children's Rights from Below: Cross-Cultural Perspectives* (pp. 143–161). Basingstoke, UK:Palgrave Macmillan.

Spyrou, S. (2016). Troubling children's voices in research. In F. Esser, M. S. Baader, T. Betz, & B. Hungerland (Eds.), *Reconceptualising Agency and Childhood: New perspectives in Childhood Studies* (pp. 105–118). London; New York, NY: Routledge.

The Fourth World Conference on Women. (1995). *Beijing Declaration and Platform for Action, A/CONF.177/20 and A/CONF.177/20/Add.1.* http://hrlibrary.umn.edu/instree/e5dplw.htm

Tisdall, E. K. M. (2016). Subjects with agency? Children's participation in family law proceedings. *Journal of Social Welfare and Family Law, 38*(4), 362–379. https://doi.org/10.1080/09649069.2016.1239345

Tisdall, E. K. M. (2017). Conceptualising children and young people's participation: Examining vulnerability, social accountability and co-production. *The International Journal of Human Rights, 21*(1), 59–75. https://doi.org/10.1080/13642987.2016.1248125

Tobin, J. (2015). Understanding children's rights: A vision beyond vulnerability. *Nordic Journal of International Law, 84*(2), 155–182. https://doi.org/10.1163/15718107-08402002

UN Committee on the Elimination of Discrimination against Women. (1994). *CEDAW General Recommendation No. 21 on Equality in Marriage and Family Relations, CEDAW/C/GC/31–CRC/C/GC/18.* http://www.refworld.org/docid/48abd52c0.html

United Nations Children's Fund. (2005). *Early Marriage: A Harmful Traditional Practice.* New York, NY: United Nations Children's Fund.

United Nations Children's Fund Innocenti Research Centre. (2001). *Early Marriage: Child Spouses.* Florence, Italy: United Nations Children's Fund Innocenti Research Centre.

United Nations Population Fund. (2018). *Escaping* Child Marri*age in Sierra Leone.* United Nations Population Fund. https://www.unfpa.org/news/escaping-child-marriage-sierra-leone

Van Daalen, E., & Mabillard, N. (2018). Human rights in translation: Bolivia's law 548, working children's movements, and the global child labour regime. *The International Journal of Human Rights, 23*, 596–614. https://doi.org/10.1080/13642987.2018.1541890

Varadan, S. (2019). The principle of evolving capacities under the UN Convention on the rights of the child. *The International Journal of Children's Rights, 27*(2), 306–338. https://doi.org/10.1163/15718182-02702006

Vogelstein, R. (2013). *Ending Child Marriage.* Council on Foreign Relations Press. http://www.cfr.org/children/ending-child-marriage/p30734

Volpp, L. (2000). Blaming culture for bad behavior. *Yale Journal of Law & the Humanities, 12*, 89–116.

Warming, H. (2016). Playing with socially constructed identity positions: Accessing and reconstructing children's perspectives and positions through ethnographic fieldwork and creative workshops. In F. Esser, M. S. Baader, T. Betz, & B. Hungerland (Eds.), *Reconceptualising Agency and Childhood: New perspectives in Childhood Studies* (pp. 119–132). London; New York, NY: Routledge.

Chapter 7

Conclusions

The previous chapters have guided you through the international discourse, national debates, judicial practices, local sentiments, and individual cases concerning child marriage in Indonesia. In this conclusion, we zoom out to see what this case study means for the practices of international human rights. I suggest we move back from Indonesia to Amsterdam and reflect on the story at the event held by Girls Advocacy Alliance, introduced at the very beginning of this book. When they were confronted by my question about marrying children's agency, their answer was to fight to change the local communities' customs and traditions so that girls would not want to get married. I wonder: Who, then, are these activists fighting? While they intend to support girls' choices, well-being, and rights, it seems that they could end up fighting against these very goals. The logic behind their approach, they explained, is that *all* child marriages (regardless of the presence of 'consent') are wrong since marriage means the end of formal education. However, this is not necessarily the case. Some of my informants in Bali did continue their education while being married. However, the Girls Advocacy Alliance seemed unwilling to explore the varied meanings and possibilities of 'marriage*s*' while being determined to undertake the massive task of changing the 'customs and traditions' of local communities on the African continent.

As this book has demonstrated, the international child marriage framework influences both transnational and national policies and programmes. Human rights advocates, such as the Girls Advocacy Alliance, work within this established framework. In this sense, human rights law and discourse *produce* particular practices. They provide specific rules and directions that CSOs and policymakers follow. However, these laws and discourses are *a product* of specific ways of thinking about development, progress, and freedom. This book explored the puzzle of 'agency' within this framework and tried to understand what choice means for international organizations and children themselves. It offers a perspective and creates space for discussions about this uncomfortable topic.

DOI: 10.4324/9781003184546-7

7.1. Multiple normative frameworks that relate to the practice of child marriage

To understand the meaning of choice, one must understand the influences of structures, since children's agency is intimately entangled in social and cultural institutions and norms at different levels of society. To do so, I analyzed multiple normative frameworks that child marriage practices inform and within which they are treated.

The first questions concerned the global discourse on child marriage and the influences of the international normative framework. By studying child marriage as a discursive practice, the analysis revealed that the framework had been constructed based on two assumptions: 1) What it means to be a 'child' and 2) the modern ideals of marriage (see Chapter 2). By building on these modern assumptions, the framework tends to *traditionalize* the problems. It dismisses what international institutions consider 'traditions' of 'the South' without seriously trying to investigate them. Such a process of international standard making, ignoring the diverse meanings of 'child' and 'marriage', seems to stem from a lack of dialogue, becoming 'monological'.

The influential international framework informs the state legal system since states need to adjust their legal framework once they subscribe to the international agenda. This book considered law-making and implementation in Indonesia and revealed the dilemmas and compromises in legal practice around child marriage. Law-making in family law involves conflicts between liberal and conservative ideas on marriage, family, and sexuality. The tension between these ideas was at the heart of a series of recent judicial reviews of the 1974 Marriage Law at the Constitutional Court. Following the court's decision in 2019, the Indonesian parliament has set 19 as the new minimum marital age for both women and men. While marital age laws will change, the local and religious concerns will challenge their implementation. To give an indication about the scope of such challenges, about one million marriages a year that have been legally concluded in Indonesia would be illegal once the new law comes into force.[1]

Local state legal agents, charged with implementation, deal with a complex set of normative frameworks (i.e., religious, *adat*, and state law). Our study in West Java showed that (1) judges use their discretion to achieve compromises between state laws and local norms and (2) village bureaucrats use their unofficial support system to solve legal issues following their customary and religious norms (see Chapter 3). Both in West Java and Bali, courts almost always grant marriage dispensations, and the decisions are similarly reasoned and justified, although using different (state) laws and terms tailored to each religious

1 The number is an estimate, calculated based on the total number of annual female adolescent marriages (15–19 years old) (Badan Pusat Statistik (BPS) 2016: 42).

background. For instance, while in West Java judges use the Islamic concept of '*kemaslahatan*' (common good) to explain the negative consequences of not granting dispensations, in Bali judges similarly justify their decisions by using the words 'negative impact'.

The comparison between West Java and Bali indicates that religion and kinship custom are the main explanatory factors for different motivations and impacts of child marriage. For instance, in West Java with mainly Muslim populations, the most urgent reason to marry is to avoid *zinah* (pre-marital sexual intercourse), while in Bali, pre-marital sexual intercourse is somewhat accepted and considered 'common'. And in the Balinese patrilineal kinship system, it is crucial to marry before prospective brides give birth, as newborns join their fathers' lineage. But such motivation and narratives are absent in West Java. What both areas see in common is that, in cases dealing with teenage sexuality in Indonesia, families, *adat* authorities, and state agents collaborate to find a way to maintain a moral and social order. The pressure to do so is especially strong when unmarried teenagers are pregnant. This way of dealing with sexuality results in mid-teenagers' marriage, which international institutions call 'child marriage'.

In Bali specifically, when marriage dispensation cannot provide a solution to extra-marital pregnancies, girls' families sometimes prosecute the boy for sexual intercourse. These cases indicated that the families and judges use laws to re-establish the moral order that they feel has been disturbed, often by punishing boys for pre-marital sexual intercourse. The overall analysis of both marriage dispensation cases and sex crimes suggests that judges take a pragmatic moral approach to using law to 'restore harmony and peace in the community'.

Both at the national and local levels, the process of law-making and implementation is the outcome of continuous struggles with diverse norms on marriage, family, and adolescent sexuality, in a rapidly modernizing Indonesian society. At another level, individuals also deal with the increasingly diverse normative frameworks, stemming from their various social relationships (i.e., 'reference networks'; see Chapter 5). In the analysis of individual cases of children who marry under the age of 18 in Bali, I explored the social and societal contexts in which they decide to marry. The findings showed that while international human rights institutions consider child marriage a *problem* and tend to view those who practice it as 'traditional' (i.e., insufficiently modern), for these young people 'child marriage' is actually a *solution* to navigating the modern world.

With increased mobility and educational opportunities, lifestyle norms and choices have generally diversified. Adolescents now live with different simultaneous normative frameworks, more so than their parents did. While adolescents today tend to marry later and have 'permissive' attitudes and behaviour towards sexual relationships before marriage, they are also constrained by their religious norms of piety. For example, a remark by one of the teenage girls in Bali illustrates this tension:

> *This friend of mine who got pregnant used to go home early morning, drunk, and in open clothes. Even more open than people in the West. [...] In the West they can be open about relationships between boys and girls, but here rumour can spread and taint a good name of the family.*

For adolescents caught in between ideas of sexual morality and marriage, they manage their romantic and sexual relationships by balancing modern demands within customary normative systems. 'Child marriage' is often a way to bridge the normative gap. This highlights the discourse's paradox of modernity. While international human rights actors advocate eliminating child marriage to achieve modernity's ideals, 'child marriage' is a response to modern social conditions (see Chapter 5).

Finally, case studies of 'child marriage' from my fieldwork in Bali explain how some children (particularly in their mid- to late teens) exercise their agency and capacity in deciding to marry. The case studies contrast the common image of child marriage as forced with many cases where teenagers decide to marry. The careful examination of their decision-making process shows that these teenagers can and do decide to marry, at times under relational and situational constraints.

Relational constraints are the power dynamics among children, their parents, their extended family, and local leaders. Swasti, who became pregnant at 15, felt she had to marry because of the strong social norms in her rural village. She and her family would have lost the crucial part of their relational and social life in the village if she had given birth outside of wedlock. Situational constraints are the options children had at the time of decision-making. For instance, Ayu, who married through run-away marriage, lived in a 'difficult situation' with poverty and no education. However, while the 'difficult situation' requires special attention, it is also important to acknowledge the possibility of exercising agency under such conditions. Ayu, despite the situational constraints, was proactive in deciding to marry young. "*I am more free when I am married – I do not have to work and raise money so I can be lazy at home*". She seemed to be aware of her life options and chose what she felt was her best option, even though her expectations of married life were later proven wrong.

The analysis of the general international children's rights framework showed that the current child marriage framework does not necessarily reflect children's rights as laid down in international instruments such as children's rights conventions (CRC and ACRWC). If one asks when policies and laws should intervene in children's decisions, the process of decision-making needs to be carefully assessed. This assessment should consider both how much children participate in the decision-making process and on how they make the decisions (i.e., the relational and situational constraints).

It is illuminating to see how these normative frameworks at international, national, provincial, local, and individual levels relate to each other. Relevant theories include the *socialization* of human rights norms (Ropp and Sikkink

1999) and the *vernacularization* of human rights (Merry 2006). These are what Engel (2012) calls the "vertical model" of studying rights consciousness. He points out some potential problems with the vertical model. He proposes combining it with the "horizontal perspective", "to ascertain what norms, practices, and beliefs prevail within carious social fields where ordinary people engage in everyday interactions" (Ibid). He argues that only with that combination can researchers gain some understanding of human rights projects' successes and failures in broader social contexts (Ibid).

My analysis of the multiple normative frameworks provided both the "vertical" and "horizontal" perspectives. The vertical perspective involved "tracing the flow of legal forms and practices from prestigious and authoritative centres of cultural production to local settings" (Ibid). It revealed the influences of international human rights institutions (i.e., law and discourse) and how these transnational norms may be adopted at the national level. The horizontal perspective provided perhaps the most significant findings of this study, revealing the gap between the rights that liberal legalism endorses (i.e., what international human rights aim to achieve) and the rights of the relational self (i.e., relating to other people). I will come back to this issue in Section 7.4.

7.2. Multi-layered reasons why children marry

Overall, the analysis and discussions throughout the chapters reveal the multi-layered reasons why children marry. Structural explanations (e.g., lack of opportunities and oppressive social structures) are important but not exhaustive explanations. Organizations that work within the international child marriage framework tend to focus exclusively on these structural reasons and are inattentive to the other subjective reasons why children marry. In contrast to structural constraints that individuals cannot control, subjective reasons are those an individual feels and describes.

By exploring the subjective reasons by listening to children's perspectives, this book showed that many of them decide to marry for love, desire, to belong to the community, and for new opportunities and hopes. These subjective reasons for why children marry have been largely absent from the human rights discourse because the structural reasons silence them.

Acknowledging children's agency to marry highlights that the current child marriage framework is constructed on a partial understanding of why they marry. For instance, adolescents' sexuality is missing, which is at the heart of child marriage. Social (un)acceptance of pre-marital sexual intercourse and (un) availability of tools for reproductive health are the core factors for why teenagers marry in Indonesia. Given that many adolescents worldwide live in societies where pre-marital sexual and romantic relationships are a taboo and even a crime, marriage is sometimes a way to have 'legitimate' sex, to gain sexual autonomy and moral legitimacy. In this sense, the new minimum age for marriage in Indonesia raises a serious question concerning adolescents' sexuality and age of consent (i.e., to have sexual intercourse), which was completely absent in the debates about the new law.

The control (or lack thereof) of teenagers' sexual behaviour is a common concern across countries. Even within the Western world, parents deal differently with their children's sexuality. Schalet (2011) demonstrates how American parents struggle to control their children's sexual behaviour, while Dutch parents manage it by often permitting young couples to sleep together and providing them with contraceptives. Desiring bodies and minds are universal and hard to rationalize. Conceptualizing agency as making rational decisions thus seems to leave little space for children's sexual autonomy. The question about children's sexual autonomy leads further to discussing children's consent to sexual intercourse and state regulations on this issue, which needs further exploration.

Just as norms around sexuality differ, the meanings and norms around marriage also differ in each country and society and for each individual. While marriage tends to be seen as a vehicle for individual fulfilment, the previous chapters showed that marriage in Indonesia often involves much more collective processes and meanings. These divergences in marriage and sexuality illuminate that when the human rights framework constructs an overall framework of 'child marriage', the consequences of this framework differ in each society.

This point about marriage's diverse meanings and consequences means that the strict and rigid child marriage framework to ban *all* marriages under the age of *18* is not an effective approach. In other words, legislation on the minimum age of marriage is *not* the most appropriate way to decrease the incidence of child marriage, neither to fully realize children's rights. It is understandable why this abolitionist approach is appealing for advocates since they focus on the negative consequences of child marriage for girls, as presented in their reports and campaigns. These consequences include reduced educational opportunities, reproductive health hazards (e.g., difficult deliveries, a higher risk of HIV/AIDS, and premature babies with disabilities), and intergenerational poverty. However, these consequences are mainly a discourse within the international agenda for women's rights and cannot be taken for granted. These discussions are limited because the consequences are not always well supported by evidence, and the causal relationship between child marriage and these consequences is often reversed. For example, child marriage can be a consequence of a lack of educational opportunities.

Overall, the monolithic framework based on a partial understanding of why children marry further hinders understanding the core problem. It does so by *traditionalizing* the problem: Turning a global social challenge (teenage pregnancy) into a cultural phenomenon ('harmful traditional practice') that is alien to the West or the upper-middle-class in the South. The label 'harmful traditional practice' obscures the social reality and prevents policy efforts from being effective. The focus on 'banning' or 'eradicating child marriage' will not solve the underlying social problems, such as lack of tools and knowledge about reproductive health. The data has proved that child marriage is often a symptom of unplanned pregnancies outside of wedlock, and therefore policies and programmes should be redirected to address this root cause.

7.3. Rethinking agency in international human rights

How do these answers to questions about child marriage relate to critical and anthropological studies on human rights? They clarify the position of agency, structure, tradition, and modernity in international human rights. International institutions such as the CEDAW committee typically talk about culture as a barrier to progress, based on their understanding of culture as a static tradition (Merry 2003). Under the label of 'harmful traditional practice', child marriage is paired with female genital mutilation, *sati* in India (the immolation of a widow), female abortion and infanticide due to son preferences, polygamy, seclusion and veiling, and food taboos for women (Ibid: 63).

However, this label is misleading. Under a relational understanding, agency is an ability to choose by making internal reconciliations with structure (i.e., patterned arrangements that influence or limit available choices). This is the difficult and significant boundary between consent and coercion. Importantly, the structure that actors interact with is not the essentialized 'culture' or 'tradition' but persons with whom they are in relationships. Structures do not disappear but are replaced by self-chosen ones (Bauman 2000: 8). Structures are essentially various relationships and social connections that an individual forms, which exist in any society regardless of it being 'traditional' or 'modern'. Child marriage occasionally occurs in "modern" social conditions (i.e., increased educational opportunities and mobility) to accommodate modern needs within the children's structure.

In light of this understanding of structure, what can be labelled as 'culture', 'tradition', or 'custom' is an essential part of people's lives. Therefore, it is not an obstacle to realizing human rights. On the contrary, it is an essential tool for realizing them. In legally pluralistic contexts, customary and religious laws can help external supporters of human rights understand what rights mean for their beneficiaries, and support these rights-holders in acquiring *their* rights. Such an approach also enables redirecting the current human rights framework to pay more attention to the rights of the 'relational self' (see previous chapters), which sometimes are in conflict with the liberal understanding of 'individual rights'. The protection of individual rights does not necessarily lead to the protection of the rights of the relational self (i.e., belonging to a community), and the latter often stay unnoticed within the current approach to protecting human rights.

Why do relational self rights stay unnoticed alongside modern individual rights? The reason is that the child marriage framework (and the human rights framework in general) is constructed on too narrow a vision of human agency.

As human rights are premised on the idea that human nature is individual and self-sustaining (Santos 2015: 7), they tend to focus on 'full-autonomy' (i.e., decision-making completely independent from social relationships and structures) in 'non-traditional' societies. This narrow interpretation of agency consequently produces a blind spot: Failing to respect and promote the agency of all, regardless of gender, race, religion, and age.

Just as a homogeneous and static image of the "Third World Woman" is useful for Western feminists to motivate Western support (MacDonald 2016; Mohanty 1984; Mustonen 2017), the stereotypical image of the 'child bride' in "the Third World" is appealing. The problem is that these images turn subjective beings into an 'object', producing the "third world difference" (Ibid). As the sex trafficking analysis suggests, when international institutions do not fully accommodate agency and consent, their interventions become "paternalistic control in the name of humanitarianism" (Merry and Ramachandran 2017: 255).

The increasing paternalistic control links to a "determining silence" (White 2002). White refers to the silence on the topic of race in development policies, demonstrating a neoliberal understanding of development reliant on ideas of modernity (MacDonald 2016: 6). The international human rights framework is similarly 'silent' on certain topics, informed by implicit assumptions about gender, race, and 'progress'.

International children's rights are also based on implicit assumptions about childhood and developmental psychology (see Chapters 2 and 6). While the CRC increasingly acknowledges the need to respect children's agency and stimulate their participation in decision-making, policies concerning children still tend to rely on a protectionist approach. As studies on child labour and child soldiers also indicate,[2] some of the international policies concerning children's rights currently fail to walk the thin line between the empowerment and protection of children. The international children's rights scheme tends to overshadow a child's agency when their decision *seems wrong*, from the perspective of a specific socio-economical and socio-cultural background typical in the West. One difficult question is when the law should intervene in individuals' (particularly children's) autonomous decisions, which the following section will partially explore.

7.4. Epistemologies of 'Human Rights' and functions of 'human rights'

Considering the blind spot on agency, the universality of international human rights is in a precarious position. While I do not reject the fundamental

2 See Bodineau (2014); Hanson, Volonakis, and Al-Rozzi (2015); Nieuwenhuys (1996); Saadi (2012); Van Daalen and Mabillard (2018).

normative principle that all human beings should enjoy basic human rights, the assumed universality of human rights can be a double-edged sword. Focusing too much on the means (a strict and narrow framing of human agency) fails to achieve the ends (protecting the human agency of *all* human beings).

Macdonald (2013: 26) argues that the human rights idea is flawed not because of its inherent characteristics but because of how proponents have used it. This book has shown that advocates interpret and use human rights regarding child marriage in a dogmatic, unilateral, and simplistic vision of how things should change. However, this does not mean that the ideas and goals themselves should change. Human rights can focus on the ultimate goal without being interventionist (Ignatieff 2003; the "minimalist" approach to human rights) by critically assessing how they function in practice and allowing for differentiation.

Overcoming the human rights framework's blind spot then requires a twofold shift: First, an epistemological shift to deconstruct the dominant narrative and engage with 'other' forms of knowledge, second, a procedural shift to include multi-cultural dialogues. For human rights to be truly universal, it needs a relativistic twist, not as tolerance without limits ('anything goes') but as an invitation to sufficiently respect differences and carefully access the need for tolerance and differentiation. This assessment cannot be done without considering how human rights operate in practice, in contrast to human rights on paper or as "idolatry" (Ignatieff 2003). Hopgood (2017: 259) usefully distinguishes between "Human Rights" as "universal, global and monotheistic in voice" and "human rights" as "bottom-up, interpretive and flexible in the hands of local people". In this sense, the debates on universalism and relativism in *Human Rights* are in serious need of the anthropology of *human rights*.

The anthropology of human rights enables an understanding of human rights' functions in practice, critical to understanding when laws should intervene. When does a behaviour become so detrimental to individuals and societies that laws (including human rights laws) need to regulate it? The rationale behind child marriage bans is that this behaviour is so harmful that it needs to be eradicated by all means, including laws.

Such strict rules and rights frames can have several functions. First, they can have a symbolic value by setting a normative standard for citizens. They can also have an external value by signalling a state's compliance and commitment to international goals, such as the Sustainable Development Goals. Second, laws can create an "enabling environment" (Shell-Duncan et al. 2013) for those who have fought or wish to fight against specific behaviour. Shell-Duncan et al. (Ibid) demonstrate that where FGM is being contested, legislation gave CSOs and individuals greater leverage in favouring abandonment. State legislation can also be invasive. For instance, in the fight against gender violence, state courts and legal processes can reinforce specific cultural images of femininity and masculinity (Merry 1997). On some occasions, resorting to trials in state courts can result in the loss of communal support (Strathern 2004).

One important question is whether laws act as a resource or constraint. While Merry (1997: 270) suggests that rights *generally* act as a resource, in the case of child marriage, the international framework is currently is more constraining rather than liberating. Such a framework limits its full effectiveness and emancipatory power. Other human rights issues also require a serious inquiry into and critical reflection on the functions of the propagated rights from the viewpoint of the rights-holders.

7.5. Towards an empowerment approach: Policy recommendations

If the child marriage framework remains monological and categorical, it also fails to incorporate the diverse views on what a child means. This lapse results in a protectionist approach of liberal paternalism that misdirects policy designs. Moving away from such a protectionist approach is not a straightforward journey. The child marriage framework faces a devilish dilemma between the protection and empowerment of children. The current framework focuses too much on protection, banning all child marriage regardless of the child's consent. We should also recognize that this approach unwillingly sacrifices empowerment by limiting children's freedom to marry that they could be exercising.

This dilemma goes beyond child marriage. For instance, imagine you have a teenage daughter who goes out frequently with her new boyfriend. One day, she is invited to his house for dinner, and his parent calls you and asks if you agree with her staying overnight. On the one hand, you want to give her freedom and to trust her and do not want to be seen as paternalistic or conservative. On the other hand, you worry about her. Will she be alright, does she know enough, is he the right kind of boy for her, and isn't she too young? When you want to protect her, sometimes you limit the freedom she could enjoy.

Balancing this dilemma is difficult and uncomfortable. Life is easier when things are binary, but the reality is often non-binary. Like the parent who wanders the thin line between giving and limiting their daughter's freedom, the discussions and policies on child marriage should also strive to balance protection and empowerment. The current protection-focused approach should focus more on empowerment to achieve human rights and development goals. Towards this end, it is crucial to know when rights act as a resource and a constraint. Both human rights scholars and practitioners should acknowledge that the child marriage framework could function in both ways. Therefore, they should continue to ask whether the child marriage framework and programmes function as a resource or constraint towards local rights-holders.

That concludes my theoretical considerations, which illuminate points of practical relevance. For instance, what does the empowerment-focused approach mean in a more concrete sense? First, it involves more collaborative and informed decision-making. Policies for child marriage should be designed to encourage children's participation in and collaboration with adults in decision-making, where they are informed of their decision's consequences. CSO programmes can better educate children to allow them to make more informed life decisions. That education includes focusing on what marriage would mean in their life, and how to manage their romantic and sexual lives in a way that does not unintentionally limit their choices and opportunities.

Second, empowerment means providing resilience-based support for married children. Advocacy for child marriage should invest in stimulating children's resilience towards improving their life after marriage. For instance, most schools in Indonesia do not accept married or pregnant students. One of the main reasons for campaigns against child marriage is that it deprives children of educational opportunities. Changes could occur so that married children can continue their education. Post-marital support includes vocational training, reproductive health support, and whatever else helps them lead the kind of lives they want.

On the last note, the empowerment-focused approach should go hand in hand with the community-based approach, which focuses on dialogues and awareness interventions with community leaders, parents, and peer groups.[3] In a society where children are actually 'forced' to marry, structural changes are necessary to foster children's choices. Therefore, I propose the empowerment-focused approach not as the sole approach to go forward but as a very important additional one. Only with such an approach can children, both married and not married, lead the lives they wish to live.

Bibliography

Badan Pusat Statistik (BPS). (2016). *Kemajuan yang Tertunda: Analisis Data Perkawinan Usia Anak di Indonesia*. Jakarta, Indonesia: BPS.

Bauman, Z. (2000). *Liquid Modernity*. Cambridge, UK; Malden, MA: Polity.

Bodineau, S. (2014). Vulnerability and agency: Figures of child soldiers within the narratives of child protection practitioners in the democratic republic of Congo. *Autrepart, 72*(4), 111–128.

Engel, D. M. (2012). Vertical and horizontal perspectives on rights consciousness. *Indiana Journal of Global Legal Studies, 19*(2), 423–455.

Freccero, J., & Whiting, A. (2018). *Toward An End to Child Marriage: Lessons from Research and Practice in Development and Humanitarian Sectors*.

Hanson, K., Volonakis, D., & Al-Rozzi, M. (2015). Child labour, working children and children's rights. In W. Vandenhole, E. Desmet, D. Reynaert, & S. Lembrechts (Eds.), *Routledge International Handbook of Children's Rights Studies*. New York, NY: Routledge.

3 For community-based approach, see for instance: (Freccero and Whiting 2018; Jones et al. 2015; Karolus et al. 2019).

Hopgood, S. (2017). Modernity at the cutting edge: Human rights meets FGM. In M. N. Barnett (Ed.), *Paternalism Beyond Borders* (pp. 256–291). Cambridge, UK: Cambridge University Press. https://doi.org/10.1017/9781316799956.009

Ignatieff, M. (2003). *Human Rights as Politics and Idolatry* (A. Gutmann, Ed.). Princeton, NJ: Princeton University Press.

Jones, N., Tefera, B., Presler-Marshall, E., Gupta, T., Emirie, G., Gebre, B., & Berhanu, K. (2015). *The Power of Dialogue: The Role of Community Awareness Interventions in Ending Child Marriage in Amhara, Ethiopia.*

Karolus, M. L., Dewi, S. C., & Partini (2019). "Listen, I want to tell a story": Peer group as a mean to prevent child marriage in Yogyakarta. In M. Grijns, H. Horii, S. Irianto, & P. Saptandari (Eds.), *Marrying Young in Indonesia: Voices, Laws and Practices* (pp. 263–286). Jakarta, Indonesia: Yayasan Pustaka Obor Indonesia.

MacDonald, K. (2016). Calls for educating girls in the third world: Futurity, girls and the 'Third world woman.' *Gender, Place & Culture, 23*(1), 1–17. https://doi.org/10.1080/0966369X.2014.991699

Macdonald, R. (2013). Pluralistic human rights? Universal human wrongs? In R. Provost & C. Sheppard (Eds.), *Dialogues on Human Rights and Legal Pluralism* (pp. 15–36). Dordrecht; Heidelberg; New York; London: Springer.

Merry, S. E. (1997). Global human rights and local social movements in a legally plural world. *Canadian Journal of Law and Society, 12*, 247–272.

Merry, S. E. (2003). Human rights law and the demonization of culture (and anthropology along the way). *PoLAR: Political and Legal Anthropology Review, 26*(1), 55–76. https://doi.org/10.1525/pol.2003.26.1.55

Merry, S. E. (2006). *Human Rights and Gender Violence Translating International Law into Local Justice*. Chicago, IL: University of Chicago Press.

Merry, S. E., & Ramachandran, V. (2017). The limits of consent: Sex trafficking and the problem of international paternalism. In M. N. Barnett (Ed.), *Paternalism Beyond Borders* (pp. 224–255). Cambridge, UK: Cambridge University Press. https://doi.org/10.1017/9781316799956.009

Mohanty, C. T. (1984). Under western eyes: Feminist scholarship and colonial discourses. *Boundary 2, 12/13*, 333–358. https://doi.org/10.2307/302821

Mustonen, L. (2017). Is it time for Finnish celebrities to save the black girls of a "developing country"? *Allegra Lab: Anthropology, Law, Art & World*. http://allegralaboratory.net/finnish-celebrities-save-the-black-girls-of-a-developing-country/

Nieuwenhuys, O. (1996). The paradox of child labor and anthropology. *Annual Review of Anthropology, 25*(1), 237–251. https://doi.org/10.1146/annurev.anthro.25.1.237

Ropp, S. C., & Sikkink, K. (1999). *The Power of Human Rights: International Norms and Domestic Change* (T. Risse, Ed.). Cambridge, UK: Cambridge University Press.

Saadi, I. (2012). Children's rights as "work in progress": The conceptual and practical contributions of working children's movements. In M. Liebel (Ed.), *Children's Rights from Below: Cross-Cultural Perspectives* (pp. 143–161). Basingstoke, UK: Palgrave Macmillan.

Santos, B. de S. (2015). *If God Were a Human Rights Activist*. Stanford, CA: Stanford University Press.

Schalet, T. A. (2011). *Not Under My Roof: Parents, Teens, and the Culture of Sex*. Chicago; London: University of Chicago Press.

Shell-Duncan, B., Hernlund, Y., Wander, K., & Moreau, A. (2013). Legislating change? Responses to criminalizing female genital cutting in Senegal. *Law & Society Review, 47*(4), 803–835. https://doi.org/10.1111/lasr.12044

Strathern, M. (2004). Losing (out on) intellectual resources. In A. Pottage & M. Mundy (Eds.), *Law, Anthropology, and the Constitution of the Social: Making Persons and Things* (pp. 201–233). Cambridge; New York: Cambridge University Press.

Van Daalen, E., & Mabillard, N. (2018). Human rights in translation: Bolivia's law 548, working children's movements, and the global child labour regime. *The International Journal of Human Rights, 23*(4), 596–614. https://doi.org/10.1080/13642987.2018.1541890

White, S. C. (2002). Thinking race, thinking development. *Third World Quarterly, 23*(3), 407–419.

Appendices

List of original articles

- Chapter 2: A blind spot in international human rights framework: a space between tradition and modernity within the child marriage discourse, The International Journal of Human Rights 24(8), pp.1057-1079. Copyright © 2020 Taylor & Francis. DOI: 10.1080/13642987.2019.1690468
- Chapter 3: GRIJNS, M., & HORII, H. (2018). Child Marriage in a Village in West Java (Indonesia): Compromises between Legal Obligations and Religious Concerns. Asian Journal of Law and Society, 5(2), pp.453-466. Copyright © 2018 Cambridge University Press. DOI: 10.1017/als.2018.9.
- Chapter 4: Pluralistic legal system, pluralistic human rights?: teenage pregnancy, child marriage and legal institutions in Bali, The Journal of Legal Pluralism and Unofficial Law 51(3), pp.292-319, Copyright © 2019 Taylor & Francis. DOI: 10.1080/07329113.2019.1683429.
- Chapter 5: Child Marriage as a 'Solution' to Modern Youth in Bali, Progress in Development Studies 20(4), pp.282-295. Copyright © 2021 SAGE. DOI: 10.1177/1464993420977793.

	Case	Region	Decision	Applicant	Wife candidate	Husband candidate
A	7/Pdt.P/2016/ PN/Bli	Bangli	granted	fathers of the candidates	Brahmana 19-year-old Hindu farmer	Sudra 18-year-old Hindu private employee
B	13/Pdt.P/2016/ PN.Bli	Bangli	granted	fathers of the candidates	Sudra 18-year-old Hindu farmer	Sudra 18-year-old Hindu farmer
C	60/Pdt.P/2016/ PN.Bli	Bangli	granted	father of the wife candidate	Sudra 14-year-old	Sudra 20-year-old

Reasons that the judges gave	*State Law cited*	*Adat/religious Law cited*
As the girl is pregnant, if she does not immediately marry, there will be a situation of *cuntake/leteh* according to *adat* and religion. *Adat* law does not set a certain age limitation on marriage, and it allows the marriage of children. This is because in *adat* law, marriage is not merely the union of both individuals but also the union of two families (*keluarge kerabat*). An underage marriage or a marriage of children is not a problem in *adat* law because the families will guide the wife and husband, so *adat* law does not prohibit the marriage of children. The minimum age limit provisions in A7(1) mean that married persons are expected to have maturity, mental maturity, and adequate physical strength. Due to the circumstances of a six-month-long pregnancy, it is appropriate to grant marriage dispensations. The decision also does not conflict with the rules, legislation, or *adat* law in force in the applicants' place of residence.	A6, A7, A47, A50 of Marriage Law 1974 A34 A35 of Law No.23 2006 juncto Law No.24 2013 about Population Administration	*Adat* law does not set an age limit for marriage. In *adat* law, marriage is between two families.
As the girl is pregnant, if she does not immediately marry, there will be a situation of *cuntake/leteh/kotor* according to *adat* and religion. After the discussion between the two families, they planned the marriage. There was no barrier to conducting the marriage either in terms of kinship or *adat* relationships. There is no prohibition against conducting marriage under Balinese *Adat* Law and Hinduism. If the marriage dispensation is not granted, there will be unfavourable negative impacts on both parties, so the judge believes that the best legal solution is to provide a marriage dispensation. Granting marriage dispensations has been reasoned and is not against state law.	A7 Marriage Law 1974	There is no prohibition on conducting marriages under Balinese *Adat* Law and Hinduism
They have been in *pacaran* for three months, and the relationship went over the limit (*hubungan tersebut melewati batas*). The wedding is already planned for 28th October. The girl is eight weeks pregnant. The man is ready to be responsible for his actions, and the marriage must be carried out immediately so that their child has a clear status.	A7 Marriage Law 1974	

(*Continued*)

(*Continued*)

	Case	*Region*	*Decision*	*Applicant*	*Wife candidate*	*Husband candidate*
D	104/ Pdt.P/2016/ PN Srp	Semarapura	granted	mother of the wife candidate	Sudra 14 years old at the time of marriage (2013)	Sudra
E	28/Pdt.P/2016/ PN.Srp	Semarapura	granted	mother of the husband candidate	Sudra 17 years old at the time of marriage (2014)	Sudra 17 years old at the time of marriage (2014)

Reasons that the judges gave	State Law cited	Adat/religious Law cited
As a result of a free relationship (*akibat pergaulannya yang begitu bebas*), the girl became pregnant. They already married in July 2013 and have a child without a birth certificate. When they married, the girl was underage. To now seek a marriage certificate (*akta perkawinan*), they must obtain permission from the Court. Underage marriage is strongly discouraged as it risks the reproductive health of women who are unprepared and still psychologically unstable. Thus, it should not be too easy to grant dispensations for underage marriages if there are no logical reasons for the children's interest. Their marriage (pregnancy) was caused by their social freedom and lack of supervision from parents, so the future of the newborn baby requires a complete family consisting of a father and a mother to raise, care for, and devote love to the baby's growth. Child protection aims to guarantee the fulfilment of children's rights to live, grow, develop, and participate optimally in accordance with human dignity and values, and to be protected from violence and discrimination. Their marriage was a lawful marriage carried out by the Hindu religion, so it has fulfilled the provisions of A2(1) of the Marriage Law.	A2(1) A6 A7 Marriage Law 1974 A3 Law No. 23 of 2002 on Child Protection	
As a result of a lack of supervision by the parents, the girl and the boy had a free and spouse-like relationship (*hubungan layaknya suami istri*), and the girl became pregnant. When the baby was born (December 2015) the boy was still underage (under 19), so they needed permission from the court to marry. They were married in October 2014. At that time they were both 17 years old. As they obtained their parents' permission for the marriage, and as their marriage was based on mutual love and not coercion, the marriage was lawful.	A2(1) A6 A7 Marriage Law 1974 A34(1) Law No.23 2006aboutMarriage Administration of the Population	

(*Continued*)

(*Continued*)

	Case	*Region*	*Decision*	*Applicant*	*Wife candidate*	*Husband candidate*
F	20/Pdt.P/2017/ PN Srp	Semarapura	granted	parents of the husband candidate	Sudra 18 years old at the time of marriage (2012)	Sudra 19 years old at the time of marriage (2012)

Reasons that the judges gave	*State Law cited*	Adat/*religious Law cited*
As a result of a lack of supervision by the parents, they had a free relationship (*akibat pergaulannya yang bebas*), whereby the girl got pregnant. They had an *adat* marriage in July 2012 and had a baby. As underage marriage is strongly discouraged as it risks the reproductive health of women who are unprepared and still psychologically unstable. Thus, it should not be too easy to grant dispensations to underage marriages if there are no logical reasons for the children's interest. Their marriage (pregnancy) was caused by their social freedom and lack of supervision from their parents, so the future of their newborn baby requires a complete family consisting of a father and a mother to raise, care for, and devote love towards the baby's growth. Child protection aims to guarantee the fulfilment of children's rights to live, grow, develop, and participate optimally in accordance with human dignity and values, and to be protected from violence and discrimination. Their marriage was a lawful marriage carried out by the Hindu religion, so it has fulfilled the provisions of A2(1) of the Marriage Law.	A2(1) A6 A7 Marriage Law 1974 A3 Law No. 23 of 2002 on Child Protection	

(*Continued*)

(*Continued*)

	Case	*Region*	*Decision*	*Applicant*	*Wife candidate*	*Husband candidate*
G	84/Pdt.P/2017/ PN Srp	Semarapura	granted	parents of the husband candidate	Sudra 16 years old at the time of marriage (2015)	Sudra 16 years old at the time of marriage (2015)
H	47/Pdt.P/2016/ PN.Srp	Semarapura	granted	parents of the husband candidate	Sudra Was 15 years old at the time of marriage and was still in school (2013)	Ksatria Was 15 years old and still in school at the time of marriage (2013)

Reasons that the judges gave	*State Law cited*	Adat/*religious Law cited*
As a result of the lack of supervision by the parents, they had a free relationship (*akibat pergaulannya yang bebas*), whereby the girl became pregnant. They had an *adat* marriage in 2015. Underage marriage is strongly discouraged as it risks the reproductive health of women who are unprepared and still psychologically unstable. Thus, it should not be too easy to grant dispensations to underage marriages if there are no logical reasons for the children's interest. Their marriage (pregnancy) was caused by their social freedom and lack of supervision by the parents, so the future of the newborn baby requires a complete family consisting of a father and a mother to raise, care for, and devote love towards the baby's growth. Child protection aims to guarantee the fulfilment of children's rights to live, grow, develop, and participate optimally in accordance with human dignity and values, and to be protected from violence and discrimination. Their marriage was a lawful marriage carried out by the Hindu religion, so it has fulfilled the provisions of A2(1) of the Marriage Law.	A2(1) A6 A7 Marriage Law 1974 A3 Law No. 23 of 2002 on Child Protection	
Their marriage was conducted according to Hinduism and *adat*, so it is legal (*sah*). According to the Decisions (*Keputusan-keputusan dan Ketetapan-ketetapan*) of the Parisada Hindu Dharma (PHDI Kabupaten Badung, 1986), the validity of a Hindu marriage is determined by the presence of *panyangaskara* with *bhuta* witnesses and *penyaksi* (witness) from *prajuru adat* (*adat* leader) as elements from *manusa saksi*. This is what is often referred to as *tri upasaksi* in the marriage ceremony (*samskara wiwaha*);	A2(1) A6 A7 A8 A9 Marriage Law 1974 A330 Civil Code (KUHPerdata) A56(2) Law No.23 2006 juncto Law No.24 2013	Decisions (*Keputusan-keputusan dan Ketetapan-ketetapan*) of the Parisada Hindu Dharma (PHDI Kabupaten Badung, 1986)

	Case	Decision	Defendant	Victim	Pacaran
A	67/Pid.Sus/2013/ PN.Dps.	six months imprisonment with one year of probation	18-year-old boy Hindu high school student	18-year-old high school student	yes
B	1/Pid.Sus. Anak/2015/ PN Dps	one year of imprisonment and three months of vocational training	16-year-old boy Islam private working Junior high school graduate	13-year-old (the act started when she was 9 years old)	no
C	2/Pid.Sus. Anak/2015/ PN Dps	one year of imprisonment and three months of vocational training	17-year-and-9 month-old boy Hindu no job elementary school graduate	13-year-old girl	yes

Information	*Reason*	*State law cited*	*Adat/religious law cited*
The girl is five months pregnant. She did not want to marry the boy as she already had another boyfriend. Now she is married to another person, and has given birth to her baby.	Because of her pregnancy, the girl had to marry and become a housewife, and consequently, she cannot enjoy her childhood with her peers.	A81(2) Law No. 23 of 2002 A14(1), A22(1) KUHP A29(1) Law no.3 of 1997 A143(2), A193(1), A222(1) KUHAP	religious norm to not have sexual intercourse outside of the husband/wife relationship was violated
The defendant masturbated onto the victim and put his penis into her mouth and butt. The victim and the defendant were in the same foster care facility.	The victim and her family do not condemn the defendant. The defendant himself has experienced sexual harassment at the age of 7. The defendant's action against the victim occurred not only once but continued over 3–4 years.	A82 Law No.23 of 2002 A64(1), A289 KUHP A6(2) UU No.48 of 2009 A193(1) KUHAP	'religious norm' and 'norm in community': the sexual act is only for legally (*sah*) married adults
The defendant started sexual intercourse while watching TV with the victim in his dorm.	The defendant lured the victim into sexual intercourse with deception and lies, knowing that the victim was younger than 16 years old and could not yet be married.	A81(2) Law No.23 of 2002 A6(2) Law No.48 of 2009 A193 KUHAP A71(3) Law No.11 of 2012 A287(1), A289 KUHP	

(*Continued*)

(*Continued*)

	Case	*Decision*	*Defendant*	*Victim*	Pacaran
D	4/Pid.Sus. Anak/2016/ PN Dps	two years of imprisonment and three months of vocational training	16-year-and-10-month-old boy Islam technician vocational school student	16-year-and-5-month-old girl	yes
E	7/Pid.Sus. Anak/2014/ PN Dps	two years of imprisonment and three months of vocational training	17-year-old boy Hindu student	16-year-old girl	yes

Information	Reason	State law cited	Adat/religious law cited
When the victim was reluctant to start sexual intercourse, the defendant convinced her by promising to take responsibility and saying that he wanted sex as proof of her love towards him. The defendant sent SMS messages, including "just come to my room", "let's play", and "come on".	The defendant caused shame on the victim among her community and school. He damaged her future. His action disturbed society. The defendant is still young, and he can still reflect on his actions and continue his education. Peace has been made between the families of the victim and the defendant. The victim's family has forgiven the defendant's act.	A81(2) Law No.23 of 2002 A332(1) Law No.11 of 2012 Law No.8 of 1981	
The defendant invited the victim to his room ("if you do not come in, I will not take you back home") and started sexual intercourse. When the victim said, "it hurts", the defendant immediately took out his penis, but the victim was bleeding. The boy told the girl "do not tell anybody. Do not tell your parents that we slept together. Tell them we just took walks". It is a '*suka sama suka*' case. The boy invited the girl to his room because he heard from his friend that she was not a virgin. Pregnancy test: negative.	Though intercourse was based on mutual willingness and without compulsion, the action of the defendant negatively impacted the victim amidst her community. The victim's reputation was tainted. She is scorned by the surrounding community as she is not a virgin. This has resulted in prolonged shame on both the victim and her extended family. The defendant's act is not a good example for other children. His act has caused trauma and shame on the victim among her communities and schools. His act damaged the victim's future. His act disturbed society.	A81(2) Law No.23 of 2002 A193(1) KUHAP A6(2) Law No.48 of 2009 A71(3) Law No.11 of 2012	sexual intercouse without legal marriage (*sah*) is against the 'norm of decency' and 'legal norms' that damage the reputation of the girl even if it was *suka-sama-suka*

(Continued)

(*Continued*)

	Case	*Decision*	*Defendant*	*Victim*	Pacaran
F	32/Pid.Sus. Anak/2016/ PN Dps	one year of imprisonment with two years of probation	16-year-old boy Hindu vocational school student	14-year-old girl	yes
G	1042/Pid.Sus. Anak/2013/ PN Dps	three years and four months of imprisonment and a fine of Rp. 60.000.000	18-year-old boy Islam private worker	14-year-old girl	yes

Information	*Reason*	*State law cited*	*Adat/religious law cited*
The defendant and the victim were in the same SMK. The victim first refused to have intercourse, but the boy threatened not to take her home if she refused. She was afraid of not being able to go home, so she accepted. After the act, the boy sat down and did not take her home. One hour later, he said, "I want it again". The girl replied, "I do not want it", but the boy insisted "yes one more time. Then you can go home directly after".	The defendant's act is not a good example for other children. His act has caused trauma and shame for the victim among her communities and her schools. His act damaged the victim's future. His act disturbed society.	A 332(1) KUHP A 193(1) KUHAP A1(1), A81(1) Law No.23 of 2002 A6(2) Law No.48 of 2009 A71(3) Law No.11 of 2012	
The girl first refused to have sex because of a fear of pregnancy, but the boy insisted and convinced her by telling her that he would take responsibility and marry her if she became pregnant. Pregnancy test: negative.	The defendant's act damaged the victim's future.	A81(2) Law No.23 of 2002 A1(1) Law No.3 of 1997 A22(4), A193(1), A222(1) KUHAP A332(1) KUHP	

Index

Note: Page numbers with "n" indicates the end notes in the text.

For Product Safety Concerns and Information please contact our EU representative GPSR@taylorandfrancis.com
Taylor & Francis Verlag GmbH, Kaufingerstraße 24, 80331 München, Germany

www.ingramcontent.com/pod-product-compliance
Lightning Source LLC
LaVergne TN
LVHW011133300926
849160LV00008B/626
* 9 7 8 1 0 3 2 0 2 6 7 2 5 *